Stacking the Decks

A study of race, inequality and council housing in Nottingham

Alan Simpson

Nottingham CRC

Photographs — Nick Oldham and Polly Griffiths

Illustrations — Navvie Brick (Graphics), 48 St Mary's Gate, Nottingham

Published 1981

ISBN 0 9507627 0 9

©NDCRC 1981

Nottingham and District Community Relations Council,
37 Mansfield Road, Nottingham (0602) 49861

Printed by the Russell Press Ltd., Gamble Street, Nottingham.

Contents

Dedication

Dedicated to the Memory of Peter Price . . . whose principles and sheer presence still remain at the centre of the struggle against inequality.

Peter Price died, tragically, only weeks before this book was published. He was one of the Labour Councillors represented on the CRC's Executive Committee and had, throughout his life, been a persistent campaigner against inequality and discrimination. His longstanding involvement in housing issues, particularly when Vice-chairman of Nottingham's Housing Committee, provided a wealth of experience which he had intended to throw behind this study.

His death takes away not only a courageous advocate and ally, but also a source of inspiration and a warm and generous friend.

Acknowledgment

We wish to acknowledge our thanks to the Commission for Racial Equality, the Hilden Trust and the late Miss Dorothy Marion Wood, without whose generous financial support the publication of this study would not have been possible.

Miss Wood was a stalwart campaigner on race and community relations issues in Nottingham for many years. The use of part of her bequest to Nottingham CRC for the publication of this study is, we hope, consistent with the work she helped to promote.

Foreword

At a time when, nationally, council housing and race relations are in such a critical and uncertain state, this report offers one of the most far reaching and positive policy studies
to have emerged in recent years.

At last someone has set out the central links between housing policy decisions (i.e. on sales, improvements, the building
programme, etc) and the prospects of black families getting a
square deal through a Council's own allocations process.

I have supported the research because, as an Authority, the
City Council is committed to pursuing equality of opportunity in Nottingham. We ourselves needed to know how far our
own policies and procedures met this objective.

When an Authority takes such an honest look at itself,
inevitably it will not like some of the things it sees. This does
not mean that I necessarily agree with all the comments in the
report. It must also be remembered that officers are there to
implement and work within the policies laid down by the
elected members in power for the time being. This is why the
present City Council has called for a review of housing
allocation policies. One of the bodies we will consult is the
CRC.

Nevertheless, the production of this report provides a
thought provoking opportunity of looking closely at council
housing policy which will benefit not only the black community but all families who are in search of decent council
housing in Nottingham.

The crippling effect of current government housing policies
limit the options open to any Authority genuinely committed

to tackling inequalities. However, this must not prevent us from attempting to correct any injustices which have arisen out of our own local housing policies and practices, whilst, at the same time, pressing for more sweeping changes at a national level.

The CRC in Nottingham have provided us with a valuable tool for examining our approach to housing and race.

In its most constructive sense, this is what CRC's throughout the country ought to be doing. Nottingham deserves to be congratulated for the thorough and positive way in which this work has been carried out.

Racial equality is one of the most important issues of our time. Housing, and in particular council housing, is a cornerstone upon which good community relations are built. I hope Authorities up and down the country will benefit from the exercises carried out in Nottingham.

John Carroll
Leader of the Nottingham City Council

LIST OF TABLES

LIST OF MAPS

LIST OF PHOTOGRAPHS

Outline map of Nottingham — location of key estates and flats complexes

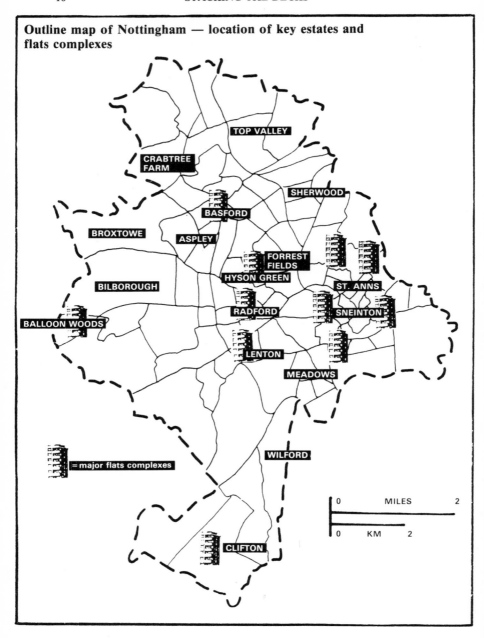

TOP VALLEY

CRABTREE FARM

SHERWOOD

BASFORD

BROXTOWE

ASPLEY

FORREST FIELDS

HYSON GREEN

BILBOROUGH

ST. ANNS

RADFORD

SNEINTON

BALLOON WOODS

LENTON

MEADOWS

= major flats complexes

WILFORD

0   MILES   2

0   KM   2

CLIFTON

Background to the Study

". . . at no time over the past two hunderd years has Nottingham been free of a severe housing problem. It is amongst todays victims of the problem that most of the city's coloured immigrants are to be found.
(Lawrence, 1974 p.74).

The last half of the 1970's saw massive changes in government policies on housing. Behind the flamboyant facade of a 'choice of housing wider than ever before', there remained a strong feeling within inner city housing areas that what was really happening was the exact opposite. Far from an extented choice of housing tenure, local housing groups increasingly expressed the view that low-income urban families were progressively being denied 'choice', and denied access to decent housing. The 'sale of the century' of council houses and severe cuts in council house building, improvement work and land acquisition were all part of a process which was to 'free' money and property for the private sector by effectively starving the public sector.

If the general prospects for council housing were grim, those facing black families appeared even more ominous. Discriminated against in the private sector — whether as prospective tenants or buyers — what chances would they then have in the public sector; even in an authority which *wanted* to offer equality of opportunity? This, in essence, was what the research sought to find out. Not simply on a 'who got what' basis, but also by examining the effects of various changes in housing policy on the real 'choices' which remained open to people.

The actual origins of the research were, however, rooted in earlier studies and issues relating to housing in Nottingham.

Comments such as that quoted above from Danny Lawrence's *Black Migrants: White Natives*, were amongst those which, during the mid-1970's, prompted and prodded for a systematic examination of Nottingham's council housing policies. The feasability of doing so, however, owed its origins to two previous decisions relating to race and housing which were taken in the city. The first was that of the Housing Department which, in 1968, began to implement a policy of including ethnic origin in its housing records. These records, *collected at the point of allocation*, made it technically possible for monitoring to take place of the racial consequences of council housing policy.

The second important contributory factor was a small scale study undertaken by Muhammed Ajeeb, the city's Fair Housing Group Worker, into the rehousing experiences of a number of black families in Nottingham. The study — *Somewhere to Live*, (1971) — followed through the difficulties which a sample of 47 black families faced on being rehoused in predominantly settled, white, council estates. Ajeeb's legacy to the Nottingham CRC was the result of an agreement he had reached with the Housing Department. In order to make his own study possible the Department had agreed to send him their weekly allocations details. Long after Ajeeb had selected the particular families in his study, these weekly print-outs continued to arrive at the offices of the CRC. Eventually these took up so much space that questions began to be asked about why we had them, and what was going to be done with them if they were not to be thrown away. Analyse them. The penny had dropped.

It was at this point that the CRC locally, and the Commission for Racial Equality nationally, became particularly conscious of the fact that although Nottingham included ethnic origin in its allocation records, no systematic use had ever been made of this in terms of its housing policy discussions. With financial support from the Commission, Nottingham CRC then attempted to look at the differing patterns of rehousing experienced by black families within the council house sector.

The original plan was for a study far grander than this. It was intended that the changing fortunes of the black communities in the council housing sector, would be examined over a period of some six to eight years. Financial constraints would in any case have made this difficult, but the overriding reason for confining it to a 3 year period was the source material itself. Gaps and inaccuracies in the Housing Department's records covering the early 1970's meant that any thorough-going analysis would have been considerably undermined before it got off the ground. It was only in the mid-1970's that a much tighter system of record keeping seemed to emerge, and that more effective (though generalised) use of these records was made by the Department itself. At the other end of the time period, we were restricted by a change in the practice of record keeping in 1978, which prevented the precise identification of allocations made to the council's flats complexes. The council itself has acknowledged that, at any point in time, flats account for some 70% of the properties which it has available for letting (even though they comprise little more than 20% of its total housing stock). Flats complexes are not only the most readily available sources of relet property but, almost axiomatically, they are amongst the least popular of the council's housing stock. To be unable to distinguish between allocations to flats as opposed to houses closed many of the most important avenues of investigation for an allocations study.

Rather than get into the most broad and tenuous generalisations after this point, it was decided to restrict the allocations analysis to the period in which we could confidently and precisely identify where people had been allocated to.

Within this three year period, we then set about analysing all of the council's allocations which went to black households and set this against a sample of an equivalent number of allocations going to the white community. In all, this involved cross checking and analysing the previous tenure, family size, eventual rehousing and (in some cases) declared housing preferences of some 2,400 households.

One important feature of our research was that the analysis which we undertook was based upon an examination of the *total* council allocations made during the period. As such it included both moves *into* the system as well as those *within* it

— i.e. by way of transfers and exchanges. Some of the studies previously undertaken on race and council housing had dealt only with what they referred to as 'primary access to the council house system'. The exclusion of transfers and exchanges from such analyses seemed to impose major limitations in their ability to identify how far discrimination or disadvantage, resulting from earlier 'primary access', was being counteracted or reinforced by local authority transfer policies. In examining the total allocations made by Nottingham's Housing Department we sought to avoid this pitfall.

In addition to this we sought to build in a specific dimension to our analysis of race and council housing which virtually all previous reports seem to have studiously avoided. This involved examining differential patterns of allocation *in the light of housing policy changes* during the period of study. It seemed to be ludicrous for us to examine ways in which racial inequalities in the allocations process might be removed, if the whole direction of the main housing policy itself was to extend or entrench such discrimination or disadvantage. However flawed the outcome of this approach might be, we were convinced of the importance of setting the racial aspects of council house allocations within such a broad framework.

Towards the end of 1979 the funding of this research from the CRE ran out. Cuts in their own budget, as well as practical difficulties in the relationship between them and the research project, dictated that another way of completing the research had to be found. In this case, the 'seventh cavalry' came in the form of the Hilden Trust who financed a further 6 months of work on the data by Stephen King who was then the researcher. Without his persistence, and the 'deep and meaningful' relationship which he developed with the computer, the research would have remained a morass of unintelligible figures. As part of the agreement with the Hilden Trust, the Nottingham CRC also seconded me to work full-time on the research for 6 months. These 6 months eventually turned into almost a year and a half's work of analysing and writing up. Their patience as well as the unlimited, unpaid and unflinchingly critical support of Danny Lawrence (as research supervisor from Nottingham University), have been largely responsible for bringing the report to fruition.

Many important issues have remained untouched or inadequately considered in this study. Nothing whatsoever has been examined in relation to changes in coucil house rents. Some racial aspects of the sales policy still remain to be explored, as does any look at possible discrimination in the length of time spent waiting/queuing for different types of council housing. And the particular influences and value positions of Nottingham's allocations staff and housing visitors have only been dealt with in the most circumspect terms. But then it's always easier to find more areas which need examination than it is to present what you have unearthed so far. The report is in any case, far longer than anticipated. In part this has come as a defence mechanism following earlier discussions with housing department staff. Nottingham, perhaps like other authorities, has steadfastly held to the line that it doesn't matter what discrimination or inequality exists anywhere else in the country — 'Nottingham's Nottingham . . . and it doesn't happen here.' The detailed, step by step, dismantling of the city's housing allocations policies had to be a feature of the report if it was to command any serious recognition. For those less burdened by the need to defend traditional procedures at all costs, this will inevitably make the report heavier going that it might have been. As a partial appeasement for this, brief summaries have been provided wherever possible. Some may find it useful to read these before (or instead of . . .!!) the main sections themselves.

For those interested, an appendix has been added to the report setting out details of the way in which the Housing Department organised its record keeping and how sampling from within the total of white allocations was organised and followed through.

Alan Simpson (April 1981).

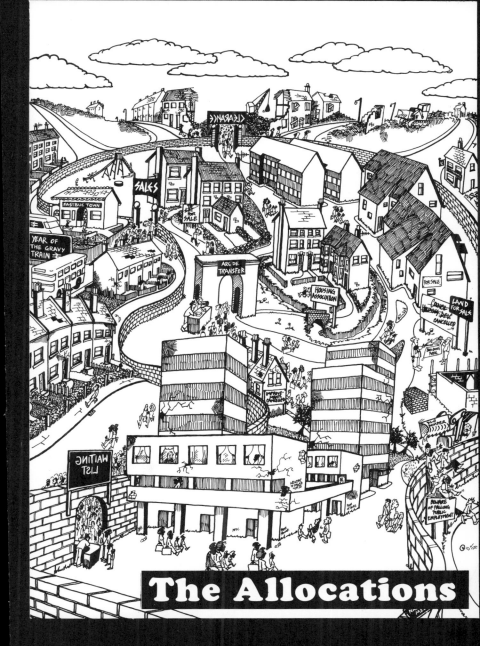

The Allocations

1

The Allocations — A Broad Outline

"The essence of the situation is still that there are a number of ethnic groups engaged in conflict over the allocation of housing, and though their conflict may not be carried through to the point of violence, it remains the centre of the overall interaction system."

(Rex, 1968, p.227 (in Pahl, *Readings in Urban Sociology*).)

Between 1st January 1975 and 1st January 1978 a total of 1,217 black households were allocated council properties through Nottingham's Housing Department. Of these, a total of 1,066 were categorised, by the Department, as West Indian, and 151 as Asian. Such categorisations immediately demand both qualification and explanation. The Council's approach to ethnic identity has been rudimentary. They have used 3 categories of ethnic origin — Asian, West Indian and white. All successful applicants had to be coded into one of these categories. The coding was done by housing officials who larged based such classifications on their own judgment. There seems to have been a simple, if flawed, process for doing so. All those who were obviously not white were coded in two easy steps. Irrespective of place of birth, all those of African or West Indian origin were classified as 'West Indian'. Then everyone who was obviously not 'West Indian' and not 'white' had to be 'Asian'. At one stage in the research this raised particular difficulties in relation to a set of 'Asian' allocants who, on examination, turned out to be mainly students from the Middle East. In addition, and in broader terms, the definitions allowed for no distinctions to be drawn in respect to European minorities — such as the Poles and the Irish, both of which had significant sized communities in Nottingham.

Despite the limitations of such broad categories, it was on this basis that our study had to operate. The analysis which follows is based on all 1,217 black households. The comparisons with allocations to white households are based on a random sample of their total allocations during the same period. This sample of 1,183 households is in fact slightly smaller than the total of black allocations. The reason for this is that, of the original 1,217 households which were selected, some were subsequently found to have important errors or omissions in the Housing Department's records relating to them.

Once these had been accounted for we found that Nottingham's extensive list of rehousing categories provided a valuable base upon which to analyse the workings of the Council's housing policies.

Before we do so it is perhaps worth making clear the broad framework within which these allocations took place. The city's population during this period was in the region of 300,000. Of these it was estimated that some 4,000 were Indian, 5,000 Pakistani and between 15,000 and 20,000 were West Indians. The Council's housing stock amounted to approximately 54,000 properties (about half of the total housing in the city) though obviously only a small percentage of these were available for letting at any point in time. It was within these boundaries that the allocations, below, took place. This table allows us to set Nottingham's housing programme within the context of the national picture in respect of council housing.

> "In England during 1975, of the 260,000 households entering the council sector, 18 per cent came via slum clearance activities, 9 per cent were rehoused as a consequence of homelessness and 64 per cent from the ordinary waiting list. The remaining 9 per cent consituted 'key workers' and other priority groups."
>
> (Merrett, 1979, p.215).

Whilst the position nationally in 1975 may well be similar to that of Nottingham in the early 1980's, it bore only limited resemblance to the local situation between 1975 and 1978.

A much greater proportion of Nottingham's allocants came in via clearance rehousing. This mirrored the extent to which the City's clearance programme, which began fairly

TABLE 1.1
Total Allocations — by rehousing category

Category	Asian	West Indian	White
Clearance	51.5	27.7	28.8
Direct Exhange	0.7	2.3	8.1
Deferred Exchange	1.3	—	0.2
Multiple Exhchange	—	—	0.5
Private Exchange	0.7	—	1.7
Transfer — ordinary	2.0	14.8	25.2
Transfer — Modernise	0.7	2.4	2.8
Waiting list — general	15.2	33.8	18.8
Secondary list	—	—	0.7
Supplementart list	0.7	0.2	—
Aged Persons list	—	—	0.6
Forces list	—	0.2	0.8
Urban Aid	6.0	11.4	1.4
Special Case	3.3	2.5	4.0
Homeless Families	1.3	3.3	2.3
Victoria Centre — city	6.0	0.8	2.0
Victoria Centre — county	4.6	0.1	1.1
Victoria Centre — other	6.0	0.3	0.5
Staff housing	—	0.1	—
Other allocations	—	0.1	0.5
TOTAL	100.0	100.0	100.0
N =	151	1066	1183

late in national terms, was still in full flow in the mid 1970's. In fact, a straight comparison between the figures quoted above and those in table 1.1 understates the contrasts between the local and national situations. Table 1.1 includes the internal movements within public sector housing. When we re-calculated the relative percentages, omitting transfers and exchanges, the differences were much greater. Some 55% of Asians, 35% of West Indians and 47% of whites came into the system via clearance. This was between twice and 3 times the national rate.

Conversely, only 16% of Asian allocants, 42% of West Indians, and 30% of white ones came in via the general waiting list — significantly less, in each case, than the national proportions. One important qualification to this, which we examine in detail later, is the extent to which Nottingham's 'waiting list' allocations, for West Indian households at least, would have conformed more closely to the national figures, had one or two somewhat ambiguous categories been included under this hearing. Thus, 'Urban Aid' and (to a lesser extent) 'Special case' allocations appeared to draw people — albeit for different reasons — from the waiting list queue. The impact of including these in the 'waiting list' figures would have been to increase them significantly. This would have raised the proportion of West Indian waiting list allocations to around 60% of their total moves into the system.

Equally important however, is one of the direct features of table 0.1. Almost 40% of the allocations to the white sample in our study were internal moves within the council house sector. This compared with less than 20% of the West Indian moves and 5% of Asian ones. The sheer scale of these disparities is something which we pay particular attention to later in the section on transfers and exchanges, and it constitutes one of the most important aspects of our study.

Despite a general concern about the position of homeless families, there did not seem to be any sound statistical basis in our study for analysing the treatment of such small proportions of each ethnic group's total allocations which fell into this category. Homelessness in Nottingham did not emerge as a rehousing category of anything like the importance it has in London or some of the other major cities. As such, our comments upon the position of homeless families have been restricted to sections which examine local housing policies in their broadest sense.

Another category of allocations which requires brief but specific reference to is that of the 'Victoria Centre'. This Centre is in fact a multi-storey block of flats in the middle of one of the largest shopping precincts in central Nottingham. Although the housing department deals with the lettings of such flats, and keeps records of these, applicants did not have to come from the council's waiting list or from any other of their priority rehousing categories. In particular, one part of their operation includes a block allocation to students from the local polytechnic. It is largely for these reasons that little or no reference will be made to any of the channels of allocation into the Victoria Centre, or its relevance to the Council's rehousing programme. Whilst it was true that 16% of Asian allocations were to this Centre, considerable doubt existed about the accuracy and relevance of such a figure. It was here that classification of the polytechnic's Middle East students as 'Asian' most substantially undermined the usefulness of the coding system. This was, however, the only context in which such a distortion was able to be identified. It was, fortunately, within a rehousing category which had only limited relevance to the rehousing prospects of either of the other two groups.

What must also be noted at this stage is the extent to which the contrasts in housing allocations which we have been able to examine are those between West Indian and white households respectively. Only in the area of clearance rehousing were Asian families significantly involved in the Council's allocation processes. Consequently, it was only in this particular section that pattern of Asian council house allocations could be seriously woven into the total picture.

Before moving on from Table 1.1 it is worth touching upon some aspects which become more apparent in subsequent sections. Nottingham has for some time worked on a 3 tier priority system for allocations. Clearance rehousing has had top priority, transfers and exchanges second, and allocations from various waiting lists third. Statutory responsibilities in respect of the homeless have over-ridden these priorities in terms of the speed, if not the quality, of rehousing. These distinctions are of enormous importance in determining the pattern of allocations, since they set out the order of choosing from the properties which the council has available. Within this 'pecking order', the gate through which you enter the allocations arena largely defines the rehousing opportunities you are faced with.

Within this study and under this priority system it might be said that Asian households entered the system through the only gate worth using. Such a statement would, however, have to be qualified by a recognition that, even here, the actual numbers involved were very limited. Between whites and West Indians a different balance existed. Their proportions coming in via clearance were similar, but thereafter wide disparities appeared, with whites receiving a high proportion of transfer moves whilst West Indians were heavily dependant on allocations from the waiting list. Excluding transfers and exchanges did not narrow these disparities. It merely accentuated the gap between the greater numbers of whites coming in via clearance and West Indians via the waiting lists. This was the first and most obvious, form of insitutional inequality which emerged. The problem with such priority categories is that they primarily reflect administrative priorities rather than housing need.

> "To ensure the smooth running of slum clearance schemes and because of the statutory obligations imposed upon the local authority by central government legislation, families living in compulsory purchase order areas are usually given priority over the two other groups for rehousing. This situation is an example of enforced institutionalised queue-jumping over other households who may have been waiting for many years for the tenancy of a council house and be in great housing need."
>
> (Gray, 1976, p.40).

Our own view is that waiting time is in fact a far less substantial reservation than the failure to respond to extreme housing need. In this respect, Lawrence has already demonstrated that Nottingham's waiting list system has been a far from effective means of identifying such need, let alone responding to it

> "there is clearly little correspondence between the number of families registered for council housing and the number who are in need it. The 1966 Census indicated that about 40,000 households did not have the exclusive use of a hot water tap, bath and inside toilet. Yet in the same year there were less than 5,000 names on Nottingham's council house waiting list."
>
> (Lawrence, 1974, p.96).

We return to this aspect specifically in the section dealing with waiting list allocations but its general context needs to be established here. Under the system of priorities which existed during this study, being on the waiting list did not necessarily imply that applicants had only limited housing needs. What it guaranteed was the groups seeking council housing in this way had to wait longer and then face more restricted choices than either of the other major allocation categories. Thus the disproportionate number of West Indian families who entered the system in this way did so with an immediate and equally disproportionate disadvantage.

Returning to table 1.1, it might appear from the absence of

allocations under the 'Aged Persons' list, that the elderly did not figure in any significant numbers in the council's allocations during this period. Table 1.2 makes it clear that this was not the case. What it does do is to illustrate the extent to which the Local Authority used other channels rather than this list as the means of rehousing the elderly.

TABLE 1.2
Total Allocations — by household designation

	Asian	West Indian	White
Pensioner	4.0	1.6	20.6
Handicapped	—	—	0.7
Problem Family	—	0.1	—
Check Visit Advisable	4.0	5.2	6.0
Not Applicable	92.0	93.1	72.7
TOTAL	100.0	100.0	100.0
N =	151	1066	1183

In fact, table 1.2 outlines some important features which influenced the conduct of our research. To begin with, the disproportionate involvement of pensioners within the white sample has had to be accounted for throughout the study. The importance of this lay not in the extent to which it was unrepresentative of total white allocations, but in the extent to which it restricted comparisons between the West Indian allocations and those of the white sample. We have attempted to draw distinctions throughout the study between those situations where it seemed appropriate to include figures for the elderly in our comparisons, and those from which they were excluded. Sometimes we have included both. The other side of this coin, however, was the extent to which the very different family size and age of West Indian households has had to be recognised time and again as having profoundly influenced their rehousing prospects.

It is worth mentioning in passing that the overwhelming majority of allocants in each ethnic group were classified as ordinary families (i.e. simply as 'Not Applicable') and that virtually no families were recorded as being 'problem families'. This did not mean that the Housing Department considered Nottingham to have an exemplary population. Rather it merely indicated that officials within the Department did not *use* this part of their coding system to identify the families they found difficult or undesirable. Such references more regularly appeared upon the personal file cards of the households concerned. The 'check visit advisable' coding was the nearest that the Department came to any formal identification of problem families but even here it would be unwise to read too much into the coding. Our limited examination of personal record cards revealed some diversity in the use of such coding. In some cases it had obviously been used to identify households who were confused or uncertain in the choices they were attempting to express. On the other hand it had also clearly been used where a family were suspected of having poor housekeeping standards or being of dubious virtue as tenants. Overall it is easiest to conclude simply that neither of these codes were systematically used to identify problem families. Whatever methods existed to do so were of a more discrete character. In fairness, however, it is important to set out the Housing Department's explanation of this. Their own view is that the clearance programme in particular necessitated such speed of rehousing that problem families and ordinary ones were offered the same unrestricted choice of properties. It then became pointless to classify problem families as such since this would have had no impact. Whatever the validity of this in respect of clearance, such an explanation would not apply to either transfer or waiting list allocations.

However, turning attention back to the main body of allocations, we need to consider carefully the important differences in the family sizes of the 3 ethnic groups. Tables 1.3a and 1.3b set these size patterns out, first of all including the elderly and then excluding them.

Whether pensioners were included or excluded it is fairly clear from these tables that both Asian and West Indian households were far more likely than whites to be represented in family sizes of 5 or more. Even excluding the elderly, households of 5 or more comprised 37% of the Asian allocations, and 24% of the West Indian ones, but only 15% of the white allocations. Before the elderly were taken out of the calculations, there were twice the proportion of West Indian households of 5 or more persons as there were white ones,

TABLE 1.3a
Total Allocations — by family size

Family Size	Asian	West Indian	White
1 person	6.0	20.3	28.2
2 persons	30.5	25.4	27.7
3 persons	9.9	20.2	18.8
4 persons	17.2	10.5	12.8
5 persons	11.9	9.7	7.8
6 persons	9.9	6.8	2.3
7 persons	8.6	3.8	1.4
8 persons	2.1	2.3	0.8
9 persons	2.6	0.8	0.1
10 persons	1.3	0.2	0.1
TOTAL	100.0	100.0	100.0
N =	151	1066	1183

TABLE 1.3b
Total Allocations — by family size, exluding pensioners

Family Size	Asian	West Indian	White
1 person	6.2	19.4	19.7
2 persons	28.3	25.4	27.2
3 persons	10.3	20.4	21.7
4 persons	17.9	10.7	15.8
5 persons	12.4	9.8	9.7
6 persons	10.3	7.0	2.9
7 persons	8.3	3.9	1.6
8 persons	2.1	2.3	1.2
9 persons	2.8	0.9	0.1
10 persons	1.4	0.2	0.1
TOTAL	100.0	100.0	100.0
N =	145	1050	939

and the proportion of such Asian families was 3 times that of the white groups. Without doubt the number of pensioners affected the relative proportions in white family sizes quite significantly. Far less easy to account for was the absence of black elderly in the allocations of the time. Although it is not something which we were able to effectively pursue, it is worth noting that members of the Afro-Caribbean Community have suggested that this does not correspond to the numbers of black elderly living in the city.

Additional differences in the background of allocants can be seen in table 1.4a and 1.4b detailing their previous housing tenure.

TABLE 1.4a
Total Allocations — by previous housing tenure

	Asian	West Indian	White
Lodgers	35.8	52.4	27.2
Tenants	38.4	42.8	68.5
Owner Occupiers	17.9	4.3	3.0
Business Tenants	5.3	—	0.1
Lodgers Outside City	2.6	0.5	1.2
TOTAL	100.0	100.0	100.0
N =	151	1066	1183

TABLE 1.4b
Total Allocations of new entrants — by previous tenure

	Asian	West Indian	White
Lodgers	37.5	63.1	42.0
Tenants	35.4	31.1	52.5
Owner Occupiers	18.8	5.2	4.7
Business tenants	5.6	-	0.1
Lodgers Outside City	2.7	0.6	1.7
TOTAL	100.0	100.0	100.0
N =	144	883	761

It seems appropriate to mention here the very different ways in which the Authority has used the word lodgers. In terms of previous tenure 'lodgers' referred specifically to those families sharing rooms in someone else's house. This was very different from its meaning when applied to the 'General or Lodgers Waiting List'. In the latter case it then embraced a variety of tenure types including tenants of unfurnished and part-furnished accommodation, as well as flats where some amenity was shared. Apart from the section dealing with the waiting list, we have referred to 'lodgers', particularly in the tables, in its earlier and more precise context.

The problem of interpreting table 1.4a lay in the extent to which it was skewed by the proportion of white allocants who received transfers and were therefore already council *tenants*. Table 1.4b compensates for this by focusing upon new entrants to the council house system. Consistent with their entrance via the clearance programme, a much greater proportion of Asian allocants were owner occupiers than either West Indians or whites. However, even for Asians this proportion was no more than half the rate at which they came in as either tenants *or* lodgers. Even discounting the transfer moves of white allocants a far greater proportion of them entered the system as tenants than either Asians or West Indians. In contrast, West Indian households were far more likely to have come in from a background of having been lodgers than either of the other groups.

Table 1.5 begins to sketch out something of the picture of the allocations themselves, and it illustrates one half of the process by which the Housing Department distinguished properties within its total stock. The data in this table is based upon differences in property age and location as well as whether they formed part of the Council's purpose built estates or were simply purchased from the private sector.

TABLE 1.5

Total Allocations — by property age

	Asian	West Indian	White
ACQUIRED			
New Non Estate	2.0	1.7	3.4
Non Estate	4.0	2.7	4.1
Inner City Non Estate	7.3	4.5	2.5
Relet Inner City Non Estate	8.6	7.4	3.5
PURPOSE BUILT			
New	29.8	21.2	23.3
Post-War Relet	41.7	54.3	47.3
Pre-War Relet	6.6	8.2	15.9
TOTAL	100.0	100.0	100.0
N =	151	1066	1183

There are important interpretive limitations of such a breakdown which require that, throughout the report, allocations by property age have to be seen in the context of 'property type' as well. We shall attempt to do so in a moment having first clarified some of the terms in table 1.5.

All of the 'acquired' properties refer to purchases from the private sector. 'New non-estate' and 'non-estate' properties are all ones outside the older central areas, with 'non-estate' properties being recently purchased existing properties as opposed to those purchased brand new (and previously unoccupied) from private sector builders. Similarly, within the inner city the distinction between the two headings is that 'inner city non-estate' refers to recent purchases from the private sector whereas 'relet inner city non-estate' refers to privately built properties which have, for some time, been within the Council's housing portfolio.

The purpose built estates are much more self-explanatory. It is here, though, that the major limitations emerge. Such an age breakdown offers no indication of the *type* of property which it refers to. This is particularly so in relation to the significance of post-war council built properties. All the other forms of classification relate to houses flats or bungalows. Post-war properties, however, include the 11,000 or so properties which are in deck-access or multi-storey complexes. These have in recent years constituted up to 70% of the properties which the Authority has had *available for letting* at any point in time. They are also amongst the least popular and most stigmatised parts of its stock. Thus whilst *houses* built in this period have been reasonably sound and popular, the more readily available flats complexes have been much less so.

Conversely, Nottingham's pre-war properties do not warrant the same automatic stigma as might be the case elsewhere in the country. Though there are one or two notorious exceptions, much of Nottingham's purpose built pre-war housing was constructed during the periods when the more generous central government building subsidies were available. As a result many of its pre-war estates, though ageing, are structurally sound, have settled communities, give reasonable access to the city and are generally sought after.

From table 1.5 alone, we are able to recognise that white families went into these pre-war housing estates at almost twice the rate of either Asian or West Indian families. We can also establish that all 3 groups went into new properties — houses, flats, bungalows — at roughly the same rate, though with Asian families appearing to have fared particularly well (probably again as a result of coming in via the clearance programme). In terms of allocations to 'acquired' properties, 22% of Asians, 16% of West Indians and 14% of whites went to these, although the overwhelming majority of both Asian and West Indian moves of this sort were to inner city properties (mainly relets) whilst the majority of such white allocations were to council properties on private estates *outside* the central areas. This still leaves us with the problem of the Council's post-war relets which made up the majority of West Indian allocations and only slightly less so of both white and Asian ones. Table 1.6 sheds some light on this.

TABLE 1.6
Total Allocations — by property type

	Asian	West Indian	White
Aluminium Permanent Bungalow	—	—	0.8
Bungalow	—	0.2	2.5
Deck Access Flat	2.6	6.9	6.0
Deck Access Maisonette	9.9	24.1	10.1
Flat	7.4	14.8	15.7
House	55.6	42.2	48.8
Multi-Storey Flat	4.6	7.1	4.1
Multi-Storey Maisonette	—	1.2	0.6
Short Life Property	2.0	1.9	1.0
Temporary Bungalow	—	—	0.3
Warden Aided Bungalow	2.0	—	0.8
Warden Aided Flat	0.7	—	5.2
Victoria Centre Flats	15.2	1.6	4.1
TOTAL	100.0	100.0	100.0
N =	151	1066	1183

For West Indian households, moves into flats complexes* made up 40% of their total allocations, as opposed to 21% and 17% of white and Asian totals respectively. These all came within the category of Nottingham's 'post-war' properties. When we talk, then, about allocations to post-war properties, it is important to realise that for West Indians, 4/5 of these allocations will have been to flats complexes, as opposd to roughly 2/5 for both Asians and whites. Allocations to post-war properties thus assumed a very specific significance. For West Indians it became synonymous with some of the poorest, least desirable sections of Nottingham's council

* The term 'flats complexes' is used, throughout the report, to refer to both *multi-storey* blocks (normally serviced by a central lift system and internal corridors) and *deck-access* developments (usually of 3-6 storeys, and where access is via a series of open and interconnecting walkways which run the length of each level in the block). The term does not include the council's category of 'flats', since these normally refer to single or paired units within a housing estate, or to converted units within large older housing.

housing. The extent of West Indian allocations to post-war properties provides one measure of the relative disadvantages they encountered in pursuit of decent public sector housing.

A similar direct correlation for white or Asian allocants would not be anything like as valid. For each of these groups, they were far more likely to obtain post-war *houses* than accommodation in flats complexes. This was not consistently so for all the categories of allocation. However, as we shall see when we examine each category separately, this relative disadvantage experienced by West Indians was maintained across the whole spectrum of council allocations.

In its own right, table 1.6 offers some important evidence about the racial impact of the Council's allocation policies. West Indians were the least likely of any group to be allocated houses, irrespective of their age, quality or location. When pensioners were excluded from these figures, the disparities were even greater. Some 57% of white households obtained houses as opposed to 43% of West Indians.

Given the data in the earlier tables it is reasonably evident from table 1.6 that the majority of white pensioners went to bungalows, warden-aided properties or flats. Very few allocations of any sort went to short life property; and the Victoria Centre, apart from its contingent of middle-east students, was only significant (and then to a limited extent) in the white allocations. *Most striking of all, however, was the extent of West Indian allocations to flats complexes.* Deck access masionettes — frequently derided as the Council's white elephant or booby-prize housing — provided a stark example of this. Going beyond the normal disparity in allocations, West Indian households were rehoused in such such properties at almost 2½ times the rate of either whites or Asians.

Summary

The broad picture of Nottingham's council house allocations over the research period includes a number of fairly distinct features. Asian families only obtained council housing on a very limited scale. Where they did so, however, it was primarily through the most advantageous of re-housing categories — clearance. The experience of West Indians was almost the opposite of this. West Indians came into the council house system in far greater proportions than whites or Asians (42%, 30% and 16% respectively) through the low-priority gateway of the waiting lists.

The disadvantages and inequalities created by this pattern were then compounded by the extent to which blacks failed to obtain transfers at anything like the same rate as whites. There was virtually no involvement of Asian families in the transfers process, and West Indians only received such moves at just over half the rate of that of white households. Important differences existed in the family structure of the different groups of allocants. A significant proportion of white allocants were pensioners (20%), whereas virtually no pensioners were independently re-housed within the Asian or West Indian communities. On the other hand, larger family units (i.e. 5 or more) were much more common amongst Asians and West Indians re-housed than whites (36%, 24% and 13% respectively). In consequence, the size, age and location of appropriate council properties available for letting, will have had an important differential impact upon the re-housing prospects of the 3 ethnic groups.

In terms of the moves which did take place, the majority of West Indian re-housing was to post-war council built estates. However, some 80% of these moves were to deck-access or multi-storey flats complexes. These complexes were (and are) amongst the least popular and most stigmatised parts of the council's housing stock. Although similarly large proportions of Asians and whites went to post-war properties, in each case the majority (i.e. 60%) of such allocations were to post-war *houses*.

This disparity between allocations to houses and flats complexes formed an important part of the total allocations picture. West Indians were the least likely of the 3 groups to obtain houses (43% of their total allocations as against 57% for both whites and Asians). Conversely, they were far more likely to be allocated to flats *complexes* (as opposed to ordinary flats or bungalows). Some 40% of West Indian allocations went to such complexes compared with 21% of whites and 17% of Asians. The most marked contrast of all emerged in allocations to the highly unpopular *deck-access* maisonettes. West Indians were allocated to these maisonettes at almost

2½ times the rate of white or Asian households.

Within the allocations to houses themselves, it was also important to note that, whilst 22% of Asians, 16% of West Indian and 14% of white allocants went to houses which the council had *bought* rather than built, roughly 75% of these Asian and West Indian moves were to older, inner city properties. The majority of whites moved to 'acquired' properties outside the central areas of Nottingham — properties much less likely to present substantial rehabilitation needs.

Clearance

2

Clearance Rehousing
— *the chance of rags to riches?*

However late Nottingham grasped the nettle of post-war slum clearance and re-building, by the late 1960's it had committed itself to a programme which would stretch well into the 1980's before completion. The sheer scale of this commitment necessitated major changes in the administration of its public housing. Not least of these changes was in the Housing Department's capacity to rehouse large numbers of families from clearance areas quickly and efficiently.

Delays in moving families from their old houses, ran the risk of contractors invoking penalty clauses against the Authority. Even without these, any delays in the schedules of rehousing, demolition, and rebuilding involved considerable costs to the local authority. Such financial incentives (as well as a recognition of the extreme needs of many families in clearance areas) established clearance as the major platform of Nottingham's housing policy and elevated it to the top of the Council's list of rehousing categories.

A commitment of this scale brought about organisational changes which substantially countered the earlier criticism that,

> "for a city the size of Nottingham, the administrative machine was still a fairly primitive one, with few of the advantages or disadvantages of departmental interplay in the housing and planning field."
>
> (*Burney,* 1967, p.198-9).

Clearance families, then, got the pick of whatever council housing was available. How privileged a position this was to be obviously varied through time. Cuts in the building programme, a policy of council house sales rather than letting, or a large volume of families seeking moves at any one time, would limit the scope of individual choice. On the other hand, a policy of buying houses from the private sector, or a large scale building programme would widen it.

The benefits of being in this highest of priority categories did not fall uniformly on all of those within it. Family status, existing housing conditions, area of preference and type of property required offered as many variables to be accounted for as in any other category of housing. Such variables have to be carefully considered when examing differences in the pattern of clearance allocations.

During the 3 year period of our study, Nottingham completed the rebuilding of its first major clearance area (St Ann's) and began rehousing from the earliest phases of its second (the Meadows). In addition, clearance also took place in a number of other central parts of the city, including areas of Sneinton, Kirkstead Street, Raleigh Street, Basford, Salisbury Street and North Sherwood Street.

However, the major area from which clearance allocations were made from the beginning of 1975 to the beginning of 1978 was the Meadows. This was doubly significant for us, since it was also a major area of concentration of black

'Those who live by the sword . . .' — clearance in Lenton.

families. 55% of all Asians rehoused under clearance came from the Meadows, along with 38% of the West Indians and 40% of the white sample. The Raleigh Street and Kirkstead Street clearance areas accounted for a further 17% of the clearance allocations of Asians; 35% of the West Indians and 25% of the whites. At the end of this section we examine more closely the allocations from Phase 3 of the Meadows clearance and the whole of the Raleigh Street clearance, in order to consider the relationship between allocations and 'choice' within the clearance programme.

The nature of properties which were allocated under clearance during this period is set out, below, in table 2.1.

TABLE 2.1
Type of Property allocated to clearance area residents

	Asian	*West Indian*	*White*
Bungalows	—	0.3	5.4
Deck Access Flats	—	5.8	5.6
Deck Access Maisonettes	2.6	7.1	4.4
Flats	7.6	7.9	14.3
House	87.2	75.2	65.2
Multi storey Flats	1.3	2.4	2.7
Multi storey Maisonettes	—	1.0	0.6
Short life Property	1.3	0.3	0.3
Warden Aided Bungalow or Flat	—	—	1.5
TOTAL	100.00	100.0	100.0
N =	78	294	336

The most striking confirmation of the priority given to clearance families is the high proportion of allocations to houses. In the general breakdown of allocations from all categories of rehousing roughly 56% of Asians, 42% of West Indians and 49% of whites received houses. The comparable figures under clearance of 87%, 75% and 65% respectively were thus considerably in excess of this average rate. In addition, it appears that under the clearance procedures both West Indians and Asians received houses as a higher rate than white families. This picture is slightly distorted, however, due to the numbers of white pensioners who were rehoused. Table 2.2, detailing the 'personal code' of households rehoused under the clearance programme some idea of how

Fig.2.a **White Clearance Allocations**

Shaded areas constituting **49.2%** of white clearance allocations

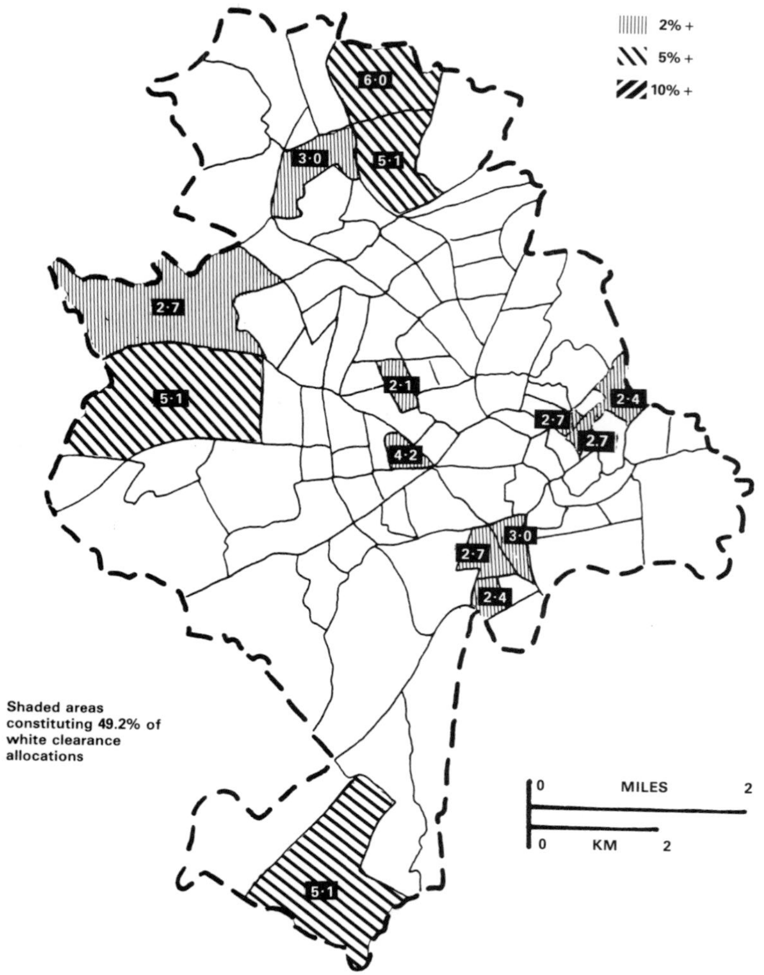

Fig.2.b West Indian Clearance Allocations

Legend:
- ||||| 2% +
- \\\ 5% +
- /// 10% +

Shaded areas
constituting 62.8% of
West Indian
clearance allocations

MILES

KM

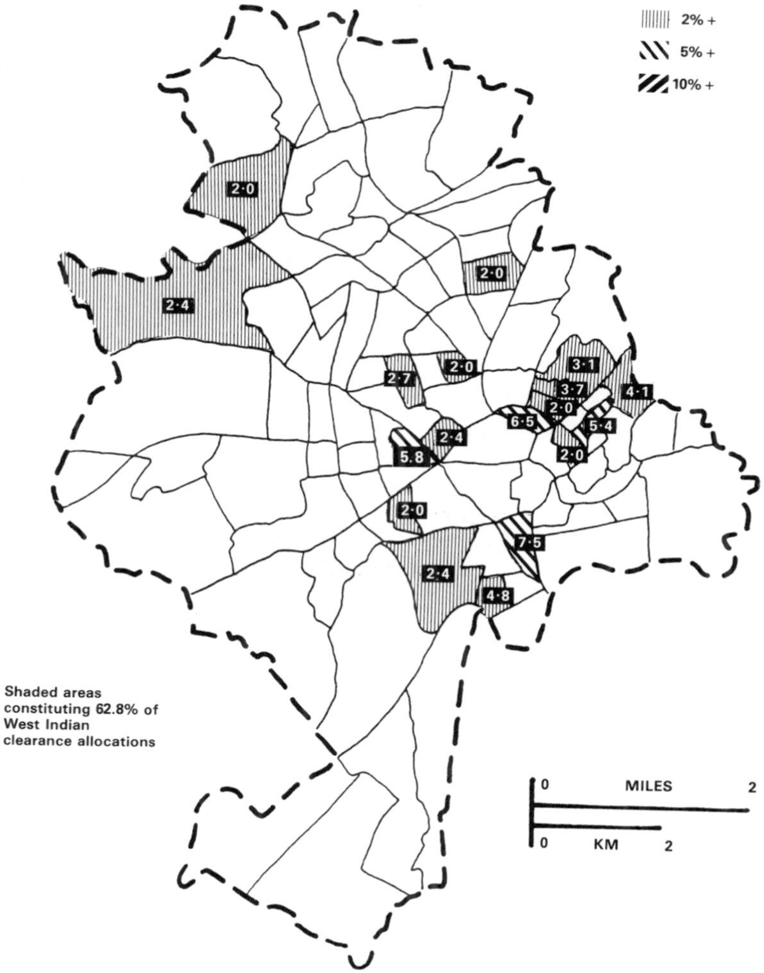

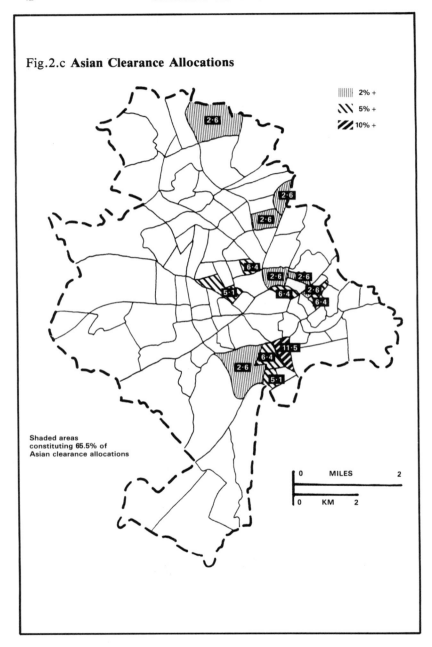

Fig.2.c **Asian Clearance Allocations**

||||| 2% +

\\\ 5% +

//// 10% +

2·6

2·6

2·6

6·4

2·6   2·6

5·1   6·4   2·6

6·4

11·5

6·4

2·6   5·1

Shaded areas
constituting **65.5%** of
Asian clearance allocations

0   MILES   2

0   KM   2

significantly the elderly figured in the pattern of white rehousing.

TABLE 2.2
Personal Code of Allocants from Clearance Areas

	Asian	West Indian	White
Pensioners	1.3	1.0	28.5
Handicapped	—	—	0.9
Check visit advisable	2.6	4.1	7.4
Not Applicable	96.1	94.9	63.2
TOTAL %	100.0	100.0	100.0
N =	78	294	336

The vast majority of these pensioners were allocated to one bedroom flats or bungalows. When this is taken into account the pattern shown in Table 2.1 changes significantly. The proportion of white families then receiving allocations to houses emerged as just less than 90% of their total allocations. In one respect this merely gave further confirmation of the high status of clearance. However, in doing so it also highlighted two other features. First of all, it confirmed that even at the top of the pile white families maintained a relative advantage over black families in gaining access to *houses*. Second, it also showed an increased disparity between West Indian and white clearance allocations to flats complexes.

There is, however, a broad picture of clearance families, irrespective of colour, being allocated principally to houses. Within this, important spatial and quality differences can be identified. Figures 2a, 2b and 2c outline these broad patterns of clearance movement of the 3 different ethnic groups.

Quite clearly the patterns of movement under clearance differed considerably between the 3 groups. The pattern for white households (fig. 2a) was noticably one of movement out to the new housing estates in the north of the city, and to the more established ones in the West and South. Where concentrations emerged in the Central part of the city the actual locations were fairly important. Those areas most commonly understood to comprise the central areas of Nottingham are in fact fairly close the City's eastern boundaries. Thus two clusterings of white allocants in the east and south-central parts of the map represent movement into the new St Ann's estate and various parts of the Meadows respectively. New St Ann's was (and still is) a popular and much sought after new estate. Significantly, the parts which white households generally went to were in the earlier, more settled and more desirable phases.

In amongst the winners — new housing in the Meadows.

It is difficult to say for certain whether movement into the Meadows area was from Meadows people wanting to remain local, or from other clearance areas. Almost inevitably, however, some of this will have represented moves which kept people one step beyond the bulldozer. The nature of our research has not made it possible to trace the full extent and implications of this. Certainly at the time, considerable pressure was being brought to bear upon the local authority by local residents in the Meadows, to give them the right to remain or return there. *The Meadows is our Home*, a detailed and well argued document published by the local tenants association MATAR (Meadows Association of Tenants and Residents), clearly articulated the desire of many local people to remain local. We are, however, unable to say precisely how far rehousing in the Meadows was a conscious and positive response to this as opposed to a convenient staging post for some households in semi-permanent transit.

The two other groupings of white households in the very centre of the map are in flats complexes. Given the fact that the vast majority of flats allocations amongst the white sample were to pensioners it is unlikely that any such moves involved white *families*.

What is also important to note in this pattern of white allocations is that added together these concentrations of 2% or more comprised only 49% of the total white allocations. Much less distinguisable, but no less important, was the general spread of the remaining white allocations throughout a band of intermediate estates in the city whose principal characteristics are those of being stable, respectable and desirable residential areas. Such a broad dispersal amongst these estates was an important characteristic of white rehousing under clearance. This was not reflected in the pattern of moves for either Asians or West Indians.

By comparison, West Indian clearance moves were much more focused around the central housing areas of the city. Very few were involved in the outward movements to the north, south and west of the city. Instead, there were much heavier concentrations of West Indian households in the old and central housing areas. Much of this movement was to areas which were to be affected (in whole or in part) by further clearance schemes, with the Meadows and Radford figuring significantly in this category. It is important to note, however, the significant allocation of West Indian households to the new St Anns estate in the eastern part of the city centre. The spread of West Indian allocations here, was right across the various phases of the estate, giving West Indian families access to the whole range of property types and sites available. If there are to be any reservations about this it can only be on the basis that the heaviest concentrations of West Indian allocations went to those phases which included the much stigmatised St Ann's Phase 10 and an older part scheduled for improvement. In the latter case in particular, the quality of the rehousing will obviously have been largely determined by the effects of the council's improvement programme. However, given the timescale of the improvement programme and the Council's switch of emphasis towards a policy of selling off its housing stock rather than improving it, it may well be that those who moved into such houses expecting imminent modernisation were not always particularly fortunate.

Concentrations of West Indians rehoused under clearance were more identifiable than those of white households. This might simply reflect the wider network of social contacts traditionally attributed to the indigenous (and in this case, white) population, and a greater preparedness on their part to disperse. On the other hand, it could also have been indicative of a greater diversity of housing 'offers' made to white as opposed to West Indian households.

Both of those explanations have to be born in mind when we begin to evaluate the fact that West Indians were rehoused within the central areas at more than twice the rate of white households (a disparity made even more obvious in the pattern of Asian moves).

For Asians (fig. 2c) over 55% of their clearance moves were into/within the central areas of the city. Again there was a significant clustering within the Meadows (in the south) and St Ann's (in the east). St Ann's would have offered the greatest prospect of new housing, but again there have to be doubts about the extent to which allocations in that area were either to the older retained parts or to new housing in the less popular 'Phase 10' part.

TABLE 2.3
Property Age of Clearance Allocations

	Asian	West Indian	White
Acquired Properties			
— New non-estate	1.3	1.0	1.8
— Non-estate	7.7	4.1	6.2
— Inner city non-estate	15.4	6.5	4.2
— Relet inner city non-estate	7.7	9.9	5.1
Purpose Built			
— New	48.7	35.0	30.1
— Post war	11.5	32.3	33.9
— Pre war	7.7	11.2	18.7
TOTAL %	100.0	100.0	100.0
N =	78	294	336

Almost 50% of the Asian and 35% of West Indian allocations under clearance were to new purpose built properies. In addition to this, 32% of West Indians were allocated to post-war estates. Even allowing for the proportion of allocations going into deck access accommodation, this meant that a considerable proportion of West Indian and Asian clearance allocations went to houses which were amongst the most desirable of the council's existing stock. However, the most important qualification about such a picture is the fact that, when deck access allocations are taken out of this analysis, both Asian and West Indian allocations to post-war estates and pre-war estates fell significantly below the rate of such allocations to white households.

The other side of this coin can be seen in terms of the clearance allocation to non-estate properties. 23% of Asians, 16% of West Indians and 9% of whites went to inner city non-estate property of one sort of another. In making qualitative assessments of this we have been hampered (throughout the report) by the council's apparent inability to produce coherent information about the size of its inner city non-estate housing stock and the proportion of it which has been fully modernised. This is despite the fact that such information would seem to be central not only to formulations of its housing policy but also to any meaningful development of its Inner City Programme.

The greater proportion of Asians and West Indians who went to inner city properties, lends some weight to the arguments of those who stress the positive attractions of living within familiar and supportive communities. Such notions may be reinforced by the data breakdown in table 2.4 which shows a larger proportion of both Asians and West Indians being rehoused on parts of the same estate from which clearance was taking place.

TABLE 2.4
Rehousing of Families from Clearance Areas

	Asian	West Indian	White
Same Estate	33.3	25.5	19.9
Adjacent Estate	20.5	28.2	22.8
Further away	46.2	46.3	57.3
TOTAL %	100.0	100.0	100.0
N =	78	294	336

The confirmation in table 2.4 of the greater propensity of white households to move away from their previous area of accommodation and the greater propensity of black households to remain 'local', raises questions about why this should have been so. Such questions are particularly important since roughly half of the 'local' moves by Asian families, and at least a third of those of West Indians, will have been to older properties within the central area — even in this highest of priority rehousing categories. Since this is a pattern which repeats itself throughout all the allocation categories it is worth considering some of the possible arguments which might be advanced as explanations.

i. Family Size — The argument about family size and housing concentration is that post-war building programmes have mainly catered for smaller size family units; that larger accommodation has become concentrated within the stock of older housing; and that this is turn has become increasingly confined to the declining inner city areas. Large families are then compelled to exercise 'choices' within a constrained geographical and quality range of houses in these central areas.

Despite Nottingham's policy, throughout the 1970's of ensuring that 5% of their 'new-build' properties were specifically for larger families, the bulk of its larger housing stock still fell within the central areas. The question then becomes — does such a situation disproportionately and/or disadvantageously affect black families.?

Table 2.5 sets out the differences in family sizes between the white sample and all the Asians and West Indians rehoused from clearance areas during the 3 years of our study. Almost 57% of the white allocations were to one or 2 person households, with pensioners figuring significantly in this. The corresponding figures for Asians and West Indians were much smaller (i.e. 15% and 33%). In the case of 3 and 4 person households the proportions were very similar (i.e. 28%, 31% and 28% respectively). Amongst larger families, however, the differences were again very marked. Only 15% of white families were of 5 or more persons, compared to 54% of Asians and 39% of West Indians). Clearly the shortage of larger properties affected greater proportions of Asians and West Indian families. It must also be said, however, that even with 15% of the white households comprising 5 or more persons, the policy of building only 5% of new properties for larger families looks quite inadequate.

TABLE 2.5
Family Size of those rehoused under Clearance

	Asian	West Indian	White
1 person	3.8	15.3	28.3
2 ,,	11.5	18.0	28.6
3 ,,	10.3	15.3	13.4
4 ,,	20.5	12.2	14.6
5 ,,	14.1	12.2	8.6
6 ,,	12.8	11.9	3.5
7 ,,	16.7	7.9	1.5
8 ,,	2.6	4.5	1.2
9 ,,	5.1	2.4	0.3
10 ,,	2.6	0.3	—
TOTAL %	100.0	100.0	100.0
N =	78	294	336

Since our study dealt with the total black allocations during these 3 years some important inferences can be drawn from these particular figures. The inferences are made all the more important by the fact that these differences emerged *within* the category of clearance allocations. In all the other categories the Allocations Section of the Housing Department has a greater degree of control than under clearance. In other categories, applicants are organised into more or less orderly queues; with allocations being made as and when appropriate properties come available. The actual allocations therefore need not exactly reflect differences in family characteristics between applicants of different ethnic backgrounds. The importance of clearance is that the Authority has no real choice of whom it rehouses. Irrespective of size, all households living in a clearance area at the time the compulsory purchase orders are made, have to be rehoused by the Authority. The picture which emerges from this process (in respect of family size) will be much less distorted by the local authority's own flitering mechanisms.

In many ways it is the extent to which larger families figured in both Asian and West Indian clearance allocations which raises the greatest misgivings about equality of opportunity in council housing. The limited supply and uncertain quality of the city's larger housing stock will then have meant that:

a. large families were considerably restricted in their 'locational choice' of rehousing.
b. both Asian and West Indian families were restricted to an even greater degree than whites if only because of their greater demand for large houses.
c. the concentration of larger priorities within the central areas must have played a large part in both Asian and West Indian rehousing patterns.
d. greater freedom of movement for black families could not have been guaranteed merely by changes in the allocations procedures. (Clearance being in any case the highest priority category).
e. the Authority's building programme, sales policies, contracts with housing associations, and their own council house improvement strategies will have been the major determinants, of the degree of racial disadvantage in this part of its public housing policy.
f. the picture of black family sizes rehoused under the clearance programme may have been more representative of the pattern of all black *applications* for council housing. (The extent to which *allocations* to black families in other rehousing categories differed significantly from this possibly being indicative of the extent to which the council's own filtering mechanisms worked against larger families).
g. any concentration of larger families into older central housing areas will have provided the basis of tomorrow's rehousing problems. The margins of flexibility, for both the Authority and such families themselves, narrowed in line with the contraction of the stock of decent large housing.

Many of these propositions are not solely or wholly confined to the pattern of allocations which emerged from Nottingham's *clearance* programme. They cut across the boundaries of all categories of housing allocation. Whilst final judgement upon their validity cannot be made until we have analysed the total allocations picture, such propositions ought to provide a critical touchstone for our analysis of each of the subsequent rehousing categories.

At this stage however we can at least be clear that family size was an important area of difference between white and Asian or West Indian families involved in the clearance programme. This inevitably had some influence on allocations, and was probably an important deterimant of the spatial pattern of rehousing which emerged.

ii. Employment — it is often argued that black families remain 'local' because of the ties of their workplace. Our own study did not provide us with information which could directly confirm or refute this argument. There are, however, a number of other studies which would suggest that such explanations have a greater place in folklore than reality.

The GLC in their own detailed study of 1976, concluded that:

> "the fact that more white workers moved out of inner London cannot be explained in terms of employment . . . The idea that non-white workers are locked into the inner city because of their employment does not stand up in this case."

> (Parker & Dugmore, 1976, p.46).

A year later, in her report on rehousing from Moss Side, Manchester, Flett took this a step further. Her findings were that:

> "black Moss Siders are *less* likely to work locally than white, and more likely to work . . . several miles away . . . Of the whites, those working locally are more likely to stay local, but for the black sample workplace has no effect."

> (Flett, 1977, p.32).

The nature of economic decline in Nottingham also raises doubts about the attractiveness of the central areas as a focus for employment opportunities. Reference to a local study done in 1978 highlights this:

> ". . . between 1964 and 1975, 18,000 manufacturing jobs have been lost in Nottingham . . . Significantly 64% of the City's manufacturing employment is located in the inner city."

> (Simpson *et al.,* 1978, section 1.4 & 1.6.)

During the period of our current research, the growth in unemployment in Nottingham reduced job prospects of inner city residents even further. Between 1975 and 1977 local unemployment within the manufacturing industry increased by 26% (Simpson, *et.al.*, section 7.7). The particular significance of this decline to inner city residents is that in at least one of the specific clearance areas which we consider later, 42% of those in active employment at the beginning of the decade had been in this manufacturing sector. (Simpson *et.al*, section 7.5). In a study of their own the County Council conceded the disproportionate impact that this was having upon the local black population —

> "For the young immigrant, without qualifications, living in the worst of the inner city areas, the picture is far worse."
>
> (Notts. County Council, 1977, section 2.2).

Given all of this it would seem unlikely that employment ties played a major part in central area rehousing patterns during this period. The only rider to this may stem from the demoralising logic of oppression so graphically set out in Burney's description of Nottingham in 1967:

Home and garden — quality housing in Aspley.

"In the slum districts of central Nottingham not even the wages are enough to give anyone big ideas — and anyway, outside these districts the women could not find the same easy casual employment. The effect is almost uncanny: a slice of old-fashioned proletarian life right next to the tidy commercial heart of the city centre, like a strip of old film cut into a modern 'glossy'."

(Burney, 1967, p.187).

Female employment has always played an important part in Nottingham's economy. However, we were unable to find any reliable source of data on such casual or part-time female employment. Thus, whilst recognising its importance, we are in no position to assess the extent to which this affected either black or white rehousing patterns in providing any positive attraction to central area housing.

iii. Previous Tenure — Suggested links between previous tenure and post-clearance housing patterns appears at best to be somewhat idiosyncratic. Flett, in her studies of Manchester (1977) and Birmingham (1979) found major differences in the relative importance of previous tenure groups.

"Tenure is the most revealing variable we have examined. Whereas most black people stayed local whatever their tenure, with white people tenure was highly significant. The proportions of lodgers staying local are high (almost as high in 1971 as for black people); most tenants and owner occupiers on the other hand moved away."

(Flett, 1977, p.33).

and then two years later . . .

"So lodgers, who played such an important numerical and explanatory part in my analysis of rehousing from clearance areas in Manchester, scarcely feature in Birmingham."

(Flett, 1979, p.26)

Nottingham's picture of previous tenure within the clearance programme was different again.

Unlike Manchester (where 41% of blacks and 32% of

TABLE 2.6
Clearance Areas: Tenure Prior to Rehousing

	Asian	*West Indian*	*White*
Lodgers	7.7	6.8	2.7
Tenant	57.7	77.6	88.7
Owner	34.6	15.6	8.6
TOTAL %	100.0	100.0	100.0
N =	78	294	336

whites from clearance areas were lodgers) the proportion of lodgers in Nottingham's clearance programme was very small. For black families this was smaller even than their significance in Birmingham's clearance programme (11% in 1976). Clearly in Nottingham's case it was not 'lodgers' which was the most important category. Tenants were un-doubtedly the most significant group in the tenure breakdown. Despite this the major difference between Asians, West Indians and whites was largely in the degree of private ownership amongst the 3 groups. Asians were twice as likely as West Indians to be owners and 4 times as likely to be so as whites. Knowing as we do the pattern of clearance rehousing, this may well be consistent with some of Flett's findings in Manchester, that *for whites . . .*

> "most tenants and owner occupiers, on the other hand, moved away."
>
> Flett, 1977, p.33)

It does not in itself however, offer anything which explains the pattern of Asian or West Indian rehousing.

iv. *Previous Housing conditions* — the GLC found that

> "previous housing conditions do influence differential allocation. Households who previously had exlusive use of the four facilities listed (hot water, bath/shower, flush toilet, kitchen) secured accommodation much above standard, while those sharing those facilities secured ac-commodation which was below average. Similarly, households with more than 1.5 persons per room secured accommodation of below average standard."
>
> (Parker & Dugmore, 1976 p.50).

It is easy to see how this happens. The worse your initial conditions, the greater is your need to move sooner rather than later. You are then less able to confidently reject offers, and more vulnerable to the quality of first offer you receive.

Nottingham's coding system pays no attention to previous housing conditions. However, because of the significant dif-ferences in family size between black and white clearance households, it is likely that both Asians and West Indians were disproportionately affected by overcrowding problems. The PEP Reports, as well as studies based on the 1971 Census data (the Runneymede Trust, and the GLC itself) have all clearly established the over-representation of black families

living in houses lacking one or more of the basic amenities.
We were unable to identify anything which would suggest
that this was not equally true of Nottingham. As such, this
too would have had an inevitable (if incalculable) effect on
the pattern of rehousing.

v. Wages — Differences in the wage levels of allocants have
been seen as influencing council house allocations. This is a
complex notion only in that councils rarely have an income
scale which directly defines the property range tenants might
choose from. There may be rule of thumb guides to this in
each authority but these are hard to identify. Harder still is
the identification of subjective assessments by housing
visitors about relationships between the level of income and
the tenant's *attitude* to future rents. (For a useful illustration
of this see Flett, Henderson and Brown, 1978). All that we
were able to do was to examine the wage breakdown of
clearance families in our study.

TABLE 2.7
Clearance Areas: Wage Breakdown (Heads of households)

	Asian	*West Indian*	*White*
Under £20	21.8	22.4	42.6
£20-£30	21.8	21.4	14.3
£30-£40	26.9	34.0	23.8
£40-£50	3.8	1.8	3.3
£50 +	1.3	2.4	3.8
Not known	24.4	18.0	12.2
TOTAL %	100.0	100.0	100.0
N =	78	294	336

Great care must be given to any conclusions being drawn
from this data. In the first place there are opposing biases
which might have lead people into 'adjusting' their wage level
appropriately — i.e. to either conceal some of their actual
earnings or to inflate their earnings so as to be considered for
better quality properties. Second, even though this was the
only rehousing category in which, for analytical purposes,
sufficient numbers identified themselves as being within any
particular wage bracket, there were still large numbers who
chose not to answer this question (or who were never asked).
    All that can be said is that a large proportion of whites

were in the lowest income brackets. This disparity was largely accounted for by the numbers of white pensioners involved in clearance. Apart from these, few differences in 'declared' wage levels emergede as important distinguishing charcteristics between the 3 groups.

vi. Choice — this seemed to be such an important notion that we have devoted a separate section to it later on in the report. What we have done at this stage, however, is examime patterns of stated preferences amongst the different groups rehoused in two specific clearance phases.

Stated Preferences and Rehousing Patterns in Raleigh Street and The Meadows (Phase 3)

Two of the clearance areas during this period proved to be of particular importance to black families, and also provided sufficient numbers of the white sample for a basis of comparison between all 3 ethnic groups. The two areas involved were Raleigh Street and the Meadows (Phase 3); each of which is little more than a ten minute walk, north or south respectively, from the Council House at the heart of the city. In all 120 West Indian and 34 Asian families were rehoused from these areas. Ninety five families from the white sample also moved from there. The actual division between the two schemes is set out below in table 2.8.

TABLE 2.8
Rehousing from Meadows (Phase 3) and Raleigh Street Areas

	Asian	West Indian	White	Area Totals
Meadows (Phase 3)	24	50	62	136
Raleigh Street	10	70	33	113
TOTAL NO.	34	120	95	249

As with the clearance programme as a whole, the bulk of the families who were rehoused were previously tenants, though the proportions of West Indian and white home owners were slightly less than in the general picture for those rehoused through clearance. Again whites were least likely to have previously been lodgers.

TABLE 2.9
Meadows (3)/Raleigh Street — Previous Tenure

	Asian	*West Indians*	*White*
Lodger	8.8	5.0	2.1
Tenant	55.9	85.0	93.7
Owner	35.3	10.0	4.2
TOTAL %	100.0	100.0	100.0
N =	34	120	95

The picture in relation to family sizes was also consistent with the pattern for clearance as a whole. Larger family sizes formed a particularly important part of both Asian and West Indian allocations, with 53% of Asians, 41% of West Indians (as against only 15% of whites) comprising families of 5 or more persons. Pensioners again figured significantly in the white sample but not in either Asian or West Indian allocations.

The type of propery that they received was also similar to the allocations within clearance as a whole. If anything the allocations to houses were at an even more advantageous rate in these two areas. 94% of Asians, 80% of West Indians and 67% of whites obtained houses. However, when the allocations to pensioners (predominantly bungalows, warded aided or flatted accommodation) were excluded from the white allocations it emerged that well over 90% of white *families* were also allocated houses.

TABLE 2.10
Meadows (3)/Raleigh Street — Area of Clearance Movement

	Asian	*West Indian*	*White*
Same Estate	35.3	17.5	16.8
Adjacent Estate	14.7	24.2	30.6
Further away	50.0	58.3	52.6
TOTAL %	100.0	100.0	100.0
N =	34	120	95

The spatial pattern of movement was slightly more complex. Whilst the majority of each group moved further away from their original area, the proportions of Asians and West Indians doing so were greater than under clearance as a whole. For whites it was less so. At the same time white

families were more likely to move to an adjacent estate and
least likely to remain on the same estate. For both whites and
West Indians their rate of remaining on the same estate was
significantly less than the rate for all clearance areas, whereas
for Asians it was slightly higher.

Some of these differences could be seen in relation to the
age and nature of the property they received.

TABLE 2.11
Meadows (3)/Raleigh Street — Allocations by Property Age

	Asian	West Indian	White
Acquired Properties —			
New non-estate	2.9	0.8	2.1
Non-estate	14.7	2.5	4.2
Inner city non-estate	2.9	6.7	3.2
Re-let Inner city non-estate	11.9	15.0	8.3
Purpose built —			
New	52.9	33.3	25.3
Post War re-let	5.9	26.7	35.8
Pre War re-let	8.8	15.0	21.1
TOTAL %	100.0	100.0	100.0
N =	34	120	95

With families in each group having gone primarily to
houses, Asians were distinctly the most likely to have received
new ones. Behind them, roughly one third of both West Indian and white families (once the elderly had been accounted
for) received new houses. The major differences from the
general pattern of clearance movement were quite important:

—more than double the proportion of Asians went to the
   generally better quality acquired non-estate properties outside the central areas;
—in contrast, their movement into recently acquired inner city non-estate properties dropped to almost one fifth of
   their general clearance rate. The bulk of non-estate rehousing of Asian families was therefore to relet property, most
   frequently *outside* the central areas.
—for West Indians the bulk of movement into 'acquired'
   properties was not necessarily to relets in a general sense,
   but to inner city properties where the *emphasis* was upon
   relets. It was their moves into inner city non-estate proper-

ty which marked the distinct difference between West Indians and other groups.

—white allocations to acquired properties were closer to the pattern of Asian moves with the exception that there was no movement to relet non-estate properties in the outer ares of the City which corresponded to the extent of Asian moves there.

—white movement into relet properties was much more significant in relation to allocations to the Council's purpose built post-and pre-war estates.

—Asians generally moved at a far lower rate to post-war and pre-war council housing estates than either of the other groups.

Making the most of it . . . children in Caunton Avenue flats

We wanted, however, to go one step further than this analysis of actual allocation patterns and relate it somehow to 'preferences' held by the families before moving. Within the time availabe to us, the nearest we were able to get to this was an examination of the 'personal' file cards retained centrally within the Allocations Section of the Housing Department. The cards themselves were of a predominantly functional, factual nature; recording details of family size, current accommodation, period of tenancy, etc. There were also sections for information which was less obviously relevant. For example, people receiving unemployment benefit or social security payments had this recorded on their card. Details of any rent arrears in the current or previous tenancies were also recorded. At the most subjective end of the scale there was a chart for recording a 'tenant assessment' and space for additional comments either by the Housing Visitor or other departmental staff. The tenant assessment chart required comments on the *type* of applicant, the state of his or her *furniture* and the degree of *cleanliness* of the property. Under each of these headings Housing Visitors were required to grade applicants into one of five categories — 'good', 'medium', 'supervise', 'poor' or 'not suited'.

In addition to this there was space for details of the applicant's areas of preference (identified as 1st choice, 2nd choice, 3rd choice, etc). and for details of their 'stated requirements'. It was upon this framework that our subsequent analysis took place.

The limitations of such an approach are manifold. To begin with it is totally incapable of assessing or evaluating what happens between the Housing Visitor and the applicant. This is a crucial area, but the general importance of it has only recently been articulated and observed.

> "It is the way, then, in which the visitors culturally perceived the applicant and his/her family that had a crucial effect on the nature of the visit, and also on the visitors comments recorded on the application form . . .
>
> In general, the nature of the visit and the visitors comments recorded on the application form depended on the sympathy which the visitor had with the applicants situation."
>
> (Flett, Henderson & Brown, 1978 p.11 and 12).

The study in Birmingham upon which these comments were based has at least begun to help that Authority appreciate the broad (if unconscious) cultural bias which had become embedded in the work of Housing Visitors — asking to see Asians' passports; 'marking down' different decorative tastes; frowning upon 'deviant' family structures (i.e. the extended family, the single parent family); 'pulling up short' where communication difficulties arose; and often failing to supply the necessary information upon which real choices

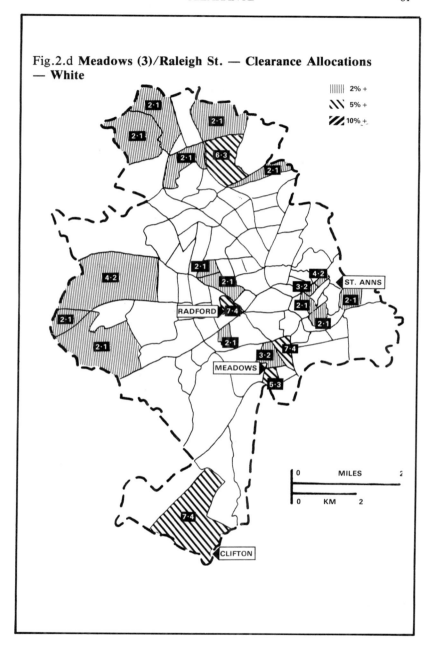

Fig.2.d **Meadows (3)/Raleigh St. — Clearance Allocations — White**

Fig.2.e **Meadows (3)/Raleigh St. — Clearance Allocations — Asian & West Indian·**

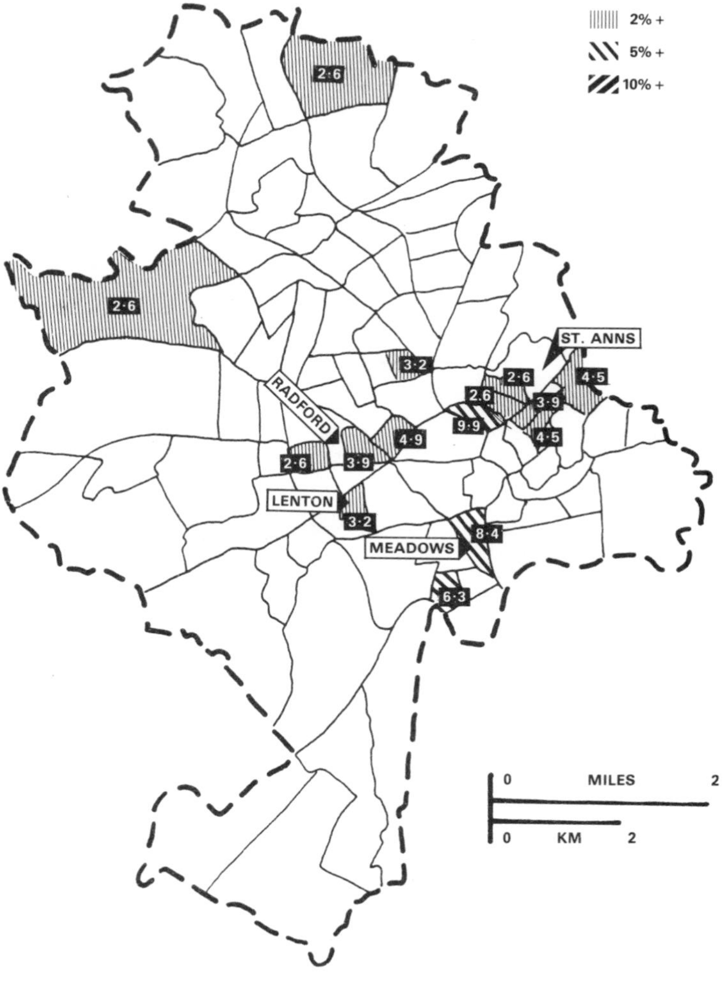

could be made by applicants. It is doubtful if any housing authority escapes such practices. They have grown up less through overt racism than the mono-cultural basis of housing departments working in increasingly multi-cultural urban areas. Personal file cards of any sort offer no real basis for evaluating this in action.

Quite apart from any such status grading done by Housing Visitors we were completely unable to assess how far other Departmental pressures inclined them to influence the actual preferences expressed by tenants. From an earlier survey done in Manchester, we were aware that Housing Visitors quite possibly encouraged tenants to express preferences which they were not committed to and/or the Visitors failed to accurately record the actual preferences which were stated:

> "... when we asked people, three months later, about their preferences, less than three in five said they would make the same choice that they had made during the Investigation. Moreover, when we checked what the Investigator had recorded against what the household told us they had asked for, we found some differences in two out of five cases."
>
> (Bull, 1971, p.13).

Such situations are clearly as vulnerable to the inconsistencies of tenants as those of Housing Visitors. Weighing this, without witnessing the interactions themselves, can be little more than speculation. Going through the 'personal' cards, however, we were struck by the number of times we came across comments such as '. . . would consider Balloon Woods' (a somewhat unpopular flats complex). We were by no means clear how such comments might have been arrived at. On the face of it there seemed to be a much greater likelihood that such a proposition would have arisen from the Housing Visitor than from the family being interviewed. At this stage, however, we would be content merely to register this as an open issue, in which important differences about perception and influence have yet to be clarified, let alone ironed out.

At a more mundane level, one of the other limitations of this exercise resulted from gaps in the data. Thus, 8.8% of Asians in the sub-sample were untraceable. So too were 7.5% of West Indians and 3.2% of the whites. The most likely explanation of the missing data was loss arising out of the age, bulk and complexity of the filing system itself (a defect which the Department is in the process of rectifying).

In analysing the data which was available, the pattern of Asian preferences so closely followed that of West Indians that we decided to put the two together and concentrate on a direct comparison between black and white stated preferences.

The first thing that we did was to take the stated 'first' preferences of all households in the sub-sample. Then, separating the votes for different areas into black preferences and white preferences, we were able to see how far the different groups sought moves to similar or different parts of the city. Set out below are details of the four most 'preferred' areas for each group.

TABLE 2.12
Meadows (3)/Raleigh Street — stated 'first' preferences

Area Popularity	Black	White
1	St. Anns	Meadows
2	Meadows	Radford
3	Lenton	St. Anns
4	Radford	Clifton
Combined % of all 1st preferences	61.7%	61.8%

Before commenting upon the most popular areas of preference some mention must be made of the preferences *not* outlined in Table 2.12. The remaining 40% of declared preferences of each group were similar in both their range and dispersal. In all, 19 areas of preference were cited by white households and 21 by blacks. Apart from the 4 most popular locational preferences expressed, no other single area was of particular significance for either group. Both groups expressed only limited desire to move to the new estates in the north of the city, although some interest was expressed by white households in moving to the highly prestigious Wollaton Estate in the west. Interest in the settled estates surrounding the central areas was similar in both groups. On the other hand there was a slightly greater interest declared by Asians and West Indians in the more central areas of Forest Fields and Hyson Green (though no interest was expressed in any of the flats complexes).

Where the wasteland ends . . . Raleigh Street during redevelopment.

The most significant feature to emerge was in the similarity of the most popular choices declared by both black and white households. With the exception of Clifton in the white 'top four', all of the areas were inner city ones. Each of these central areas were mixtures of purpose-built estates and council 'acquired' properties — although St. Anns was primarily a new and very large housing estate, and the Meadows was in the process of following suit. Clearly in terms of stated preferences alone there was little which supported our earlier proposition that whites saw advancement in terms of abandoning the central areas. On the contrary, *whites expressed almost as great a desire to remain local as blacks.* In doing so they undermined the most simplistic explanation of the differential allocation patterns.

That such differential patterns existed can best be seen from figures 2.d and 2.e, showing the *actual* moves which were made by white and black households respectively. On the one hand the major areas of preference are clearly identifiable in the distribution of both white and black moves. For white households and pattern of movement in fig 2.d identifies St. Ann's, Radford, Meadows and Clifton as major focal points for rehousing. Such concentrations were,

Older housing in the Meadows.

though, balanced by a more general and dispersed movement out of the central areas.

In the rehousing of black households Radford, St. Ann's and the Meadows were again clearly visible in the pattern of allocations. The surprising thing was that greater proportions of black households moved there than had declared any desire to do so. In addition, little could be gleaned from fig. 2.e of the proportions of blacks households declaring an interest in moving to houses in the intermediate or outer housing estates.

Such figures then suggest a picture of white families being much more outwardly mobile than black ones. When we tried to relate this to stated preferences however we discovered that outer estates (such as Top Valley, Highbury Vale, Clifton, Edwards Lane and Bulwell) appeared amongst black first preferences in much the same sort of proportions as they had in white ones.

What emerged as being of potentially much greater significance was that more than 90% of black families received allocations in the central areas of Nottingham *whether they asked for this or not.* Some information as to why this might have been so, emerged when we attempted to relate declared preferences to acutal allocations.

TABLE 2.13
Meadows (3)/Raleigh Street — Allocations in Relation to Preferences

	Blacks	*Whites*
1. — % rehoused in area of 1st choice	51.3	56.3
2. — % refusing offers in order to obtain housing in area of 1st choice	39.0	54.0
3. — % going to areas *not* of their choice	27.8	24.0
4. — % accepting 3. without any refusal	62.5	68.5

The most immediate impression to come from Table 2.13 is the broad similarity in the figures for both black and white households. The high proportions who received allocations in areas of their first choice confirmed the high priority and positive advantage conferred upon people rehoused within a clearance programme. From this it appeared that relative disadvantages between blacks and whites *within* this category were 'small beer' compared with the disparities in treatment between clearance and other categories.

Having said this, whites were slightly more likely to obtain their first choice than blacks. A partial explanation of this may be that whites were much more prepared to reject offers in order to get the accommodation that they wanted. In many cases such refusals were *within* the area of their first choice. This may also have reflected a broader understanding amongst white tenants of the extent of their rights to choose. Additionally, (or alternatively) it could have reflected the stronger initial bargaining position of whites — less likely to have been living in housing conditions where *any* offer might have been considered 'to good to refuse'.

Such reasoning must also be applied in respect of those who were rehoused in areas which were *not* amongst their stated preferences. Black families were marginally more likely to be rehoused outside their areas of preferences than whites (28% to 24%). However, whites were more likely to accept this without making any refusal. Our first inclination was to see this as a reversal of the successful first choice situation — with white families displaying a more passive acceptance of their 'lot'. On examination this proved to be a wholly inadequate explanation. Real differences emerged amongst those who accepted first offers outside their areas of choice.

The majority of the white families received offers of good (frequently 'new') houses which correspond to their 'house' requirements though in a different (but equally high status area). The remainder of white families accepting unrequested offers were the exact opposite. There were all families graded, at best, as 'medium/medium/medium' and were either receiving DHSS payments of one sort or another and/or classified as 'check visit advisable'. Because of the demands already being made upon Housing Department staff, it was unlikely that this could have brought 'support' mechanisms into operation within the department. Rather it was more generally taken to identify families which were likely to present management problems to the Authority. All such families were offered, and accepted, poor quality accommodation.

For black families in this group the picture was slightly different. Though they received a mixture of 'gradings' the properties they were allocated were of the generally poorer quality. Families graded as 'good/good/good' appeared to fare no better than ones with lower ratings. There was, however, some pattern to this.

Some of the black families were certainly graded as no more than medium quality tenants. As with the whites, some were also on DHSS payments and/or had rent arrears. Along side these (though occasionally overlapping) were the tenants with better grades but 'deviant' family structures. Larger families and (to a lesser extent) single parent families were the most noticeable group with good grades to receive poor properties.

One example graphically illustrated the difficulties confronting the department even where it wanted to act promptly and positively. One black, seven person, family with two of their children being mentally handicapped, had their case taken up by the Social Services Department. The problems arising from their existing accommodation brought forth an intervention by Social Services in August, 1974, urging rehousing as a matter of great priority. The housing department concurred with this and instructed that an offer be made as soon as possible. That the family were highly graded and were in any case seeking central area rehousing ought to have made the matter that much easier. As it was, the first offer came 9 months later. Even though this offer was of a large house (centrally heated), the property was old and unmodernised. The offer was rejected. Two months later the family agreed to consider a move to anywhere in the city. They were quickly offered a large, good quality house in one of the outlying estates. This was accepted. It was, however, another 3 months before the council were in a position to make this house available. Thus, despite being in the highest category for rehousing, and having additional (official) support from both Social Services and Housing, *it still took some 14 months for the Department to make available the first good quality, large house it could find.*

We need to remember that this was so for a family classified as 'good' tenants, whose urgent need for rehousing had been acknowledged, and who had eventually agreed to consider a move anywhere in the city. If this was the sort of difficulty faced by the Department in providing decent large houses (for rental) then, for the Council as much as the applicants, the notion of housing choice becomes, not so much constrained as emasculated.

This provides an important additional perspective on one of the conclusions reached by the GLC in relation to the working of their own allocation processes. They noted that,

> "the most interesting finding is that the average quality of first offers accepted is significantly lower for the non-white applicants than for whites in all applicant categories except the homeless. It is the quality of the first offer which is the all important factor."
>
> (Parker & Dugmore, 1976 p.56).

In so far as this also applies to Nottingham, two important variables have to be assessed in terms of their influence upon 'tenants choice'. In the first place we need to bear in mind the influence that housing department officials might themselves have in manipulating choices expressed by applicants. (This would have to include an examination of the value judgements upon which such manipulation is based.) On the other hand, however, this has to be weighed against the extent to which housing officials are themselves constrained; being unable to offer properties which simply do not form part of the council's housing stock.

Since it has only been in two selected areas of clearance that we have had access to information about offers and applicant preferences, we are no position to say whether the GLC observation applies in equal measure to Nottingham's allocation policies. However, what we do know is chat within these two clearance schemes, black families were to some extent more likely than whites to accept the first offer made to them. If this was a general feature of the allocations process in the city, then the nature of first offers will have been no less significant in Nottingham than it was for the GLC.

As it was, the nature of offers made to black and white families, respectively, appears to have had a considerable influence on the different patterns of movement which resulted. Concentration of black families in the central areas and the movement of whites outward could not be adequately explained without reference to the offers they received from the Housing Department.

Within the whole category of clearance allocations, however, it is important to remember that such differences were limited. Their significance lies mainly in the extent to which small scale disadvantages at the top of the pecking order for council housing, established a pattern of racial disadvantage which was to become more obvious and pervasive in categories of lesser priority.

Summary

In national terms, Nottingham's clearance programme began quite late and was still in full flow by the mid-1970's. Of particular significance was the completion, during our research period, of large numbers of new houses in both the St Anns and Meadows areas of central Nottingham. These offered considerable opportunities for families to remain in or near familiar areas whilst at the same time obtaining new houses to live in.

The high status of clearance re-housing was reflected in the fact that almost 90% of white and Asian re-housing was to *houses*. Whilst 75% of West Indians also received houses through the clearance programme, they remained at an important relative disadvantage. When such allocations were broken down further — to identify age and locational differences — blacks (both Asian and West Indian) obtained new or post-war houses at a lower rate than whites.

In part this was accounted for in family size differences. With 54% of the Asian allocants, 39% of West Indians, but still only 15% of whites, comprising families of 5 persons or more, the disparities in family size were wider than in any other re-housing category. As a result black clearance households, despite their priority, faced re-housing choices which were directly limited by the amount, quality and location of new properties which Nottingham had produced for larger families. The limited amount of such larger housing which Nottingham possessed was clearly insufficient to meet even the needs of white households, let alone those of West Indians and Asians.

Evaluating the impact of other variables proved particularly difficult. Employment ties offered little to account for differences in black and white re-housing patterns. So did declared statements of income levels. Apart from family size differences, the only other obvious distinction between black and white clearance allocations, was that Asians were twice as likely as West Indians (and four times as likely as whites) to have previously owned their own houses rather than rented them. As a group, clearance households obviously benefited both from the rate at which clearance was being organised, and by the quality and location of the new properties being built. However, not all of this picture offers unqualified optimism. Greater proportions of both Asians and West Indians went to predominantly older, central area housing which the council had at some time acquired. It is not at all clear how much of this remained unmodernised. Similarly, although the numbers were limited, there were disparities between the rates of West Indian and white allocations to flats complexes.

From the limited examination of stated preferences which we were able to undertake it became clear that, whilst no desires for flats complex accommodation were expressed by any of the groups, the majority of both blacks and whites expressed a preference for remaining 'local'. In fact the complete patterns of housing preference expressed by both blacks and whites were remarkedly similar. This included the specific concentrations of area preference as well as the range of more dispersed preferences set out by the differnent groups.

What did emerge was the fact that 90% of the black allocants were re-housed centrally *whether they had re-quested it or not*. Both the distribution of housing stock and the workings of the allocations procedures need to be considered in attempting to account for this. Within the arena of 'choice' it appeared that whites were slightly more successful than blacks, although the general success rate for both was high (56% of whites and 51% of blacks going to housing in their first choice area). Where housholds went to areas unrelated to their stated preferences, very different patterns emerged. Amongst white allocants, households with 'good' grades went to good quality houses which met their specific housing requirements, albeit in different (but equally popular) estates.

The white allocants who went to poorer properties were generally those given 'poorer' grades by the Department and/or who had some record of rent arrears. For black allocants the gradings did not appear to have the same relevance. Those going to areas not of their choice, generally went to poorer properties irrespective of the grades they had been given. What did seem to be the case was that 'good' black families re-housed in this way were often the larger families from within the particular clearance areas. In part this must reflect the general difficulties over the supply of large, good quality accommodation.

What was absolutely clear was that the expressions of individual preference did not effectively correspond to the actual pattern of clearance re-housing. In the top priority re-housing category, where the general quality of re-housing was extremely good, such disparities have to be assessed with caution. However, accounting for them, particularly in respect of black families with 'good' grades, cannot adequately be done without examination of both to the distribution of the council's housing stock and its mechanisms of allocation. That black households were more likely than whites to accept the first offer of re-housing which was made to them, illustrates how critical is the quality of this offer in determining the pattern and nature of eventual re-housing.

Transfers

3

Transfers and Exchanges

The workings of a local authority's transfers and exchanges mechanisms throw a great deal of light upon the 'qualitative' factors which come into play during the housing allocations process. By and large, people looking for transfers or exchanges are already *within* the system. Their bargaining positions are reasonably strong by virtue of being existing council tenants, and they will be 'negotiating' a move from a relatively stable and secure housing position. At the same time the tenants, as a group, may be more easily compared in terms of the treatment they receive since all have already passed through the first set of 'eligibility' filters (Gray, 1975) by which the relative worth of prospective tenants is judged before allowing them into the council housing system. Thus, all of those who apply for transfers have at least been recognised as having had a legitimate claim to council housing in the first place.

It is possible, therefore, to examine the working of the allocations process in respect of those already within the council house system to see how far ethnic minorities receive similar treatment to the majority population. Such an analysis would also make it possible to see whether the opportunities open to minorities for 'betterment' once they were in, differed from those available to other council tenants, or for that matter, from those of the remaining black or white households seeking council housing for the first time.

It is important to emphasise that dissimilarity in treatment 'per se' need not necessarily constitute direct discrimination. It might reflect, for example, different ways in which families entered the council house system, or alternatively, the efforts being made by the Authority to redress any such inequalities which this created in the past. On the other hand, it might also be part of the way in which the Council seeks to make use of its mechanisms of 'internal adjustment' to free those types of property for which there is a particular unmet demand.

Within a situation of at least a short term relatively inelastic supply of housing, the ways in which an Authority seeks to use these internal mechanisms of adjustment serves as an important test of the integrity and commitment behind the declared housing objectives and priorities which the council has set for itself. It is also a measure of the Authority's commitment to creating conditions of equality of opportunity in the field of public housing.

Although transfers and exchanges both constitute movement within the system, the similarities in their mechanisms of operation virtually end there. In the case of exchanges the Housing Department has limited control, whereas the system of transfers is entirely determined by the Department itself. Because of this we have examined transfers and exchanges separately, retaining exchanges within the terms of our research brief partly to see how the privately organised movement within council housing worked out, and partly to see in what ways, if at all, the Department was inclined to so arrange its transfers system so as to supplement or counterbalance the movement taking place via exchanges.

a. Exchanges

As we have said, the Council normally has little or no control of the exchanges which take place amongst its tenants. The fact that it keeps detailed records of them is largely a byproduct of the fact that it has to register the change of tenancies which are taking place, and the easiest way of doing this is by using the existing personal records system which operates for all council tenants. The Council could in theory veto an exchange but Nottingham shows little evidence of seeking to regulate this aspect of people's housing movement. By and large the mechanisms for organising an exchange are done privately. Personal adverts in shops and post offices appear to be the most widespread method of communicating a general desire to move into a particular area. It then depends upon how enticing the neighbourhood and/or accommodation being offered in exchange is to tenants in the canvassed area as to whether an exchange takes place or not.

TABLE 3.1
Exchanges as a % of Total Allocations

Type	Asian	West Indian	White
Direct	0.7	2.3	8.1
Deferred	1.3	—	0.2
Multiple	—	—	0.5
Private	0.7	—	1.7
TOTAL %	2.7	2.3	10.5
N =	4	24	125

Table 3.1 indicates that, compared with whites, in numerical as well as proportional terms, very few Asians or West Indians were involved in exchanges during the 3 years 1975-78.

We are certainly not in a position to do more than suggest hypotheses for this under-representation, but the whole area is one which the Housing Department might find it useful to investigate further; not least because it has implications for the working of the transfers system which the council controls directly.

Exchanges are normally bilateral relationships in which (even for multiple or deferred exhanges) the numbers of people coming from a given area or type of property do not exceed the numbers doing in. Given that the Housing Department's own policy on transfers facilitates most forms of movement other than 'like to like' transfers — i.e. between similar properties — it is worth bearing in mind that exchanges probably represent movement *within* categories of property type, size, age, or area as much as *into* them.

Table 3.2 gives us some limited idea of the sort of exchanges taking place at the time. Such a table must be viewed with considerable caution. Because of the limited number of West Indian exchanges we have included the actual members along side the percentages in each sub-category. Asian exchanges were so few that they have been omitted altogether.

TABLE 3.2
Exchange Allocations By Property Age

Property Age	West Indian %	White %
Acquired		
Non Estate	—	5.6
Inner City non-estate	—	0.8
Relet innter city non-estate	16.7 (4)	3.2
Purpose Built		
New	—	1.6
Post-war relet	75.0 (18)	66.9
Pre-war relet	8.3 (2)	21.9
TOTAL %	100.0	100.0
N =	(24)	125

Because of the small numbers of West Indian exchanges no worthwhile comparisons can be made directly with the exchanges undertaken by white households. The figures, in the main, serve only as simple statements. No black households exchanged into a new house; none were to acquired properties outside the central area; the majority of black exchanges were to post-war relet properties. Whilst post-war relets were also the most important sub-category of white exchanges, significant proportions also went to pre-war relets on council estates and (to a lesser extent) to acquired properties outside the inner city.

A sense of space — new St Anns.

Probably the most significant comments we are able to make about the importance of exchanges to black households stems from the 'before' and 'after' picture of the exchanges they were involved in. (See figures 3a and 3b which follow.)

A room with a view — Balloon Woods.

Given that these figures map out the total numbers of black households involved in exchanges, it is striking that there was such an unusual similarity between the 'before' and 'after' situations. Without providing absolute proof, it does lend support to the notion that black households were primarily involved in exhanges with other black households; and quite possibly that any geographical movement emerging in this way was also contained within similar property types.

Even bearing in mind that we were only dealing with a sample of the white population, when we look at their pattern of exchanges, nothing like the same sharpness or starkness emerged. In the first place there appeared to be no such geographical boundaries for movement. Unlike the exchanges affecting black households, white moves were not confined to two of the older inner city areas, to the areas with deck assess accommodation or to the newer estates on the northern outskirts of the city. A far more varied pattern emerged for whites in which the buffer zones of the city (the established and respectable estates which encapsulate the older inner city areas and separate them from the new estate

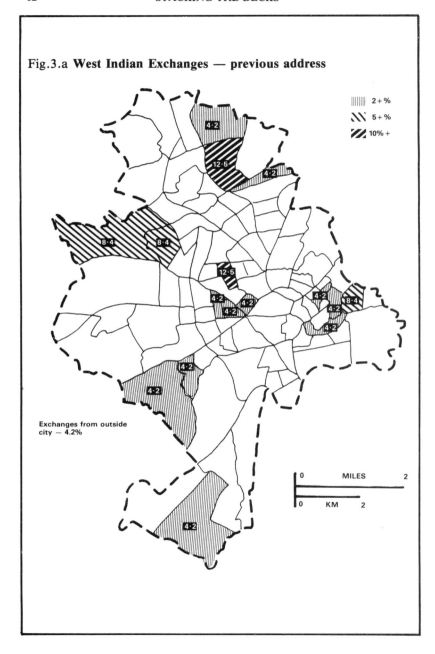

Fig.3.a **West Indian Exchanges — previous address**

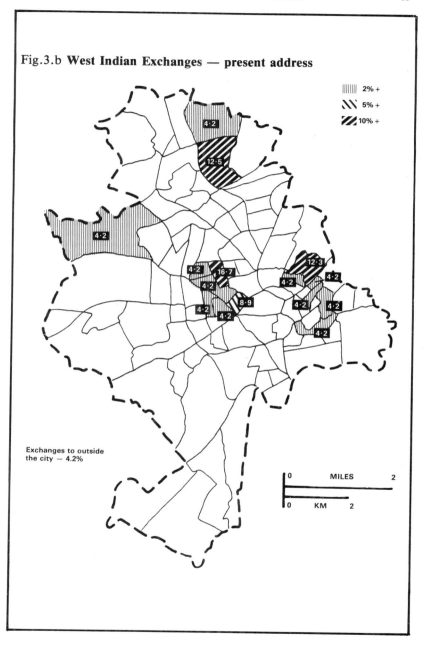

Fig.3.b **West Indian Exchanges — present address**

developments on the periphery) played a far more significant part.

In addition to this, numerical (as well as zonal) concentrations were less noticeable for white households. There was nothin which approached any general inward moving pattern which might be associated with the moves of West Indian households. For whites, the picture reflected a more open and flexible pattern of mobility which if anything, took place within or between zones of comparative high status council housing.

TABLE 3.3

Exchange Allocation by Property Type

Property Type	West Indian %	White %
Aluminium Permanent Bungalow	—	1.6
Deck Access Flats	8.3 (2)	4.8
Deck Access Maisonettes	12.5 (3)	8.9
Flats	16.7 (4)	7.3
Houses	54.1 (13)	71.0
Multi storey flat	—	5.6
Multi storey maisonette	4.2 (1)	—
Short life	4.2 (1)	—
Temporary Bungalow	—	0.8
TOTAL %	100.0	100.0
N =	(24)	125

Almost half of the West Indian exchanges were into flats complexes (irrespective of whether this was within a complex, between different ones or from a house to a flat). Exchanges to houses were in the main restricted to ones on the peripheral estates or to older housing in the central areas.

For white households exchanges to flats were much less significant than to houses. This becomes even more pertinent when related to the location of such houses. Thus, while the white households in our sample were involved in housing moves into, between, or within popular estates, the same could not be said of West Indian moves. Even the houses to which black families exchanged failed to gain them access to such estates. Rather, such housing was either in the peripheral council estates or it was amongst the older acquired housing stock which the Council possessed in the inner city.

Ignoring the argument that, within exchanges, black people are directly discriminated against by a host population still besotted with stereotypes of racial prejudice, an important pattern of inequality can still be identified in the workings of these exchange processes. Bearing in mind the generally limited numbers involved in exchanges, two very different sets of experiences can be catalogued. On the one hand there were those offering good quality housing in the more sought after parts of the city. On the other there were those seeking exchanges from poorer housing and/or from less desirable areas.

Given the 'like to like' basis of exchanges — in which the status 'gains' of a move for any household are very limited — the strength or weakness of each houshold's starting position becomes crucial. Even from the limited data above it is clear that, as it stood, the system of exchanges offered black people no real prospect of breaking out of the cycle of poor housing in which they were confined. It is against this that the more substantial data relating to transfers must be weighed — if only to assess how far the Department's direct control of moves within the system sought to redress such disadvantage.

b. Transfers

Unlike exchanges, transfers within the Council's housing stock offer the Authority a direct means of manipulating the existing pattern of stock allocation. It can use the transfer policy as a way of responding to changes in public demand for housing and/or to reinforce any shifts in its own system of priorities.

In terms of the various steps involved in the transfers process, Nottingham seems to have followed a roughly similar course to many other Authorities. In her study of Harlow, Niner spelt this process our very clearly:

> "All tenants seeking transfers fill in an application form, though it is stressed that this gives no automatic right to transfer. On the basis of information on this form, an interview/inspection, a doctors report where appropriate, and a check on the history of the tenancy, the Transfer Officer must decide which cases to refer to Central Office for allocation. For the tenant, Area Office referral is an essential step towards a transfer. For the local authority this is the first step in determining both

transfer eligibility and priority. The decision seems to be taken after consideration of the tenants need to transfer, his eligibility for transfer in the sense of meeting basic conditions for decorative standards and rent payment, and the wider context of local authority letting requirements."

(Niner, 1980 p.4).

Whilst such processes do not determine where within the hierarchy of priorities transfer applications actually come, they do set out the imporant role that the Transfer Officer (the equivalent of Nottingham's area based Housing Officers) has in the process. The actual significance of this role is something which we return to later.

There appears to be an even division throughout the country between Authorities which operate a formal points system for deciding on priorities between transfer applicants, and those which do not. This was highlighted by the Housing Services Advisory Group in 1978. (See para 2, 46 of their report *Allocation of Council Housing*, (DoE) 1978.)

This division reflects some important conceptual differences in the approach to transfers. The formal system allows allocants to know precisely where they stand and enables policy changes to be clearly reflected in terms of the points system. The informal system allows for discretion and flexibility in responding to housing need. Each approach has its own limitations. Flexibility itself raises issues of credibility and accountability:

"While those who have no formal scheme may make transfers impeccably in accordance with need consideration, there is always the possibility . . . of abuse."

(Niner, 1980 p.86).

The importance that such an approach raises in terms of training, accountability and supervision, is something which we also return to later.

In Nottingham no points system for transfers operated as such. All existing tenants were entitled to register for a transfer. The Transfers Section within the Housing Department kept details of all tenant applications which had been forwarded from Area Offices and the properties available at any point in time. The sytem worked loosely on the basis of 'priority categories which were then subject to tenant matching'.

From discussions with Housing Department officials, it appears that the priority categories for granting a transfer at the start of our research worked out roughly as follows:

1. where the properties (for whatever reason) suited the housing department.
2. medical or social grounds.
3. overcrowding.
4. under occupation.
5. families in flats.
6. social preference (proximity to work, etc).
7. 'like to like' transfers.

This order was, however, not a strict one. In addition, some of the categories themselves require explanation. For instance, in the category of 'under occupation', the size of the property rather than the degree of under occupancy determined how much of a priority the transfer application was given. So, where the property involved had four or more bedrooms, the application was generally treated as a higher priority than ones say from families in smaller units, even where the degree of under occupancy might have been the same. This reflected the extent to which the Authority sought to recognise the limited choice of property which was open to larger families. Giving a greater priority to transfers from larger properties, maximised (as far as possible within the existing housing stock) the arena of choice available to larger families. Transfer policy also followed this line in other ways, especially in terms of the Council's approach to elderly council tenants. The current leader of the City Council recently explained that the Authority,

> "did discover that we had a lot of under-occupation of properties, and so the building of warden-aided accommodation was intended to encourage elderly people living in large houses to transfer out of these properties and free them for families."
>
> (John Carroll, Leader of Nottingham City Council, 1980).

This policy of freeing larger properties has to be understood particularly in relation to the policy which was introduced after 1975, of transferring families out of flats complexes. The short term inflexibility of housing stock raised very real problems in making such transfers more than a paper commitment. Again the current leader of the (now Labour controlled) Council summed up the difficulties involved:

> "The Labour group are on record as saying that families with children should not have to live in flats complexes and shall therefore be a priority for decant — but to where? We're short of 4 bedroom houses and it's even hard to build 4 bedroom houses within existing government cost limits."

> (John Carroll, *ibid*).

What must be clearly understood in relation to these two aspects of the policy on transfers is that they have in fact been applied or interpreted very differently over time. The two quotations we have just used refer in part to the policy of the out-going Labour controlled Council in 1976, and its restatement when they regained control in 1979. In the intervening period of Conservative administration locally, it has to be remembered that whilst the warded-aided complexes were already open or in the pipeline, the policy on council house sales made it unclear whether the properties vacated by the elderly were relet to larger families, as previously planned, or sold off on the open market. When we examine the actual data on transfers this is an important point to bear in mind. Although we deal with the impact of the sales policy in a separate section, it is worth registering here a sense of regret that, despite repeated approaches, no one from the Conservative administration of 1976-1979 was willing to comment on this (or for that matter any other) aspect of our reseach.*

Irrespective of which party was in power locally, all priority categories within transfers were affected if there was any evidence of rent arrears. Whilst a clear rent book was not exactly a 'sine qua non' for a transfer it did exert a considerable influence on the treatment you were likely to receive. Its in-

---

*   The approaches made were by letter to the Leader of the Council and the Chairman of the Housing Committee. Both were asked for interview time, both declined. Both were sent copies of questions we were looking into. We invited their comments or observations; none were forthcoming.

fluence has also grown considerably during this research period:

> "at one time transfers were not allowed uhtil the arrears were paid off. This has been tightened up in that now no one is allowed on the transfer list with any arrears, *or with a recent history of arrears.* This means that people are not allowed simply to pay off their arrears in order to get a transfer. However, this ruling is not rigidily applied either in cases of medical transfers or under the policy of moving families out of flats. When we bend the rules in such cases though, we do take account of the new rents which the tenants will face.
>
> A good tenant obviously has a better chance than a bad tenant. Where there has been a history of rent arrears we would be unlikely to direct a family towards high rent property thereby increasing the problems which the family and the Department might face. Similarly, if it was felt likely that the family would damage or abuse the property they moved into, then we would obviously be happier if they were in properties where the cost of such repairs could be kept within manageable limits."

(Malcolm Magee, Deputy Director of Housing, 1980).

This sort of tenant assessment or grading is not a phenomenon which is unique to Nottingham. Such processess appear to be part of the essential character of local authority housing departments throughout the country. In a study of the workings of the housing department in Hull in 1975, Gray concluded, in respect of transfers, that:

> "the major criteria for determining whether the request for a proposed move is granted are the characteristics of the family applying and, in particular, the nebulous factor of the 'status' or 'quality' of the household. The grading of the status of a household is related to the officials' interpretations of the extent to which a household will aid or hinder the Department in carrying out the various management functions . . . Factors such as relationships with departmental officials, police, the social services department, and neighbours, the cleanliness of the house and extent of rent arrears, determine the assessment of a tenant . . . in the majority of cases the assessment of status provided the basis for determining whether an application is successful."

(Gray, 1976, p.39).

This sort of picture has also been confirmed or elaborated upon in similar studies of areas such as Manchester and Birmingham. The problem about this kind of information is that although it is an important part of the workings of a housing department, it is extremely difficult to quantify its impact. Nor is it as straightforward as the above quote might imply, for it is not confined to decisions as to whether an application is succesful or not. It also relates to the *quality* of allocations received by those who are granted a transfer. The process of tenant grading does not restrict itself to a simplistic division of applicants into 'deserving' and 'undeserving' categories. The gradations continue even amongst those who are successful; resulting in high status tenants receiving better quality housing and low status tenants being restricted to less desirable properties. By its very nature this builds in a differential rate of advancement up the ladder of Council housing; a process which is based increasingly upon tenant status rather than housing need.

Although quantifying the impact of this is virtually impossible, what we can do is to examine the result of transfer allocations in Nottingham during the 3 years of our study to see whether any identifiable disparities emerged, and if so whether they appeared to have any racial or status charcteristics. In doing this, two additional problems have at least to be understood. In the first place Nottingham has never kept detailed ethnic records or transfers *applications*. Any reference to race only emerges (on record) at the point of allocation. Thus we were unable to obtain any data about the racial characteristics of the outstanding transfer applications. Such information might possibly have explained a great deal about the differences in family characteristics, status, geographical dispersal, and existing housing conditions of all such applicants. As well as causing us some difficulty, the absence of this kind of data would appear to make informed foreward planning within the department somewhat limited.

The second complication about Nottingham's procedure for transfer allocations is that, so far as we have been able to determine, transer applicants were hardly every formally rejected. In itself this could have been simply a tribute to the Department's flexibility. However, in the absence of any details of those with outstanding transfers applications, and their length of waiting, it also increased the risks and fears about chances of unpopular, 'undeserving' or ill-informed applicants being marooned within the filing cabinets of the

Housing Department.

In many ways the scope for personal discretion by staff in the transfers section in their treatment of applications was illustrative of, rather than an exception to, the way in which the allocations system works.

> "Matching tenants to their dwellings in allocation is a major art of housing management. It is an art, and not an exact science."
>
> (Niner, 1980 p.11).

> "Since the system relies on personal judgement rather than rigidly applied rules there is obvious scope for personal differences. While the system itself does not inevitably mean that applications will be treated differently in different areas, it does little to ensure that such disparties do not arise."
>
> (Niner, 1980 p.10).

Such a process always leaves applicants perilously vulnerable to the idiosyncracies of Housing Department officials. One way in which this vulnerability aroused continuing hostility from tenants, was in that aspect of the allocations process which was itself peculiar to transfers. Each tenant was visited before any offer was considered, and they were advised, on the basis of this visit, as to whether they had to redecorate any (or all) of their existing property before a transfer would be sanctioned or forthcoming. This was the only allocation category in which such a requirement existed.

Looked at through the eyes of the Department it is perfectly understandable that his should have been so. Good management practice dictated that the number of voids (properties standing empty at any point in time) should be kept to a minimum. Properties in states of disrepair and/or poor decoration involved time and money being spent on them (as well as loss of rents) before they could be brought back into public use after a tenant had moved out. In this respect, Nottingham's approach to transfers appeared to be similar to that more formally identified in Harlow, where it was. . .

> "Council policy that transfers should only be given where the dwelling to be vacated is in a state of decoration allowing it to be immediately relet without further work."
>
> (Niner, 1980, p.6)

On the other hand such a policy unduly favoured those already in good quality accommodation and imposed additional pressures upon those in poorer Council properties. Apart from this the actual amount of choice involved in the allocation process was, as ever, limited within the boundaries of the family characteristics (and aspirations) of the applicant, the available housing stock, and the dynamic which existed between the applicant and department officials.

It was within this framework that we examined the ethnic breakdown and pattern of transfer allocations which took place in Nottingham.

TABLE 3.4

Transfers As Part Of The Total Allocations

	Asian	West Indian	White
Numbers involved in Transfers	3	158	298
Transfers as a % of each group's total allocations	2.0	14.8	25.2

Table 3.4, above, illustrates something of the significance of transfers for the 3 different ethnic groups. The most striking feature is the extent of disparities which emerged. That only 3 Asian households in the whole of the 3 year period received tranfers, is not something which can easily be discounted or ignored.

The explanation most readily advanced for this rests on the assumption that Asians have avoided council houses; preferring instead home ownership or living with other Asian families. Such an argument proceeds to suggest that, in the main, Asians only reluctantly become council tenants as a consequence of clearance programmes. To that extent Asian council tenants have been untypical and so unlikely to apply for transfers in the same way as West Indian or English tenants.

That Asians were relatively uninterested in becoming council tenants was certainly an assumption of Nottingham's Town Clerk and its Director of Housing when they gave evidence to the Select Committee on Race Relations and Immigration in 1971,

"one feature of immigrant housing attitudes, whilst not being based on any factual evidence, is that West Indian immigrants appear to look upon Council housing in much the 'conventional English manner' and

the Asian population tends more to look to owner occupation.''
(Nottingham City Council, 1971 p.3).

It is true that large numbers of Asians only came into consideration for council tenancies at the time of Nottingham's clearance programme. However, our own figures suggest that most Asians then affected by the clearance programme did look to the council for rehousing. By 1976 the council itself seemed to have tacitly accepted that there had been such a shift.

"Experience has shown that over the last few years the proportion of families making their own arrangements . . . (for rehousing) . . . has dropped considerably. For the purpose of forward programming it has been assumed that *all** occupants of clearance areas will require to be rehoused by the council."
(Hammond, Nottingham City Council, April 1976, p.6).

Since the period of our study followed on so closely to the significant movement of Asians *into* the council house system via clearance rehousing, it is possible that very few families could then have been prepared to contemplate another move by way of transfer. Thus, it is possible that the traditional assumptions about Asian families not being in public sector housing could account for their lack of involvement in transfers at this point in time. However, any subsequent analysis of transfer allocations in Nottingham which revealed a similarly low level of Asian involvement would raise serious questions about the extent of direct and indirect discrimination against them in the transfers process.

Ironically, if the Council's 1971 assessment accounted for the position of Asians, it also raised doubts about the small proportion of West Indians who received transfers. It would have been expected that a group which, in 1971, was already seen as having a traditionally English approach to council housing would, by at least 5 years later, be featuring in transfer allocations in similar proportion to white households.

One way of accounting for at least part of the disparity between white and West Indian households receiving transfers may again relate to family size.

*Our emphasis.

TABLE 3.5
Family Size

Family Size	West Indian	Whites
1	5.0	27.2
2	12.7	16.8
3	22.7	25.2
4	19.0	17.0
5	18.4	8.1
6	8.2	1.7
7	8.9	2.0
8	3.2	1.7
9.	1.3	—
10 or more	0.6	0.3
TOTAL	100.0	100.0
No.	158	298

Quite clearly, a large proportion of the allocations to white people went to single person households and, between them, alloations to one and two person white housholds accounted for 44% of their total transfer moves. Given the declared policy of freeing larger properties, and the availability of warden aided accommodation, these figures are not surprising, and seem to confirm that at least one important part of the local authority's policy committment was being followed through.

Equally important, for the West Indian community at least, was the proportion of larger families which figured in transfer allocations. Thus, 41% of all such allocations to West Indian households were to families of 5 or more persons. The fact that this compared with a figure of 14% of the white allocations going to larger families, appeared to reflect the tendency for West Indian families to be larger than white ones. It also suggests that the transfers system offered a positive response to the generally limited choice faced by such larger families in other categories of the Council's allocations procedures.

In order to adequately recognise the impact of transfer policy in respect of the larger families, we sought, for a number of reasons, to take into account the allocations to the elderly. The results, set out initially in terms of a family size breakdown (in table 3.6), are extremely interesting.

TABLE 3.6
Family Sizes (Excluding The Elderly)

Family Size	West Indian	White
1	4.5	9.7
2	11.6	12.1
3	23.2	34.3
4	19.4	24.6
5	18.7	11.1
6	8.5	2.4
7	9.0	2.9
8	3.2	2.4
9	1.3	—
10 or more	0.6	0.5
TOTAL	99.9	100.0
No.	155	207

When seen in relation to each other, tables 3.5 and 3.6 bring out at least 5 clear features.

i. although almost twice the *proportion* of whites to West Indians received transfers, a large amount of the white allocations (almost one third) went to pensioners.

ii. having taken pensioners out of the analysis, single persons were still a higher proportion of white transfers than West Indian ones.

iii. without the elderly, there was a greater disparity between the proportions of small families (3 and 4 person) involved in West Indian and white transfers respectively.

iv. in terms of larger families (five persons plus), whilst the proportion of transfer proportions to West Indian households remained at 41% when the elderly were omitted, the proportion of larger white households still amounted to only 19% of their transfer allocations.

v. that in terms of the involvement of larger families, the tranfers system appeared to offer far more opportunity and access than any of the other allocation categories with the exception of 'clearance'. (This is itself further confimation of its position within the hierarchy of allocation categories).

Nothing useful can be said about the income characteristics of the two principal groups involved in transfers, since 97% of the whites and almost 90% of black households had been classified as income 'not known'. This is not to suggest that income did not play a part in the allocations process. It merely recognises that it did not enter into the record keeping process in any systematic way. Our own work did not extend to sitting in on the interviews or visits done by the Department for transfer applications. Work done elsewhere, however, suggests that assessments of income levels do play an important part in the general assessments made by housing departments of all transfer applicants. In Birmingham, this emerged in respect of assumptions about the ability to pay of each household which applied for rehousing:

> "... the problem of rent did result in a racial bias on the part of most of the visitors. One question the visitor invariably raises is the amount of rent the applicant will be able to afford once they are housed by the Corporation. The question is always phrased in one of two ways; either '... rents are between £X and £Y, is that OK? or, alternatively, '... how much rent can you afford?' Where the visitor put the first form of question the figures quoted were invariably £8-£12 per week. That range was acceptable to the majority of applicants ... if the visitor used the second form of question, a common response from the applicant was '... how much are the rents?' The visitors response to this question depended not so much on how much she thought the applicant was able to afford ... but rather on how much she thought they would be willing to pay ... There was a general assumption amongst the visitors that the Asians were keen to save their money and hence did not want to pay high rents. Where the Asian applicant did not volunteer a sum in the £8-£12 range, the visitors frequently quoted the £5-£8 range. What the visitors never explained was that having the lower rented range indicated on their record, it was possible that they would only be considered for the poorer properties in the Council's housing stock."
>
> (Flett, Henderson & Brown, 1978, p.14).

The extent to which an applicants 'ability to pay' enters into the reckoning (formally or informally) of their standing with the Department, will clearly influence the nature of any offers being made to them. This applies not only to transfers but to every category of allocation which a Department uses. Such considerations were likely to have formed as important a part of Nottingham's assessment procedures as in any other major authority.

Table 3.7 begins to set out some of the detailed result of the transfer allocations which took place. Again, this does not include the white pensioners who received transfers. The vast majority of transfers going to pensioners were in any case to warded aided accommodation, bungalows or flats. Comparison between the two major groups receiving transfers is therefore less distorted by dealing with pensioners separately.

TABLE 3.7
Transfers By Property Type Received (Excluding Pensioners)

Property Type	West Indian %	White %
Bungalow	—	2.4
Deck Access flats	0.6	1.9
Deck Access maisonette	9.1	3.4
Flats	3.9	9.2
House	84.5	78.8
Multi storey flat	1.3	0.5
Multi storey maisonette	0.6	—
Victoria Centre	—	1.9
Short life	—	0.5
Warden Aided	—	1.4
TOTAL	100.0	100.0
N =	155	207

The most striking feature of this breakdown is the large proportion of families who received houses. This supports, to a limited extent, findings from elsewhere that . . .

"location was not generally given as the reason for wanting a transfer .. . the most frequently mentioned reason was the type of accommodation: most tenants wanted houses not flats, and wanted gardens for the children."

(Flett, 1979, p.58).

More tersely, it bears out the locally held assumptions about flats complexes, viz:

"the ambition of most reasonable tenants is to get out".
(Social Services Committee Report (specifically referring to Old Basford Flats)8th August, 1975).

Furthermore, in a local study of two 'problem' estates, one of which was a flats complex and the other a highly stigmatised housing estate, it still emerged that half of the allocations to the housing estates came as transfers wheras only 5.5% of all allocations to the flats comlex came in this way. Further analysis of these figures made the picture even starker. Almost 40% of transfers into the 'problem' estate were from flats complexes, whereas the overwhelming majority of transfers in the flats complex were of households actually moving *within* the complex. That transfers from flats complexes on to a 'problem' estate should appear so acceptable to households is a fair indication of the extent to which such estates:

> "although considered undesirable, rank much more highly than the concrete jungles of the 1960's."

(Tate, 1979 p.83).

However, such explanations of preference ought not to detract from any recognition of the very positive treatment which 'successful' applicants received within the transfers system. The proportion of *houses* going to both ethnic groups was extremely high. Black households in fact gained access to houses at a higher rate than white households. And even though they still went in greater proportions to deck-access maisonettes than whites did, the actual scale of such moves was much more limited than in most of the other allocation categories. Allocations to deck access flats, multi-storey flats, and multi-storey maisonettes were insignificant. Even the solitary allocation of a white household to short life property was illustrative of a recurring feature of our analysis: assuming that the transfer was not an 'enforced' one (in lieu of eviction) the fact that the particular household involved 10 or more persons, shows something of the difficulties which the Department faced in dealing with large families.

TABLE 3.8
Transfer Allocations By Property Age (Excluding Pensioners)

	West Indian	White
Acquired		
New Non Estate	3.9	11.1
Non Estate	1.9	4.3
Inner City Non Estate	5.2	0.5
Relet Inner City Non Estate	3.9	1.0
Purpose Built		
New	32.8	30.5
Post War Relet	32.3	35.7
Pre War Relet	20.0	16.9
TOTAL	100.0	100.0
N =	155	207

The picture in relation to property age to a large extent adds further confirmation of the positive position of those receiving tranfers.

For both black and white households there was a very high allocation to new properties. More than 30% of each group received these whereas in the general analysis of allocations as a whole it must be remembered that only just over 20% of each group went to new properties. Equally positive for black families, was the extent to which they were able to gain access to the pre-war relet properties, generally found on the city's more settled estates. The 20% of such allocations to blacks within this category was more than twice the rate which they generally experienced across all of the allocation categories. For the white allocants, transfers to pre-war properties were consistent with their general rate of access to such estates.

Less reassuring was the detailed breakdown of the allocations to post-war properties. In broad terms it is often difficult to distinguish between houses and flats complexes in this category: the former being largely desirable and the latter being less so. It became particularly significant then that we were able to establish that 25% of all black transfers to post-war estates were to deck access maisonettes in comparison with only 7% of whites. This cannot be easily explained in terms of individual preferences.

Equally complex was the pattern of transfer allocations to the city's 'acquired' properties. The 14% of black transfers and 17% of white ones going into acquired property was similar to the overall picture of allocations to such properties in our study (although the relative percentages were reversed in the latter case). Within these broad figures the pictures changed dramatically. The overall similarity in the proportions of families going to acquired properties divided starkly between the inner city and outer city areas. Black households went to non-estate property in the inner city at a much higher rate than their moves outwards (9.1%:5.8%). The nature of Nottingham's inner city housing stock meant that such non-estate properties would inevitably have been substantially older than that in the outer areas.

In terms of quality, such properties were heavily dependent upon the improvement programme and policies which the City pursued in relation to its own central area stock. Although we consider later the impact of cuts in public spending on council housing, it is worth bearing in mind that, in general, it was the inner city non-estate properties which presented the greatest claims for extensive rehabilitation.

In contrast, non-estate properties outside the central areas tended to be new or part of comparatively recent private developments. It was essentially good quality, high status property; almost the exact opposite of its inner city counterparts. This distinction becomes important when related to the fact that 15% of white transfer allocations went to non estate-property *outside* the inner city whilst only 1.5% went to the inner city. This contrasts sharply with the allocations to black households and is also very different from the *overall* pattern of white allocations to non-estate property (7.5% to the outer city, 6% to the inner city).

Various (conflicting) hypotheses can be put forward to account for this. They include possibilities that:

—allocations directly reflected the status of the tenants (in the eyes of the Housing Department).
—they represented the area preferences of different tenant groups.
—the larger properties sought by black families were themselves principally concentrated in the inner city areas.
—white households were more outwardly mobile than black ones.
—if inner city non-estate properties *were* generally poorer quality ones, black households accepted transfers to them because they still constituted on improvement on their existing accommodation. This would contrast with the notion that white transfers more often began from positions of strength, and consequently families were able to stick out for/demand more desirable properties.

The evidence emerging from this and other studies suggests that, despite the contradictions, all of these factors were probably involved in creating differences in the pattern of allocations between black households and white ones. What cannot be discounted is the notion that, even within this highly favoured category, the position of relative disadvantage from which black families entered council housing in the first place restricted their chances of advancement within it. That black households only received transfers at half of the rate of white households; that they then went at over twice the rate of white transfer allocants to deck access maisonettes; and that they received such a disproportionate share of the older inner city non-estate properties, have all to be seriously considered in terms of continuing disadvantage within the system of council housing.

Unlike the other rehousing categories, transfers involved movement between existing Council properties. Frequently they also involved moves between parts of the city which were covered by different Area Offices. The interactions between tenants, the Allocations Section of the Housing Department and the Area Offices then played an important part in the transfers process. In this scenario, transactions between different parts of the Department would inevitably reflect the different priorities or values which each section worked to.

Nottingham's Area Managers have been encouraged to be 'house proud'. This meant that the building up of 'stable estates' of responsible tenants formed an important part of their value system. Elsewhere it has been found that this often presents difficulties in terms of the way in which tenants are assessed.

"Housing managers are still, in theory, expected to maintain discipline on their estates in accordance with standards set a generation ago; standards that take no account of the increasing numbers of very elderly people, or households of immigrant origin or non-family type among council tenants, or the increasing incidence of family breakdown, working mothers, psychiatric illness, or the 'anomie' that can accompany long term unemployment."

(Popplestone & Parris, 1979 p.8).

Such an approach inevitably results in a favouring the 'proven' better tenants.

"It is normal practice, if a 'very good' standard applicant and a 'less good' one are competing for a very good vacancy, to allocate the property to the higher standard applicant. Such a policy is seen to enhance estate mangement."

(Niner, 1980 p.12).

If we look at the pattern of *previous* accommodation for

Transfers and the holy grail . . . "Most tenants wanted houses not flats, and wanted gardens for the children" (Aspley).

white and West Indian groups in our study, the possible influence of this on the final pattern of transfer allocationss can perhaps be better understood. Figures 3.c and 3.d below map out the different areas of the city and from which successful transfer applicants came.

What is immediately apparent is that West Indian transfers were drawn from a much narrower range of areas than white ones; quite possibly reflecting both the shorter time that they had actually had access to council housing and the limitations in the 'range' of such access points. Closer analysis reveals how constraining this might actually have been. From the picture of previous tenure amongst West Indian transfers it is clear that the four areas from which the greatest proportions of transfers came were all major flats complex areas, with the fifth being one of the older inner city areas. For white households the picture was a very different one. The top two areas from which transfers came were again, flats complexes. However, the proportion of houslholds involved was noticeably smaller than the respective one for West Indians. After this the whole pattern was different. The next four significant areas from which whites moved were all post-war or pre-war *housing* estates. People already in modern (or relatively modern) houses would have been unlikely to even consider possible moves to properties which were other than high status ones. At the same time such tenants were likely to be doubly fortunate in that the Department itself would have been inclined to regard their existing tenure as a confirmation of their being 'good' (and therefore 'deserving') tenants. Such a reaction from housing officials would also have recognised, to some extent, that their own management pro-

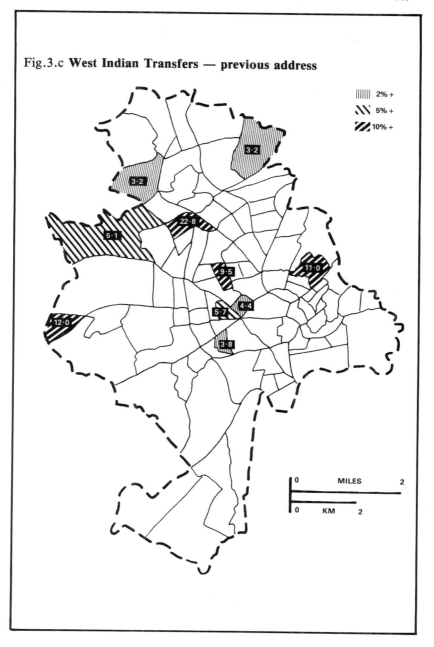

Fig.3.c **West Indian Transfers — previous address**

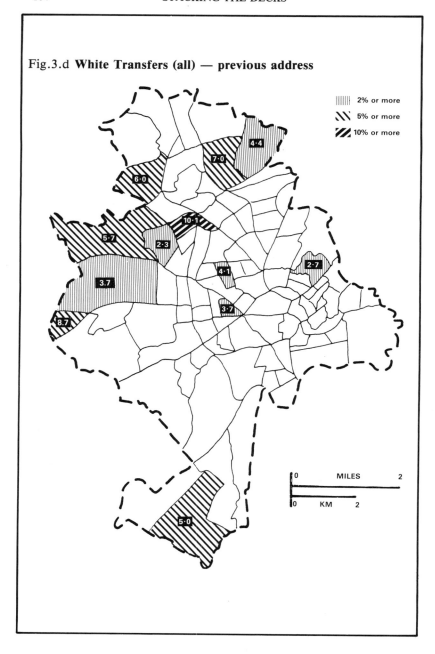

Fig.3.d **White Transfers (all) — previous address**

blems (i.e. reletting vacated properties) were much less when they involved moves from desirable properties than from undesirable ones.

There are, though, limits to what can be deduced simply from an 'initial tenure' analysis of council house transfers. We can be clear about the relative positions in the council house hierarchy from which different groups began. Interpreting the significance of this is more uncertain. For example, that over 50% of black transfers were from flats complexes might be both disturbing and encouraging. On the one hand, it could confirm that in the first instance black households were being allocated, in disproportionate numbers, to flats complexes as their only way into council housing. On the other, it could represent an official recognition that this had been the case and that greater opportunities were consequently being afforded to blacks to move out.

The city's reluctance to keep any ethnic breakdown of transfer *applications'* make it hard to see how any such recognition could have formed a consious part of its transfers policy. Other studies both in Nottingham (Tate, 1979) and elsewhere (Niner, 1980) have confirmed that a much higher than average rate of transfer *applications* are made from 'unpopular estates than 'popular' ones. Although tenants in such estates generally received an above average rate of *allocations*, the *ratio* of allocations to applications from unpopular estates were invariably below the average for the city as a whole. In view of this, a knowledge of the ethnic breakdown of transfer applications would seem to be essential to any transfer policy which purported of offer equality of opportunity.

It cannot be argued that Nottingham's policy on transfers sought (in any conscious way) to identify and/or redress racial inequalities arising out of the initial allocations to council housing. What must be recognised, however, is that at least one aspect of transfers might have done so inadvertently. Given the tendency for black families in our study to be slightly larger than white ones, the 1976 policy of moving families out to flats complexes ought to have been of considerable importance to black tenants. To a large extent this might account for the high proportion of black transfers which were from flats complexes.

This very positive policy was introduced at a time when a much harsher policy was being pursued in relation to rent arrears. A study of one of Nottingham's flat complexes pointed out that:

> "the 1976 decision to allow families with children to transfer out of the flats was ineffectual because many were in serious rent arrears. Families in rent arrears cannot transfer. This Catch-22 situation must be overcome if such a policy is to be meaningful."
>
> (Tate, 1979, p.133).

Two important inferences might be drawn from this. First, the proportions of black families who did come from flats complexes on transfers further undermined any sterotype of black people as poor rent payers. The second inference which might be much more harmful to black families, is that any such firm association between rent arrears and those who are ineligible for a move from flats complexes might only increase other harmful stereotypes being built up about the sort of people who are allocated to such complexes in the first place — irrespective of the lack of choice they might have had in such a move. This becomes particularly important later when we consider allocations from the waiting list. To an extent, even the Housing Department itself recognised the danger of this. During the period of our study, one official report referred to parts of a flats complex which:

> "are known throughout the city, and applicants are becoming more and more reluctant in finding themselves labelled as problem tenants — should they move here."
>
> (Nottingham City Council, Housing Department Report Feb. 1976).

The influence of such stereotyping needs to be seriously borne in mind when considering patterns of actual allocations, whether under transfers or any other rehousing category.

The pattern of acutal transfer allocations to West Indian and white households is set out below in figures 3.e and 3.f respectively.

Again, to compare like with like as far as possible, we have taken the elderly out of the white sample of transfers. The two Figures give a spatial dimension to the data in tables 3.7 and 3.8. A number of important features emerge when they were linked together.

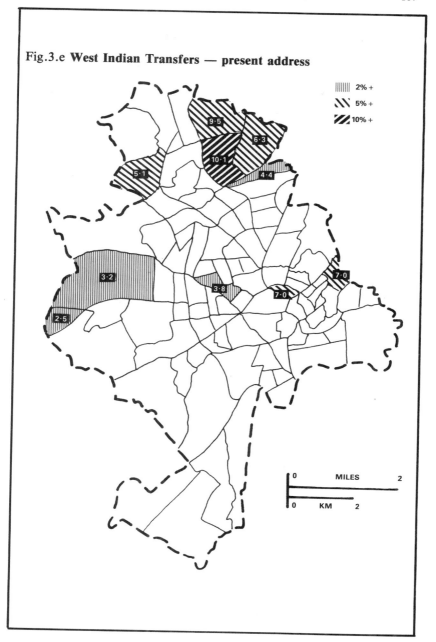

Fig.3.e **West Indian Transfers — present address**

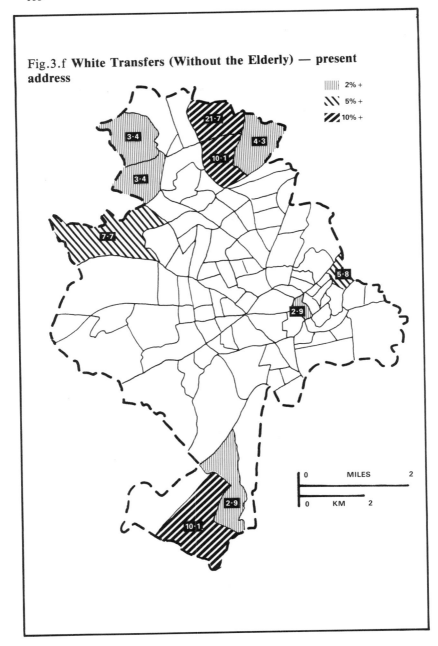

Fig.3.f **White Transfers (Without the Elderly) — present address**

1. for both whites and West Indians there was a marked outward movement through transfers. For white households this represented a distinct abandonment of the central areas.
2. both whites and West Indians moved out of flats complexes in significant proportions and were not replaced there (to any great degree) by other personal households receiving transfers.
3. a greater proportion of West Indian transfer allocations did go to flats complexes but the pattern of these also differed significantly. West Indian households were more likely to go to Central area complexes whereas whites went into complexes more towards the north of the city.
4. 2.5% of West Indian transfers went to the unpopular Balloon Woods complex on the Western boundary of the city.
5. there was no movement of West Indians which matched white transfers to the popular estates of Clifton and Wilford in the South of the city.
6. the most notable areas of transfer movement of West Indian and White households into the city centre were adjacent to each other in parts of the new St Ann's housing estate. It is significant that whereas some 3% of white transfers were to one of the settled earlier phases of this estate, the 7% of West Indian transfers were to new houses in the much less popular 'phase 10' part.
7. the other major concentration of West Indian transfer moves into the Central part of Nottingham was to older properties in the Hyson Green/Radford areas. These areas, though encompassing a number of Housing Action Areas, would have been directly affected by cuts in the rate of improvement of the Council's own properties.

It is in respect of allocations that we also need to build in a specific consideration of the part which transfers to the elderly played in the over all pattern of black and white movement. During this period Nottingham pursued what has generally been described as a "strategic lettings policy" (Bird & Whitbread, 1975) in relation to transfers of the elderly. What this entailed was the moving of non-priority applicants in order to release particular dwellings needed for higher priority cases. In Nottingham this was helped considerably by the availability of a number of new warden-aided complexes.

This policy was in response to a general recognition that the city was short of accommodation for larger families. Amongst the variety of property types, such houses were of particular importance to black families. The importance of such moves by the elderly was, however, not simply in terms of the type of property they vacated, but also its location. Figure 3.g sets out the distribution of properties from which the elderly moved under this strategic lettings policy.

A close examination of this pattern raises considerable doubts about the extent to which transfers of elderly succeeded in freeing properties needed for high priority families. Even within this however, its relevance to the redress of racial disadvantage appears even more obscure.

Virtually all of the moves from the northern segment of the city were from peripheral council estates built comparatively recently. A small proportion of large houses were only ever included in such new developments and since allocations to these estates only began in recent years it is unlikely that elderly people would have been allocated to any of the large properties in the first place. The properties that were vacated were therefore unlikely to have been appropriate for larger families.

This would not necessarily have been true of moves from the western, southern and eastern outskirts of the city. Estates in these areas are much more established ones. In these cases it is much more feasible that elderly transfers could have come from properties originally allocated as family houses, but where the children had now grown up and moved out to houses of their own. What must be said however, is that these were areas to which white families moved with far greater regularity than black ones.

Although we did not have the details of the precise properties vacated there was a good deal which suggested that possibly 10% of elderly transfers were from flats complexes. If the allocations policy in respect of families in flats complexes was being followed through, these would have been of minimal relevance to either black or white priority households.

Fig.3.g **Transfers of the Elderly (white) — previous address**

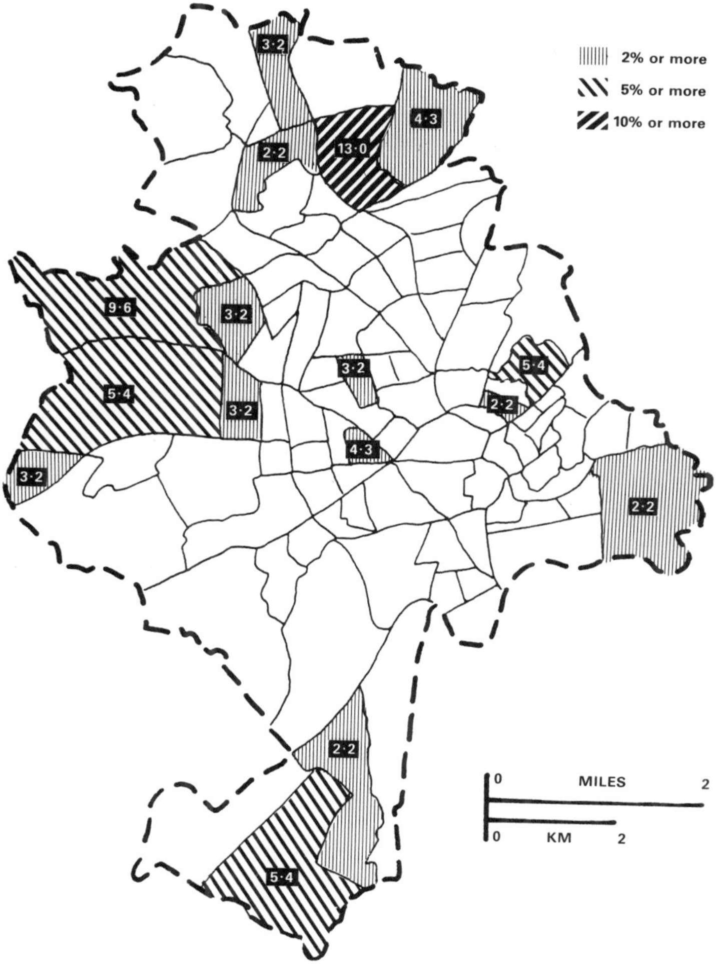

Flats apart, the diversity of properties vacated by the elderly involved in transfers can be seen to have focused around the more established intermediate estates in the city. Whilst these estates did receive allocations of white households they were largely irrelevant to the movement of black people either in transfers or in any of the other allocation categories.

Thus, when we consider the pattern of transfers of the elderly, virtally all of whom were white, it is difficult to see how they did anything more than extend the 'choices' open to other white households during our period of study. Even if we presume that a large number of these strategic transfers of the elderly did in fact free the larger properties, it is clear that they were not in the areas to which, ultimately, black people found themselves allocated in any great numbers or to any great advantage. Whatever the particularly advantages for the elderly themselves (though noticeably not the black elderly) this form of strategic intervention appeared mainly to have helped maintain the strategic advantages of the white community in terms of choice in public sector housing.

Whatever fine intentions the Authority had in pursuing this particular strategy, its workings do not appear to have ever been monitored or evaluated in any significant way. Set up in hope; pursued in naive isolation; the strategic transfers of the elderly did little or nothing to redress racial inequalities in public housing.

Having said that, it is important to restate many of the positive characteristics which did emerge from the pattern of movement under transfers:

—a high proportion of allocants (black and white) went to houses.

—to some extent transfers still catered for the larger than average family sizes of West Indian households, though not to the same extent as under clearance.

—the proportion of transfers going to deck access complexes was low, although West Indians went there at roughly twice the rate of whites.

—a large proportion of both white and West Indian transfers were to new properties or to houses in the pre-war estates.

—the transfers policy in relation to families having high priority for moves out of flat complexes did appear to be operating in a way which was of particular benefit to black households.

—some of the elderly who received transfers came from settled estates, thereby *possibly* freeing houses for larger families.

Families moving in this way did generally appear to do well out of the allocations process. However, huge gaps still remain in this picture which give grounds for some concern.

The positive treatment of those receiving transfers does not adequately explain why it is was that West Indians received transfers at almost half the rate of white tenants. This is particularly important considering how limited was the relevance of the strategic transfers of the elderly to West Indian rehousing patterns. This disparity in the rate of transfers received by black households raises difficult questions about the prospect of both direct and indirect discrimination existing within the Council's transfer process. Pursuing this proved to be extremely difficult because of the absence of records about the ethnic origin of transfer *applicants*. It might well have been the case that the rate of allocations was in line with the rate of appliations received by black people. However, it is as true now as it was in the years 1975, 1976 and 1977, that the Housing Department has no adequate mechanisms by which to judge whether its transfer policy is discriminatory or not.

The dangers of this sort of situation are that it encourages entrenchment. The absence of evidence to the contrary makes it all the more possible for black people to believe that . . .

"they do register our names but we're ignored when the houses are allocated,"
(Lawrence, 1974 p.95).

and for housing officials to argue that 'they're reasonably happy with accommodation they've got'. Within the current climate of race relations in Britain there are strong social (as well as legal) grounds for having a more detailed, open, and up to date means of scrutinising the fairness of an Authority's allocation procedures. The regular monitoring of applications for transfers would be one step in this direction.

The significance of such monitoring becomes even more important if, on examination, it appears that inequalities exist (or existed) in the pattern of initial allocation to council housing. We have already seen some of the difference in allocations between transfers and those under the clearance programme. In addition to this, allocations from the Waiting List and 'Urban Aid' also constituted important points of access, particularly for West Indians. In this particular respect, the policy on transfers will have played an important part in redressing or reinforcing any disadvantage arising from the initial access to the system which waiting list families experienced.

As a gateway into the better parts of council housing, the importance of transfers, to black families in particular, will be seen more fully as we move on to examine some of the differences in council allocations from the Waiting List, 'Urban Aid' and 'Special Case' categories. Then, even without knowing the level of transfer applications from each group, we will at least be able to identify the areas to which families were principally allocated in the first instance, and the consequent bargaining positions from which black and white families might then have begun their pursuit of a transfer. The importance of this initial point of access to the system is quite clear:

"Almost by definition, unpopular areas are typified by above average transfer requests. Since transfer applicants are normally only willing to accept an offer which represents an improvement on their previous accommodation, it follows that there will be a net transfer movement away from these areas, leaving vacancies for new tenants. This has implications for social segregation in two self reinforcing ways. The tenants who leave the unpopular areas are likely to be relatively less disadvantaged than those who remain. Those who leave have aspirations encouraging them to move, and are more likely to know about how the system operates and to have a good record of rent payment and housekeeping, than those who remain . . . The second factor is the selection of 'replacement' tenants in the less popular estates. To speak of choice either for the housing authority as landlord, or for the prospective tenant in these circumstances is misleading."

(Niner, 1980 p.87-88).

Changes in the workings of transfer procedures have distinct limitations. They would not remove inequalities or injustices created by an altogether inadequate building programme, an indiscriminate sales policy, half hearted improvement of older council housing or widespread discrimination

Another way out . . . children in Hyson Green flats.

at the point of access to the system. Without pretending to offer any such panacea, it is however perfectly feasible for transfers to play an important part in *reducing* some of any such inequalities. If, in addition, the relationship between transfers and allocations from the waiting list only appeared to extend disadvantage then there are arguments, which we must return to later, for changing both the workings of the transfers system *and* its relationship to allocations from other categories. Even at this stage we are clear that the workings of the transfer policy in Nottingham were less advantageous to black council tenants than to white ones. The question really is how far such discrimination or disadvantage merely compounded the problems experienced by blacks through their point of access to the system in the first place.

Summary

For those who obtained them, transfers offered a route into good quality council housing. The major issues concerning transfer policies, however, were about who received them and how they related to other aspects of housing allocation.

There was certainly little which linked (or off-set) the effect of exchanges with the policy on transfers in Nottingham. Exchanges did very little to alter the status quo. Those in good housing exchanged with others in good housing. Those in poor accommodation normally only found people who were similarly placed who would be willing to exhange. This had important consequences for the black community.

Their pattern of exchanges had nothing of the diversity characteristic of white exchange moves. In the main West Indians came from (and went to) flats complexes, older inner-city housing, or (to a lesser extent) peripheral estates. Although it is not altogether certain, the similarity between the pattern of black housing prior to exchange and the one after their exchanges might indicate that black families were additionally restricted to exchanges mainly with other black families.

The transfers system which, unlike exchanges, was directly organised and controlled by the Local Authority, introduced inequalities of its own. White households received transfers at almost twice the rate of black ones. That this might have merely reflected the different rate of transfer *applications* from black and white tenants respectively, was not something we could test, since the Authority has never recorded information of the ethnic origin of those with outstanding applications. The absence of such information also meant we were unable to explain why virtually no Asian families were involved in transfers.

Amongst those who did receive transfers, significant differences in family size between whites and West Indians were again apparent. Some 44% of white transfers were to 1 or 2 person households. In contrast, 40% of black transfers involved households of 5 persons or more.

Transfer moves in general reflected a desire for a house and a garden rather than flats. The high priority given to transfers was reflected in the fact that the moves of 85% of the West Indians and 79% of the whites were to houses; almost half of these moves (for each group) being to new properties. Differences in the rate of transfers to houses were, in the main, consistent with the greater proportion of black families with children who were involved in such moves.

The differences in family size were also particularly important in terms of where people were transferred *from*. More than 50% of the black transfers were from flats complexes. This was higher than the proportion of white transfers but consistent with the policy of moving families out of the complexes. Less reassuring was the sense in which, even in transfers, more than twice the rate of black moves were *into* flats complexes than that of whites (12%:6% respectively).

Transfers involving the elderly were particularly significant. This was not simply due to the availability of warden-aided accommodation, but also as part of the attempt to free larger properties for families. As a strategic lettings policy it was, however, never monitored and does not appear to have significantly increased the available stock of large houses. Even where it did so, the properties freed were in areas into which white families rather than black ones were principally moving. As an aspect of transfer policy it offered little to the re-housing prospect of blacks.

The most obvious remaining difference between West Indian and white transfer moves was in respect of moves to houses that the Council had bought rather than built. Although the general proportion of such moves was similar for each group, their location was very different. The majority of black moves into 'acquired' properties were within the inner-city, whereas the equivalent moves by white households were almost entirely to properties outside the central areas. There are important aspects of this concerning both housing quality and individual choice which we have yet to consider.

Overall, though, the picture of re-housing under transfers is one of considerable advantage. Moves were usually to high quality council accommodation; with a large proportion of people obtaining houses. Of far greater consequence than the racial inequalities which emerged within these moves, is the issue of why the rate at which black households received transfers was so much less than that of whites.

Waiting List

4

The Workings of the Waiting List

— *Waiting for Godot*

"Well, what I've heard is that they re-house white people in the modern ones and put coloured people in the old ones."

"The do register our names but were ignored when the houses are allocated."

Black interviewees   (Lawrence, 1974 p.95).

"We are accused from time to time of putting immigrant families into this type of accommodation (i.e. sub-standard). In fact they have a free choice of selecting not only the type of accommodation they want, but the estate in which they wish to live. If they are prepared to wait the necessary time for a new house — and again I stress that this is the waiting list I am dealing with — then they can wait like any other member on the list for that period of time."

Malcolm Campbell-Lee, Nottingham's Director of Housing. (Select Committee on Race Relations & Immigration, Minutes of Evidence, 1971 p.344).

Bland and undiscerning/harsh and discriminatory: such diametrically opposed views encapsulate many of the arguments about racial in equalities in the allocation of council housing. The most extreme accusations and denials inevitably came at the least prioritised points of access to the system. This invariably turns out to be the position of the waiting list and the lot (or burden) of those who seek access through it to the promised land of council housing.

In Nottingham's case the waiting list was only catered for after the prior claims of clearance and transfers had been satisfied. If only from the extent of outstanding transfer requests, it can be seen that not all of these claims were met before waiting list applicants were considered. What is the case, however, is that the nature of priorities given to clearance and transfers in Nottingham ensured that the more desirable properties were allocated before they became available to waiting list applicants. What also follows automatically from the existing system of priorities is that the greater the demands for clearance and transfer rehousing, and/or the more limited the supply of properties available for letting, the more restricted will be the choices open to those on the waiting list. What needs to be stressed is that whilst housing shortages cannot be removed at the wave of a wand, disparities in treatment between waiting list applicants and those in other categories are not a necessary feature of any system of council house allocations. Some authorities, for example, already assess transfers and waiting list applications on the same basis.

For waiting list allocations to be that much less of a priority than other categories merely added to the uncertaintities of those waiting in the queue. As figure 4.a illustrates, the whole pattern of allocations is a volatile one. For those on the waiting list it is particularly so. The 'residual' nature of waiting list allocations in Nottingham meant that its month by month fluctuations, in figure 4.a, have to be understood as being largely determined by the levels of clearance and transfer allocations (which can be seen from the graph), and the unspecified but equally variable number of new and relet properties which came available to the housing department. Thus even though new houses may rarely, if ever, have been allocated to those on the waiting list, the rate of handover of new properties to the Authority did have a considerable effect on the volume of properties which (potentially at least) remained available for waiting list applicants.

The extent of disadvantage experienced by those seeking access to the Council housing sector is well illustrated during this period. In November 1974 the City's Chief Executive spelt out one of the consequences of the Authority's existing housing programme:

> "Satisfying the clearance programme . . . will necessitate about 64% of all available property being taken up by families from clearance areas."
> (Hammond, Nov. 1974 p.2).

The immediate and visible impact of this upon waiting list allocations is also easily identifiable from figure 4.a.

Fig.4.a **Monthly Allocations, 1974/75**

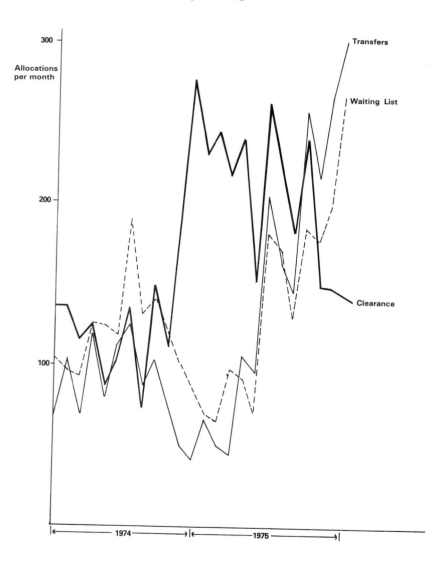

The disparity between the levels of clearance and waiting list allocations from the end of 1974 and into the early summer of 1975 shows how limited was the amount of property left over for those on the waiting list. Even after this the increase in transfers and waiting list allocations was not necessarily at the expense of clearance. More probably it resulted from extra properties coming available to the council.

The most obvious disadvantages for those on the waiting list are, then, the indeterminate duration of time in the queue and the uncertain qualitative choices which face those who eventually do get an offer. The disadvantages, however, do not end here.

The problems of those on the waiting list are only added to since the statutory responsibility for rehousing them is loose and ill defined. Once clearance and transfer allocations have been dealt with by a local authority, its housing responsibilities are merely to comply with the vague wording of Section 113 of the 1957 Housing Act. This requires them to ensure that "reasonable preference is given to persons who occupy insanitary or overcrowded houses, have large families, or are living in unsatisfactory conditions". Despite the open-endedness of this wording it is doubtful that the working of Nottingham's waiting list procedures has ever effectively provided such 'reasonable preference' for those in greatest need.

Such an assertion is not simply based upon the low priority of the waiting list itself, but upon the procedures by which waiting list applications are assessed. To begin to understand this we must first of all draw some distinctions between the diverse sub-categories which comprise the 'waiting list'. Table 4.1, below, sets out the different sub-category lists which Nottingham has used.

What is immediately apparent from the above table is that the waiting list (in its broadest sense) is made up of a number of different queues and that many of these queues don't appear to go anywhere. During the 3 years of our study, allocations to those on the Aged person, Forces, Secondary and Supplementary Waiting Lists were minimal. The only queues in which any significant movement took place were those of the General (or Lodgers) waiting list and the Urban Aid, or

TABLE 4.1

The Proportion of total allocations going to Waiting List Categories

Waiting List Category	Asian	West Indian	White
Aged Persons List	—	—	0.6
Forces Waiting List	—	0.2	0.8
Special Case	3.3	2.5	4.0
Secondary Waiting List	—	—	0.7
Supplementary Waiting List	0.7	0.2	—
Urban Aid	6.0	11.4	1.4
General/Lodgers Waiting List	15.2	33.8	18.8
TOTAL %	25.2	48.1	26.3
N =	38	512	311

Special Case sub-categories. It is then, of only limited value to talk about *the waiting list* in a generic sense. Most commonly this is taken to refer to the General (or Lodgers) Waiting List and it is this which we concentrate upon in a moment.

Before doing so, however, some outline of the rules and restrictions which have governed Nottingham's waiting list sub-categories needs to be given. The lack of allocations to some of the specific lists mentioned above illustrates the hierarchy of sub-categories existing within the total 'waiting list'. The order of priority has long been — Lodgers list, Forces list, Secondary list, Aged Persons list and finally Supplementary list. This largely corresponds with the proportion of allocations going to each sub-category. Thus, even in a broad category which was disadvantaged because of its low priority there were many people waiting on particular lists whose marginal rehousing prospects were in reality non existent.

To ensure that this was so, additional restrictions were often attached to these lists in order to make the filtering process more rigorous. Such restrictions were often very specific. On the Forces list, people would only qualify for a house if they had registered on the list at least 12 months before being discharged, and had served a minimum of 5 years in the Forces. Those who had been registered for less than 12 months (but more than 6 months) were still eligible for an offer upon discharge, but this was normally to be an offer for flat accommodation only.

On the move — Basford flats.

The Secondary list was similarly constrained in terms of the properties to which it conferred eligibility. In October 1976 the Housing Department spelt out the existing policy to its new Housing Committee:

> "Except in the cases of Caretakers of Schools with the City and members of the Police Force occupying tied accommodation in the City, applicants on this list are only eligible for multi-storey or deck-access maisonettes."
>
> (Nottingham City Housing Department, Report to Committee, Oct. 1976, Appendix p.6).

Even the two apparent exceptions to the restrictions — the police and school caretakers — were only eligible for a house providing they had registered on the list at least 5 years prior to retirement.

The same sort of restrictions were placed on allocations from the Aged Persons list. Applicants were restricted to offers within deck-access and multi-storey accommdation. However one concession which was made here, was that for those who had been registered for a considerable period of time, the allocations they received would be confined to the lower floors of such developments.

The priority attributed to the Supplementary list was so low that the Department found it unnecessary to spell out the extent of its restrictions. They merely pointed out that:

> "Very few allocations are made to applicants on this list . . . In general, applicants on this list already have satisfactory accommodation."
>
> (*Ibid*, p.7).

It is worth merely noting at this point that this list, which for lettings purposes was only likely to offer prospects of rehousing if the rest of the country decided to emigrate, was soon to be used substantially as the vehicle which the new Council used to flaunt the restrictions which required that council houses sales be limited to those on the waiting lists. You might wait forever on the list if you wanted to rent a council house, but if you wanted to *buy* one it was a different matter altogether. As the *T.V. Eye* investigators were able to demonstrate virtually anyone who fell off a bus outside the Housing Department could pay their £5 registration fee to get on this list and within days (sometimes hours) could have the keys of a house — providing they wished to purchase it*.

*See, *Beyond the Bulldozer* — Coates and Silburn, 1980, p.119-120.

On examination, it is quite clear that the city's claims to have an open waiting list, free from residence requirements, was not altogether true. In some cases residence requirements were directly required — as in the case of school caretakers or the police wanting a house. In other cases they emerged in a covert form, resulting from the low priority of particular lists. In some cases no amount of residence in the city would make you eligible for council housing, because you would be debarred from registering in the first place.

At one stage in the city's recent past there were two important barriers to registration on any of the lists. One was an income barrier and the other a tenure one:

> "Earnings must not be more than £25 per week . . . and an applicant is excluded if he is living in 'self-contained' accommodation. As a result of this latter condition there are thousands of low-income families in obviously sub-standard yet 'self-contained' accommodation who are not even able to join the queue for council houses."
>
> (Lawrence, 1974 p.96).

By the time our research started both of these criticisms had been responded to. The income barrier had been dropped altogether, and tenants of furnished, self-contained accommodation were now eligible to register on the General Waiting List. However, those living in *unfurnished* rented accommodation still had no rights of registration, and those living in part-furnished, self-contained accommodation had only conditional rights to register on the General Waiting List — depending upon the acceptability of an inventory of furniture which had to be provided by the tenant's landlord.

Those who lived in unfurnished accommodation, or who actually owned their own houses, were not exactly excluded from registering on one of the waiting lists. They were, however, restricted to being eligible for inclusion only on the Secondary list. As has already been made clear, the chances of anyone on this particular list being allocated a council house were only marginally greater than those of becoming Prime Minister.

Within a generally ill-favoured and slow moving set of queues for council housing, easily the most dynamic part of the waiting list was the General/Lodgers list. Even in this, though, the very mechanics of the allocations process, however scrupulously applied, maintained or exacerbated disadvantage. The Department has always argued that the workings of waiting list allocations are non-discriminatory. In a very narrow sense this is probably true. Applications, once they had been sorted into their respective lists, were dealt with in date order. The basis of such a system, however, has one major weakness — it has nothing whatsover to do with housing need. Those in the poorest, most desolate, private sector accommodation will only reach the front of the queue once others who have been waiting longer have been seen to. No matter how dubious a basis this provides for council house allocations, it has to be recognised that the virtues of queuing have assumed almost moral qualities in the vetting process. However comfortable their existing conditions, those who have queued longest become the most deserving. Conversely, no matter what the reason, those who jump the queue, become synonymous with the undeserving.

Such a system maintains disadvantage partly by taking no positive account of the housing 'needs' of applicants. In so doing it perpetuates the cycle of disadvantage. Those in the very worst housing conditions are the least able to wait around casually for the right house to come up. Their urgent need for rehousing increases the pressure on them to 'choose' an unpopular estate (in the hope of getting an offer quickly) and subsequently to accept the first offer which comes in.

It is against this background of restrictions and exclusions that racial inequalities in housing opportunity have to be weighed. It is common knowlege now that when black immigrants arrived in the country, public housing authorities did not exactly welcome them with open arms. The residence requirements of many authorities specifically excluded blacks from eligibility. They were forced into the private sector. Irrespective of whether they then found accommodation through private renting or house purchase, they were still effectively confined to those areas and properties which the (respectable?) white community was in the process of abandoning.

Study after study during the 1970's confimed the over-representation of black households in the poorest parts of the private sector, i.e.

". . . 33% of black households share or lack a bath compared with 12% of the rest of the population. 25% share a W.C. as against 3% for the white UK born population."

(CRC Discussion paper for Housing Directors, February 1975 p.1).

"Housing amenities, like other aspects of housing quality, are worst in the areas of high immigrant concentration. In ED's* with 20% of immigrants or more, 44% of Asian and West Indian households are without exclusive use of bath, hot water and inside W.C. . . ."

(Smith, PEP report, 1977 p.234).

Such information detailing the extent of racial inequalities in the private rented sector, presented a stark challenge to local authorities. Knowing this, any Authority which then proceeded to deal with waiting list applications simply on a date order basis, merely demonstrated its manifest incapacity to understand, let alone tackle, the problems confronting it. This applies as much to Nottingham as to anywhere else. In fact the criticisms of Nottingham's approach to waiting list allocations must be even stronger. The studies of Nottingham by Burney (in the late 1960's) and Lawrence (mid 1970's), raised grave doubts about the adequacy of existing waiting list evaluation procedures. Lawrence in particular, focused attention on the weakness of having no ethnic records of the outstanding waiting list applications. The absence of such information meant (at the very least) that the Authority could not identify the extent to which black families in poor private-rented accommodation, were either failing to register on the general waiting list, or were trapped somewhere near the bottom of it.

Whilst clearance rehousing could be seen to be largely a response to conditions of extreme housing need, and transfers (to a much lesser degree) could have been used to recognise this within the council house sector itself, it is difficult to see how the workings of the general waiting list even vaguely approached this. In fact, it could be argued that the queuing ethic is one of the least effective ways of redressing inequalities (racial or otherwise) in housing provision.

In the form in which they have existed in Nottingham, the waiting lists have served not simply as descriptions of what

* EDs = Enumeration districts, the smallest areas within a city upon which census data can be obtainined.

people are doing — viz. waiting for council houses — but actual techniques for making them do so in a passive, accepting way. They are mechanisms for rationalising the general inadequacies of state housing provision rather than for highlighting and challenging such inadequacies.

"Concrete is fine material for a place like Brazilia where it sparkles in the sun . . ." — poor relations, Hyson Green.

This was particularly so during our research period, when the politics of the waiting list took on a new form. In April 1975 the waiting list stood at 10,100 (Progress Report on the Clearance and Housing Programmes, M. Hamond, Chief Executive, Nottm. City Council, 1975). Little more than a year later, following the change in local political control, the leader of the City Council announced that the true figure for those 'in real need' on the waiting list was less than 1,000. The argument behind this was that the existing list exaggerated needs because it included people who had no *real* need or desire for immediate rehousing. In this guise the waiting list was presented as a banking or insurance system of little short term significance; the implication being that the majority of those registered on it might never actually want a council house, but were merely keeping their options open. It was an argument which also conveniently supported the new administration's policy of dramatically reducing the extent of future council housing programmes.

Many local housing groups took issue with this at the time. However, even to concede that some such 'exaggeration' exists, due to people registering who have a medium term rather than short term interest in obtaining a council house, a more substantial biasing in the opposite direction has yet to be accounted for. Writing about Nottingham's waiting list, Lawrence commented that:

". . . there is clearly little correspondence between the number of families registered for council housing and the number who are in need of it. The 1966 Census indicated that about 40,000 households did not have the exclusive use of a hot water tap, bath and inside toilet. Yet in the same year there were less than 5,000 names on Nottingham's council housing waiting list."

(Lawrence, 1974 p.96).

Whether through ignorance or cynicism there have always been considerable numbers of people living in poor quality, private sector accommodation who have not been registered on the council's waiting lists. The knowledge that this was so could easily have been used to support claims that the waiting list considerably underestimated the degree of housing need in the City. Two such disparate interpretations highlight the extent to which the evaluation of housing need has as much to do with political interest as actual housing conditions.

Whatever exclusions or inaccuracies there are in the numbers of those queuing in this way it is clear from table 4.1 that, for the West Indian population in particular, the waiting lists provided important points of access to the council house sector. In all, 48% of their total allocations came in this way, as compared to 25% and 26% of allocations to Asian households and the white sample respectively. Waiting list allocations assumed an even greater significance if (by excluding transfers and exchanges) they were seen in relation to the numbers of people *entering* this housing sector rather than moving about within it. In that context, allocations from the waiting lists made up 60% of West Indian new allocations, 27% of Asian ones, and 43% of white ones. This provides an interesting basis of comparison with the national picture for council housing at the time.

"In England during 1975, of the 260,000 households entering the council sector, 18% came via slum clearance activities, 9% were rehoused as a consequence of homelessness and 64% from the ordinary waiting list. The remaining 9% constituted 'key workers' and other priority groups.''

(Merrett, 1979 p.215).

Only for West Indians did the waiting list figure as significantly in Nottingham as in the country as a whole.

To some extent, Nottingham's clearance programme will have accounted for some discrepancy with national figures. It does not, however, account for disparities between the 3 ethnic groups.

Of all the waiting list sub-categories, clearly the *General (Lodgers) Waiting List* was the most significant. This has always been so; not simply in terms of the number of allocations going to it, but also in respect of those registered on it at any point in time. It is the allocations from this list that we have sought to examine before going on to the more specific forms of 'positive intervention' as practiced through Urban Aid and Special Case allocations. It is this which we shall be referring to as the Waiting List in the remainder of this section; beginning with an identification of its part in the total allocations going to each group.

TABLE 4.2
Allocations from the General (Lodgers) Waiting List

	Asian	West Indian	White
Number	23	360	222
% of total allocations to each group	15.2	33.8	18.8

Table 4.2 largely confirms the limited relevance of the Waiting List to Asian allocations. In addition, it highlights the disparate importance of the Waiting List to West Indian and white allocants. Almost twice the proportion of West Indians received allocations in this way as did whites. Within this, however, there was a marked similarity in the family sizes of Waiting List allocations to these two groups. This emerges quite clearly from table 4.3

Simply comparing family sizes of 5 or more, the massive disparities between clearance and Waiting List allocations are startling. From the Waiting List such families comprised only

4% of West Indian allocations and 3% of white ones. Although they accounted for 17% of Asian allocations it must be remembered that we are, there, only talking about a total of 4 families.

TABLE 4.3
Waiting List allocations by family size

No. of persons	Asian	West Indian	White
1	13.1	33.3	31.5
2	39.1	36.9	41.4
3	13.1	20.8	20.3
4	17.4	4.8	4.1
5	4.3	1.9	1.8
6	8.7	0.9	0.9
7	—	1.1	—
8 +	4.3	0.3	—
TOTAL %	100.0	100.0	100.0
N =	23	360	222

The relevance of this is, perhaps, best grasped when seen in relation to the different pattern which emerged under clearance rehousing. This is set below in table 4.4.

TABLE 4.4
Family Size of those rehoused under the Clearance Programme

No. of persons	Asian	West Indian	White
1	3.8	15.3	28.3
2	11.5	18.0	28.6
3	10.3	15.3	13.4
4	20.5	12.2	14.6
5	14.1	12.2	8.6
6	12.8	11.9	3.5
7	16.7	7.9	1.5
8	2.6	4.5	1.2
9	5.1	2.4	0.3
10 +	2.6	0.3	—
TOTAL %	100.0	100.0	100.0
N =	78	294	336

Simply comparing family sizes of 5 or more the massive disparities between Clearance and Waiting List allocations are startling. From the Waiting List, such families comprised only 4% of West Indian allocations and 3% of white ones.

Although they accounted for 17% of Asian allocations, this represented only 4 families.

Under 'clearance' the picture was very different. Families of 5 or more persons, comprised 40% of the West Indian, 15% of the white and 51% of the clearance allocations Asian respectively.

The most obvious explanation for this lies both in the different priority given to each of these rehousing categories, and in their different processes of making allocations. Under the clearance programme the Council had much less scope for selectivity. It had to rehouse households irrespective of their size, and it had to do so fairly quickly. Allocations from the Waiting List on the other hand, were almost exclusively determined by the property which the Council had available. Properties did not *have* to be found for those on the Waiting List; people could, after all, continue waiting.

The practical significance of this has long been misunderstood by the City Council. In 1971, in its submission to the Select Committee on Race Relations and Immigration, the City set out its claim to an even handed and non-discriminatory approach to waiting list allocations:

> "The method of determining allocations is basically chronological, with the waiting time being determined by the type of property requested and its availability in relation to the priority granted to Clearance rehousing cases. The applicant is visited prior to allocation time being reached and it is at this stage that the personal elements of the computer code are recorded. Sub division of the list is by familiy size grouping and type of area requested. As properties within the chosen categories become available, an offer is made. Refusal of an offer would not result in any penalty being imposed as may be the practice in some areas."
> (Nottingham City Council, Select Committee Submission 1971, Section C, p1-2).

This process, which has remained substantially unaltered, fails to adequately examine inequalities inherent in it. Within this same 1971 submission some mention was given to the position of those families who were on the Waiting List partly by virtue of being 'overcrowded'. In an almost throw away sentence about their prospects the city commented.

> "it is relevant to point out that most applicants in this category will be waiting for relatively scarce large houses."
> (*Ibid.*, p.2).

It is crucial to understand the racial consequences of this. Larger houses were particularly important in the pattern of black clearance rehousing. If this family structure were also reflected in the Waiting List then at least three things followed:

i.black families would have figured disproportionately amongst those waiting longest on the Waiting List for council housing.

ii.the allocations process itself will have discriminated against such households in so far as it failed to *identify* the racial inequalities in relative waiting time, and

iii.the capacity of the Authority to adequately respond to such housing 'need' in the waiting list would itself have been undermined both by the greater priority given to clearance and transfer rehousing, and by the bland nature of Waiting List assessments per se.

The inability to quantify this is one of the most direct consequences of the Authority's refusal to keep ethnic records at the point of application rather than allocation.

The similarities in family structure amongst Waiting List allocations would then suggest a degree of 'tailoring' by the local authority; with the properties which remained available

TABLE 4.5
Waiting list applications — by property age

	Asian	West Indian	White
Acquired properties			
New non-estate	8.7	0.8	2.7
Non-estate	—	0.8	1.8
Inner city non-estate	—	1.1	0.9
Relet inner city non-estate	4.3	2.2	1.8
Purpose built			
New	13.0	12.8	14.4
Post-war relet	69.7	79.2	70.3
Pre-war relet	4.3	3.1	8.1
TOTAL %	100.0	100.0	100.0
N =	23	360	222

for letting, determining the family size breakdown of Waiting List allocations. Whatever the disadvantages of this for larger black families, it did provide a basis for assessing further similarities (or differences) in the ensuing pattern of allocations.

The figures in table 4.4, reveal important differences between Waiting List allocants and those in other categories. Predictably, allocations to new properties were less than under clearance or transfers. The movement of both black and white families into the council's 'acquired' stock was also more limited than in other categories. In addition, the bulk of all Waiting List allocations went to council built properties, with a greater proportion of black households going to post-war relets. This was largely accounted for by the greater pro-pportion of white allocations going to new or pre-war council estates. This pattern of allocations was not significantly distorted by allocations to the elderly since there were only eight such allocations to the white sample, three in the Asian, and four in the West Indian totals respectively.

To serve any real purpose, however, information about the age of properties received by Waiting List allocants had to be linked with an analysis of the type of properties received by them. This is set out below:

TABLE 4.6
Waiting List Allocations — by Property Type

	Asian	West Indian	White
Deck access flat	8.7	11.4	13.0
Deck access maisonette	43.6	40.6	29.6
Flat	17.4	24.4	28.8
House	13.0	6.6	14.9
Multi-storey flat	13.0	14.7	8.6
Multi-storey maisonette	—	1.7	1.4
Warden aided bungalow	—	—	0.5
Warden aided flat	4.3	—	2.3
Victoria centre	—	0.6	0.9
TOTAL %	100.0	100.0	100.0
N =	23	360	222

Looked at together these two tables present some disturbing evidence about the continued disadvantage or discrimination experienced by black households. The vast majority of total allocations going to both whites and West Indians was of council built stock. This did not, however, result in them faring equally well in the properties they received. The preponderance of post-war relet properties going to West Indians almost corresponded to the proportion of their allocations to deck-access or multi-storey properties. Some 68% of West Indian allocations went to these properties. This compared with 53% of the white ones.

The allocations to pre-war properties (which in other cities have been the poorer ones) have in Nottingham, coincided with allocations to more prestigious and soundly built houses or flats. In fact, it is almost a direct corollary of the allocations to deck-access and multi-storey properties, that whites received houses at more than twice the rate of West Indian families.

When so much 'tailoring' had already been done to bring West Indian and White allocants into line, the disparities in treatment between the two groups cannot be glibly brushed aside. There is no question of differential family size producing differential allocations. It comes down to explanations based on 'choice' or 'discrimination'.

Sitting out . . . older housing in Radford.

Traditionally, the local authority has sought to explain these situations almost entirely in terms of individual choice. The rehousing patterns are then merely the result of individuals exercising their personal preferences in pursuit of rehousing. The inconsistencies in the choosing process which we outlined earlier (in the section on clearance), raise real and specific doubts about the validity of such an explanation. More substantially, the section on 'choice' later on, systematically examines how limited and constrained such notions might be.

It is our conviction that explanations based upon direct or indirect discrimination cannot be avoided. Such discrimination should not necessarily be perceived as blatant unabashed racism, but the result of in-built pressures which produce 'victims' in public sector housing provision. Such victims have to be found amongst those within the system as well as those excluded from it. As a general rule, some 60-70% of the properties which the council has available for letting at any point in time are deck-access or multi-storey ones. This was made abundantly clear by the current Deputy Director of the Housing Department:

> "You must remember that when you're talking about the allocation of relets, 60% of the relets which are available at any one time are in fact in flats complexes. This is an extremely large proportion when you consider that out of our total housing stock of about 55,000 properties only 10-12,000 of these are in flats complexes. This sort of situation restricts us as much as it restricts anyone else."

> (Magee, 1980).

The pressure upon the Department's staff is always to find sufficient properties to meet the demand for council *houses*. They must also try to let as much of the vacant property as they can. Council house sales and cuts in the building programme only increase these pressures. Those who are most vulnerable to 'offers' of less popular properties are always those whose existing housing conditions are poorest and/or whose knowledge of the workings of the council house system is most limited. Black allocants from the waiting list may well have been the victims of both. Historically, their exclusion from council housing will have restricted their ability to familiarise themselves with its workings from the inside, and their concentration in the poorest parts of private sector accommodation will have made them susceptible to the first 'offer' which the council made them. Despite the fact that black community has never expressed a desire for deck-access accommodation, it is easy to see how explanations based on 'choice' could be enthusiastically embraced by the Department. Such explanations thereby avoided the much harder questions about the extent to which the Department actually *relied* upon black families being more amenable to accept the housing which other people rejected.

It must be remembered that this all took place at a time when the Department was under considerable internal as well as external pressures. The simplistic notion of reducing the demands from the Waiting List by defining a much smaller number of applicants who were in 'real need', failed to provide any real respite for the Allocations staff. The statistical simplicity of this panacea was short lived and in the end circumvented by the policy of council house sales. As one report was soon to point out:

> "Since July 1976 the waiting list has steadily increased from 4,806 to 10,416 in December 1977 . . . The main component of the rise in numbers on the list is on the Lodgers List. It is difficult to account for this rise unless it reflects a. the difficulty of getting houses generally, and b. the effect of the sales programme reflected in a gradual decrease in properties available for relet . . . Of the relet properties other than flats, a high proportion will be sold, a proportion will be allocated to clearance, leaving waiting list families the residue. If transfers are maintained from the flats then virtually all allocations to the waiting list will be in the flats complexes."
>
> (Bishop, 1979, Sections 6 & 7).

These misgivings are, in effect, borne out by our own data. They also reinforce doubts expressed earlier about the absence of blacks moving out of such complexes by way of transfers. However, this is to digress from the limitations of the Waiting List.

The composite picture of disadvantage or discrimination perpetrated through the general Waiting List would include the following points:

a. the effective exclusion of larger families from Waiting List allocations would (on the evidence elsewhere in this report) be likely to disproportionately affect black households.

b. the absence of any credible 'need' criteria for Waiting List allocations will have worked to the disadvantage of those in the poorest parts of private sector accommodation, in which black families have been concentrated.

c. the low priority of the Waiting List will have worked against West Indian families, if only because of their disproportionate dependence upon obtaining council housing in this way.

and on top of this,

d. the eventual allocation of West Indian families in *greater* proportions to the unpopular deck-access or multi-storey accommodation, and in *lesser* proportions to the more desirable houses and estates seemed to constitute either a direct or an indirect form of discrimination.

To have gained preferential access to the 'leftovers' of council housing, is a privilege which rarely invokes gratitude. Rather it engenders a deep rooted cynicism about the conscious or sub-conscious discrimination upon which the system of public housing provision is actually based.

The examination which follows, of more specific forms of positive intervention in other waiting list categories, merely offers a cameo of the same processes at work.

'Urban Aid' and 'Special Case' Allocations —
responding to 'need' at the back of the queue

Despite a generally expressed reluctance to embark upon any form of 'positive discrimination' — for fear of it being unfair and/or inviting a backlash of public criticism — the local authority in Nottingham has used at least two forms of such intervention to speed up the rehousing of those who would otherwise have been confined to the waiting lists. These two initiatives have taken the form of 'special case' and 'Urban Aid' allocations respectively.

'Special case' allocations have generally been restricted to

"persons in private accommodation within the City who are not otherwise eligible to register on the . . . (General Lodgers) . . . Waiting List, but where the Medical Officer of Health or Director of Social Servies is satisfied that there is an urgent need for the provision of more suitable accommodation."

(Nottingham City Council, Select Committee submission, 1971, Appendix II, p.2).

This highly individualised form of provision offered a means whereby households, whose undue hardship was recognised by the Department, were able to benefit from positive discrimination. Each case was subject to individual approval by the Housing Committee, and was therefore time consuming. As a method of intervention, however, it did reflect an understanding of the fact that 'queuing' as the mechanism for allocating properties left for the waiting list — was sometimes a singularly inappropriate way of responding to housing 'need'.

This sort of understanding was also reflected in another part of the City Council's submision to the Select Committee on Race Relations and Immigration in 1971. Nottingham had previously made an application under the Urban Programme for funds which would increase its ability to use positive discrimination in the field of public housing. By February 1971, it was able to announce that an:

> ". . . Urban Aid grant has also been approved for the appointment of two additional visitors in the City Housing Department. The intention of these appointments is to conduct positive surveys in areas of the City known to contain a high element of poor housing conditions in relation to multiple occupancy, shared facilities, etc. In this way, it is hoped to extend the admission to the present waiting lists in areas where this can be of greatest help. It is almost inevitable that the trend will be for these areas to contain significant numbers of immigrant families. From information gathered from these surveys, it is possible that the corporation may consider extending its Waiting List admission rules, if this is required, as a contribution to improving housing conditions of families at present living in these areas."
>
> (*Ibid.*, p.1 of Section D).

In many ways this statement was the most positive recognition ever made by the Authority of the existence of racial inequalities in private sector housing. It was not, however, until some years later, following the publication of the 1971 Census data, that any attempt was made by the local authority to quantify this 'inevitable' involvement of black families in these areas. The census itself established that, in 1971, there were some 15,332 people living in the city whose parents had both been born in the New Commonwealth. This was the closest approximation of the size of the local black population. By 1975 it was estimated to have risen to between 20,000 and 25,000 people. Throughout the period, however, the black communities have always made up roughly 6% of the City's total population. The Council went on from there to examine the representation of these communities in the older central areas of the city. They did this by examining data on the 6 'wards' which comprised the central areas of Nottingham. Table 4.7 illustrates the size of the black population in each of these wards and the proportion which they represented of the total ward population.

TABLE 4.7

Population (by Ward) whose parents were both born in the New Commonwealth

Ward	Numbers	% of Ward Population
Bridge	1813	10.5
Forest	1397	9.8
Lenton	2864	15.1
Market	2208	20.5
Radford	1530	9.9
St Ann's	1115	18.3
TOTAL	10,927	

Thus, of a total black population of just over 15,000, almost 11,000 lived in Nottingham's inner city areas. *This constituted some 71% of the city's black population.*

The appearance of these figures, in restrospect, merely gave statistical confirmation of a situation which the Department already knew existed. The appointment of these additional housing visitors (Urban Aid Workers) formed part of a two pronged attack by the Council on the worst parts of the City's central area housing. On the one hand the large scale clearance programmes were bringing increasing numbers of people into the council housing sector. On the other, the Urban Aid workers were intended to reach out to those living in equally poor rented accommodation which, for whatever reasons, had been unaffected by the clearance programme. The initiative was both laudable in intent and entirely consistent with the original intentions of the Urban programme through which it was funded.

The job of the Urban Aid workers was fairly precisely defined. Having identified the existence of families living in conditions of housing stress, the Visitors job was to

"accelerate such families' progress through the Waiting List, or, if they were not on it, to get the family registered and included in the council house system as soon as possible."

(Magee, 1980).

An indication of how important this initiative turned out to be in providing access to council housing for black households can be seen from the figures below on Urban Aid allocations during the three years of our study.

TABLE 4.8
Allocations under 'Urban Aid'

	Asian	West Indian	White
Number	9	121	17
Urban Aid as a % of the total allocations to each group	6.0	11.4	1.4

For each group, all allocations were to 'lodgers', with only a limited number of pensioners being affected. In all only 1 Asian, 4 West Indian and 3 white allocations under Urban aid were to pensioners.

The most immediately obvious feature emerging from this table is the extent to which black households entered the council house sector in this way. Urban Aid formed a far greater part of West Indian total allocations than it did in either Asian or white rehousing. To the extent that such allocations were directed towards those living in the worst parts of the private rented sector, this confirmed many of the beliefs about the disproportionate involvement of black families in such housing. In this respect, the Urban Aid initiative obviously gave a greater number of black families access to council housing than they might otherwise have anticipated.

Figure 4.b which maps out the previous address of West Indian allocants, also confirms the extent to which the vast majority of black households had been drawn from the most central of the City's housing stress areas. Even the much smaller numbers of Asian and white allocants correspond to this pattern.

Fig.4.b **West Indian 'Urban Aid' Allocations — previous**
address

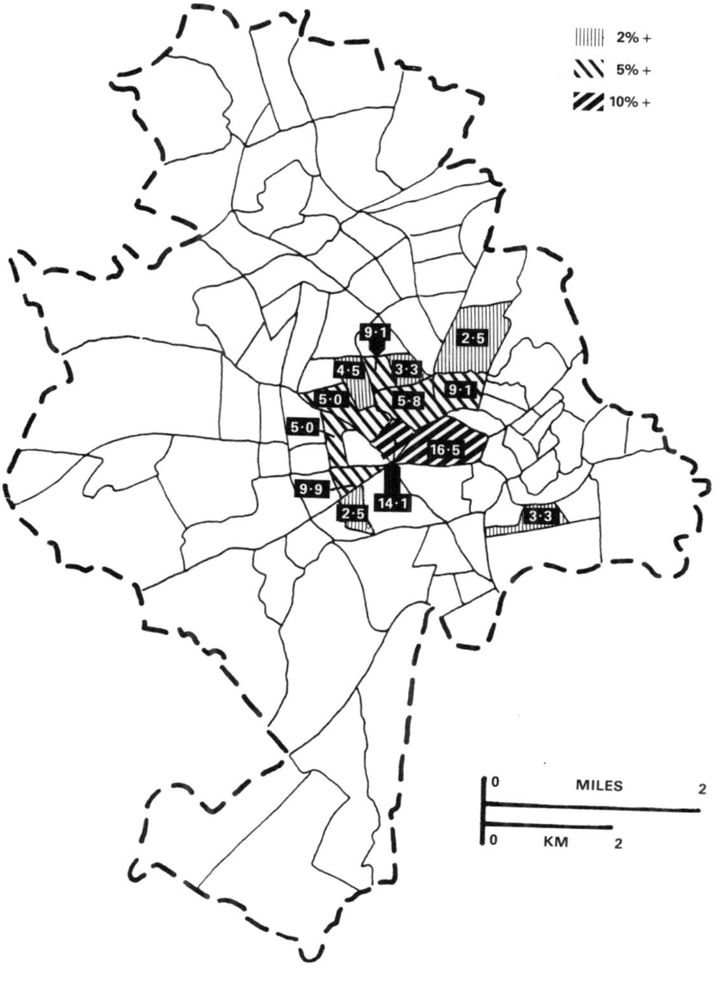

Because of the limited number of Asian and white households rehoused under this heading, considerable care must be taken when analysing any breakdown of the allocations any further. We have done so with the white ones only with considerable reservations. Within these limitations, however, table 4.9 sets out the family pattern of Urban Aid allocations.

TABLE 4.9
Urban Aid Allocations — by family size

Family Size	West Indians	White
1 person	13.3	35.3
2 persons	29.8	23.5
3 ..	35,5	41.2
4 ..	10.7	—
5 ..	6.7	—
6 ..	4.1	—
TOTAL	100.0	100.0
N =	121	17

Within this table, the larger proportion of single persons in the white sample could easily have been accounted for by the 3 allocations to pensioners within their small total. The value of this table is probably best seen in relation to the family size of allocants through the General/Lodgers Waiting List. There was little difference in the family size of white allocants between these two categories — the majority of household being of 3 persons or less. However, this was not true for the pattern of West Indian allocations. The proportions of larger, West Indian families allocated under 'Urban Aid' were greater than those within the general waiting list allocations. In fact, the whole balance of family size amongst West Indian allocants shifted upwards within the Urban Aid scheme. The effect of this was to provide openings for such households to a degree which plainly did not exist within the workings of the General Waiting List. This shift in emphasis was however confined to West Indian allocations. No significant change appeared to affect the white allocations.

In what way, if at all, did this affect the subsequent pattern of rehousing experienced by these two groups? Tables 4.10 and 4.11 set out the basic information about the properties received by Urban Aid allocants.

TABLE 4.10
Urban Aid Allocations — by property age

	West Indian	White
Acquired Properties —		
New non-estate	5.0	—
Non-estate	1.7	—
Inner City non-estate	2.5	5.9
Relet inner City non-estate	3.3	5.9
Purpose Built —		
New	9.8	17.6
Post-war relet	76.9	70.6
Pre-war relet	0.8	—
TOTAL	100.0	100.0
N =	121	17

TABLE 4.11
Urban Aid Allocations — by property type

	West Indian	White
Bungalow	—	5.9
Deck Access Flat	7.4	11.8
Deck Access Maisonette	51.3	41.1
Flats	20.7	17.6
House	9.9	5.9
Multi-storey Flat	9.9	11.8
Multi-storey Maisonette	0.8	—
Warden Aided Flat	—	5.9
TOTAL	100.0	100.0
N =	121	17

Again, these tables are best examined largely in relation to the pattern of West Indian allocations, and the ways in which they corresponded to allocations within the general Waiting List. The first point worth noting is the increased significance of West Indian allocations to council 'acquired' properties under Urban Aid. In some respects these would account for the inclusion of larger households within this category since it is almost inevitable that such properties would have been houses rather than flats or maisonettes. Few other obvious advantages for Urban Aid allocants appear in table 4.10. The proportion of houses allocated to black families actually fell, as did that of pre-war relets, and allocations were again being dominated by post-war relet properties. The full meaning of this can be seen from table 4.11. These properties were primarily the deck access and multi-storey blocks. *Almost 70% of the West Indian allocations and 65% of white ones were to properties which made up the least popular parts of the Council's housing stock.* In fact, a greater proportion of West Indian 'Urban Aid' allocations went to deck access maisonettes than did 'Waiting List' ones — surely a most curious form of positive discrimination! What emerges is a picture in which all families allocated through Urban Aid and the Waiting List were disadvantaged in the properties that they received. Within this, black families were, yet again, disproportionately allocated to these poorest, least popular parts of the Council's stock. As far as Urban Aid was concerned, the more numerous involvement of West Indian households resulted mainly in them going, more numerously, into such stigmatised properties.

It is perhaps, not immediately apparent that Nottingham's flats complexes are so ill-thought of. The basis upon which we have presented them as such, does not simply rest upon the fact that at any time 60% + of the Council's available relet properties are flats. Rather it has been based upon a series of reports both in the media and by the Authority itself, which have consistently confirmed this assessment of their status. As we pointed out in the earlier section on transfers, Nottingham's Social Services Department, in its report to Committee of August 1975, was unequivocal in its conviction that the ambition of most reasonable tenants in one of the complexes was simply to get out. In fact their report went much further than this in ascribing responsibility for much of problems and stigmatisations to the Housing Department's own lettings policy:

> "We get the feeling that, apart from the difficulties 'the flats' environment produces in the way of pressures and frustrations for young mothers and so on, the Housing Department tends to place difficult families from redevelopment areas in the complex."
>
> (Nottingham Social Services Department Report, August 1975, p.2).

Our own figures would suggest that it was families in those categories at the bottom of the housing priority list rather than clearance tenants who were allocated most consistently to these complexes. If, in addition, it emerged that 'difficult' clearance families were also allocated there, then this further confirmed the low esteem which Housing Department officials attached to such allocations.

To be fair, Nottingham is by no means alone in the burden it carries in the form of these flats complexes, and it has spent considerable amounts of money to change their image. However, the long term doubts about the viability of this show no signs of diminishing. By 1976 public scepticism was well established:

". . . Whitehall is extremely concerned at the recent deterioration of modern developments all over the country, with well-equipped flats proving unlettable as areas acquire the social stigma of being the dumping ground for difficult tenants . . . In Nottingham Old Basford is not yet unlettable, but the council suspects that it could be if nothing is done."

(*Guardian* 23rd March 1976).

Probably the most candid admission of the size of the problem facing the City in removing the stigma attached to its flats complexes, came from one of its architects during this period. Looking back at the actual structure and construction of the complexes, he commented that:

"At the time architects were a bit starry-eyed. Concrete is a fine material for a place like Brazilia where it sparkles in the sun. But it can be pretty miserable in Basford on a wet November day . . . There is no doubt about it concrete, as we used it, brings out the savagery in kids . . . The flats in Basford are drab. They lack colour and make people's lives drab and colourless."

(Quoted in Skellington, 1976 p.6).

There can be little doubt that this was (and is) how the Housing Department actually viewed its main flats complexes.

The Department's public defence of these complexes has always been half-hearted and, according to the motives you wish to ascribe to them, heavily tinged with wry humour or cynicism.

Thus, in response to the initial onslaught from Social Services in 1975, the Chairman of the Housing Committee replied that:

"We have no policy of keeping problem families together . . . There is no greater concentration of social problems at Basford than at Balloon Woods or other similar developments.'.

(*Nottingham Evening Post*, 25th November, 1975).

This was certainly a novel line of defence — not exactly a plea of innocence, but rather like asking for 6 similar offences to be taken into consideration.

Five years later the Social Services Department again returned to the attack, with headline coverage in the local press about the excessive costs facing families in flats complexes. The families were then trapped in housing they could not escape from and with heating they could not afford. The response of the City's Housing Director in this article is worth recording in detail:

> "Mr Arthur Oscroft, Nottingham's Director of Housing, said there 'must be a little bit' in the suggestion that it was poorer people who accepted flats in the high rise blocks.
>
> 'It is the people who tend to be more desparate for housing who go into high rise flats because they are more readily available and perhaps people who are under-privileged have got lower standards.'
>
> But once people get in, they are often only too keen to move somewhere else.
>
> Mr Oscroft admitted: 'A vast proportion do put themselves on the transfer list because they feel the environment is unsatisfactory. People do not like living on top of each other.'
>
> But the Council couldn't afford to have flats standing empty white it has a long waiting list for homes."
>
> (*Nottingham News*, 1st August 1980).

There we have it in a nutshell. The Council couldn't afford to have flats standing empty while it had a long waiting list for houses. However, no mention was made of the number of houses which had been sold off during the previous four years; no mention of the decimation of the council's building programme or of the development land which been dispensed with. Despite this, the statement contained two important comments. The first was the stark fact that 'it is the people who tend to be more desperate for housing who go into high rise flats because they are more readily available'. The second was the equally stark value judgment that 'perhaps people who are under-privileged have got lower standards'.

It is in this light that the positive discrimination of the Urban Aid initiative turns sour. Between them, Urban Aid and the other waiting list categories accounted for more than 45% of all West Indian allocations and 60% of their new allocations *into* the system. Of these, 70% of West Indian families went to deck-access or multi-storey complexes. In comparison, just over 40% of new allocations to white families came in through the combined waiting list categories, only half of these then went to flats complexes. If it is true that, as the Housing Director suggested, allocations to flats complexes were predominantly to those whose existing housing conditions were most desperate, what then are the racial implications of this rehousing process? To rescue people from the hovels of yesterday and confer upon them the stigmas of today is hardly a rooted commitment to equality of opportunity.

In 1971, in its Select Committee submission, the City showed that it was aware of this sort of trap. In it they commented that

> "The Corporation is aware that there is a danger of creating concentrations within new housing which might, from a community point of view, be considered little better than concentrations in bad housing."
> (Nottingham City Council, Select Committee Submission, 1971 p.3 Sec. A).

In retrospect, it must be said that the workings of the city's 'urban aid' and Waiting List allocations appear to have achieved precisely that.

Going home . . . Basford flats.

The other category in which positive intervention was used by the Authority to alleviate housing stress amongst those in otherwise low priority categories was 'Special Case' allocations. Though far less numerous than 'Urban Aid' allocations, these offered an important contrast in the value judgements about, and subsequent treatment of, applicants in each sub-category.

Tables 4.12, 4.13, 4.14 and 4.15 below set out some of the basis for this comparison.

TABLE 4.12
'Special Case'' Allocations in relation to total allocations

	Asian	West Indian	White
Number of 'Special Case' allocations	5	27	47
% of *total* allocations made to each ethnic group	3.3%	2.5%	4.0%
Equivalent % of total allocations to each ethnic group under 'Urban Aid'	6.0%	11.4%	1.4%

TABLE 4.13
Previous Tenure of 'Special Case' Allocants

	West Indian	White
Business	—	2.1
Lodgers	48.1	34.0
Tenant	51.9	63.9
TOTAL %	100.0	100.0
N =	27	47

TABLE 4.14
Personal Code 'Special Case' Allocants

	West Indian	White
Check Visit Advisable	14.8	12.8
Not Applicable	85.2	48.9
Pensioners	—	36.2
Handicapped	—	2.1
TOTAL %	100.0	100.0
N =	27	47

TABLE 4.15

	West Indian	White
Bungalow	—	4.3
Deck Access Flats	11.1	12.8
Deck Access Maisonettes	14.9	6.4
Flats	33.3	31.9
House	37.0	23.4
Multi storey flat	3.7	10.6
Multi storey maisonette	—	2.1
Temporary bungalow	—	2.1
Warden aided flat	—	6.4
TOTAL %	100.0	100.0
N =	27	47

Because of their limited numbers it is again hardly possible to say anything about the pattern of Asian allocations. The most significant feature in table 4.12 is that, the proportions of black and white households, respectively, receiving allocations was a reversal of pattern under 'Urban Aid'. Table 4.14 shows how far the category was of particular relevance to white pensioners. For white people, twice the proportion of allocations went to pensioners as under 'Urban Aid'. For both Asians and West Indians there were no allocations to pensioners at all. In addition to this, table 4.13 shows that whereas 'Urban Aid' allocations were all to lodgers, under 'special case' allocations 64% of white and 52% of West Indian allocants had been tenants. When we examined data on tenure patterns, important differences in spatial distribution also emerged. 'Urban Aid' allocants all came from within the inner city and were rehoused either there or in a peripheral flats estate. Even within the inner city, 'Urban Aid' allocants were unlikely to receive new property; especially new estate houses. On the other hand the 'special case' allocants were more generally dispersed through the city and across various property types. They were, however, more likely to receive houses or flats on council estates than 'Urban Aid' allocants.

The differences in treatment became more apparent when the breakdown of property type allocations in the Special Case category, outlined in table 4.15, are compared with the equivalent data for 'Urban Aid' allocations. Even without considering differences in treatment between black and white allocants, it is obvious that, as a category for social intervention, Special Case allocants received more favourable treatment than those rehoused under 'Urban Aid'.

Within 'Special Case' allocations, greater proportions went to houses than under 'urban aid', whilst the comparative rate of allocations to the less popular deck-across maisonettes was much lower. A spatial and property age analysis of 'Special Case' allocations merely added further confirmation of the advantages of entering the council house system in this way. On average 16% of special case allocants did not merely receive houses but did so on the more desirable of council's pre-war estates. This compared with the 1% of such allocations under 'Urban Aid'.

Differences in the treatment of ethnic groups within this category ought not to be ignored but they did appear to balance out. On the one hand 15% of West Indians, as against 6% of whites, went to Deck Access Maisonettes. At the same time 37% of West Indians went to houses, whilst only 23% of whites did so.

Geographically, there was still a tendency for West Indians to remain in, or near, the central areas (26%) whereas only 6% of white households were rehoused there.

Finally it is worth mentioning the family characteristics of those to whom, 'Special Case' status was applied. None of the West Indian allocants were pensioners. However, 44% of them were single persons. This compared with 13% of single West Indians coming in via 'Urban Aid'.

The criticism voiced earlier about the way in which families appeared to be selected from the Waiting List, to fit the size of whatever properties were at that stage still available, did not seem to apply to the same extent in the 'Special Case' category.

In general terms, the criticisms of waiting list allocation procedures were that they failed to recognise housing need as opposed to length of waiting, and that they also gave undue weighting or preference to medium size families, if only because this corresponded to the size of properties most readily available for letting. In 'Special Case' allocations, however, attempts seem to have been made to respond to 'need' irrespective of family size. Larger families were represented in greater proportions than in allocations from either the Waiting List or Urban Aid — 37% of West Indian allocants having family sizes of between five and eight persons. In contrast, only 11% of West Indian allocations under Urban Aid and 4% from the Waiting List, were to families of 5 or more. However, given the restricted numbers that we are talking about, too much weight cannot be given to this tendency.

The most disconcerting aspect of our examination of the two different forms of positive intervention was that, when considered together, they appeared to operate in ways which largely served to reinforce existing patterns of dissadvantage and discrimination experienced by black households. 'Special Case' allocations disproportionately favoured white people, both in terms of access and urban housing quality. Urban Aid, on the other hand, principally offered blacks preferential access to the least desirable parts of the council's housing stock. Positive discrimination itself had become sub-divided; with some (predominantly white) people obtaining first class tickets into council housing, and others (predominantly black) given second class ones.

To be fair to the housing department, it must be said tht the differences between 'Urban Aid' and 'Special Care' allocations were not based upon the mere whims of allocations staff. There were important procedural differences which separated the two categories. Special case allocations all required approval by the Housing Committee; Urban aid ones didn't. More important, though, was the fact that all Special Case allocations had to carry a recommendation from either the Chief Medical Officer (now the District County Physician) *or* the Area Director of Social Services. The 'gentleman's agreement', in respect of such recommendations, has always been that they would always have established that there was a genuine case of real need before any recommendation was made. The recommendations themselves frequently specified the type of property which ought to be provided for the household. The housing department have argued that this has given them little alternative but to rehouse 'Special Cases' wherever they were advised to do so.

Considerations of this sort may offer valuable insights into the constraints under which a housing department has to operate. However, in themselves, they do not adequately explain the racial disparities which were clearly evident in this part of Nottingham's council house allocations.

Only continuous monitoring of the quality of allocations made under such initiatives would make it possible for the Department to demonstrate that its positive intervention policies were being carried out in a way which did not, even indirectly, result in many black households being trapped in the housing that most 'reasonable tenants' sought to escape from.

Summary

During the research period the waiting list was undoubtedly the residual balancing mechanism in council house allocations. It was the least favoured way into the system of council housing, and normally, only gave access to properties left over from clearance and transfer rehousing.

The waiting list was not a single list, but a series of quite distinct queues which moved at very different rates. In some sub-categories of the waiting list, the queues moved so slowly that the prospects of rehousing for those waiting in them were remote.

In general, the waiting list allocations which did take place were based upon a date order of application. As such they took little account of the housing conditions in which people on the list were having to live. The two most notable exceptions to this, were 'Urban Aid' and 'Special Case' allocations; each of which sought to recognise aspects of housing 'need' and thereafter to give some priority to rehousing the families involved.

West Indian families were at an immediate and obvious disadvantage in relation to allocations from the various waiting list categories. Almost half (48%) of the total West Indian allocations came from the waiting lists, whereas for whites these comprised only about one quarter (26%) of their total allocations. The undue dependence of West Indians upon such a low-priority gateway into council housing, will have had a considerable impact upon the total allocations pattern which emerged. The number of Asian families coming in in this way was quite small although, proportionately, it was similar to the rate at which whites did so.

One of the particular features of waiting list allocations was the extent to which they were 'tailored' to the supply of properties available to the local authority. As a result there was a strong similarity between the family sizes of both white and black allocants. This removed an important variable which, in other categories, may have significantly influenced relative rehousing prospects. The general shortage of larger properties ensured that mainly smaller size properties were available to waiting list applicants. Despite this, important differences in allocations emerged. In the General/Lodgers Waiting list (the most substantial and fastest moving of waiting list categories) the disparities were most obvious. Although the average rate of allocations to houses was quite small (and to flats complexes quite large) it affected the ethnic groups differently. White families went to houses at twice the rate of West Indians (15% to 7% respectively), whilst West Indians went to flats complexes at a much higher rate than did whites (68% to 53% respectively).

Even in the category of Urban Aid allocations, the positive discrimination practised by the Authority did not show any reduced rate of black allocations to flats complexes. Thus, in an initiative which disproportionately affected West Indian households (11% of their total allocations, as against little more than 1% of whites), 70% of their moves were to flats complexes. All that differed was that the rate of white allocations to such complexes (65%) rose to *almost* the same rate as blacks. Within the particularly unpopular deck-access maisonettes, whilst the gap between black and white allocations was no wider than under the General Waiting List, the proportion of such black allocations rose to its highest level: 51% of West Indian 'Urban Aid' allocations went to deck-access maisonettes, along with 41% of white ones.

Despite the policy of not moving families with children into flats complexes, it is clear that this is precisely what must have happened — and on a fairly extensive scale. Although the mechanics of 'special case' allocations differed in some important ways, from those under Urban Aid, they offered an illustration of a very different sort of positive intervention. The limited numbers involved in this initiative were far more likely to receive houses (and ones in popular estates). It was, however, more relevant to white rehousing than to Asian or West Indian.

For West Indians, the disadvantages of coming into the system in disproportionate numbers via the waiting list, were compounded by the disadvantage they encountered in the waiting list allocations themselves. When differences in family size have already been accounted for, it is difficult to see why West Indians should still have gone in consistently greater proportions than whites to flats and complexes.

The effect of the Urban Aid initiative seems largely to have improved the speed rather than the quality of such allocations. What the initiative showed was that black families were, in the first place, disproportionate sufferers from the worst excesses of Nottingham's private rented sector. What it achieved, however, was a virtual reconstruction of such inequalities *within* the system of council housing itself.

As such the racial disparities emerging in, or maintained by, the Urban Aid initiative and waiting list allocations in general, seemed a far remove from any convincing notion of equality of opportunity in council housing.

Choice

5

'Choice', and the Mechanics of Constraint

"You don't understand. It's got nothing to do with discrimination. In fact it's got very little to do with the housing department at all. We don't force people to live in poorer properties. They go because they *choose* to."

This comment, made by a local housing department official, concerning the over-representation of black families in some of the Council's least desirable properties, has prompted us to give considerable thought to the concept of choice and the nature of the 'choices' actually facing people in the public housing sector.

It would be either fanciful or meaningless to suggest that we are all free to choose to do what we want. Some 'choices' might be physically or practically impossible. In other areas we might not be free to 'choose' something because we do not even know that it exists. When we talk about freedom of 'choice' we are, it seems, using the work in a very restricted sense. In most instances the parameters within which 'choice' is framed are rarely spelt out. They are the boundaries of what we would normally regard as 'common sense'. However, when we try to use 'choice' as an explanation of events or circumstances, it becomes important that we spell out those boundaries within which the word can be seen to have any meaning. The setting out of these boundaries is important not only in its own right, but also as a means of going on to identify how far our ability to 'choose' changes as our circumstances change; and how various people in the same situation can perceive the choices facing them, very differently.

Normally we make 'choices' within the following objective and subjective constraints:

—what we know exists,
—what we believe to be available and what is actually available,
—what we think we can afford or obtain, and what we can actually afford or obtain,
—what we regard as socially acceptable for us, and what others judge to be socially acceptable for us,
and
—what we like (or would like to try).

Such limits or constraints apply to notions of 'choice' in council housing as much as any other aspect of our lives. People are not in any meaningful sense free to 'choose' precisely the design, layout and locality of the house they are going to live in. The boundaries of choice are in many ways already defined for them. Tenants, or prospective tenants, do not 'engage' the Council to build houses to their own specifications. Public housing in an 'off the peg' service which, even in times of plenty, offers considerably wider 'choice' to standard size family units than to ones at the much larger or smaller extremes.

The purpose of approaching notions of 'choice' in this way is to systematically explore the extent to which people, within the decision making arena of council housing allocations, are in fact free. It is not to dismiss 'choosing' as a totally redundant concept, but to identify how limited and constrained it might be in this situation. The constraints which we intend to examine do not only apply to the individual applicant for council housing. In the end it may well be that the counter staff of the Housing Department, the Allocations Section, senior officials and locally elected policy makers are similarly constrained, albeit by different considerations.

The importance of 'choice'

As a public proclamation of faith, 'choice' is a much better bet than God. No one becomes uncomfortable at a declared commitment to it. No one is likely to brand you as a fanatic or some kind of antedeluvion crank. Arguably, however, as many injustices have been perpetrated under the banner of choice as that or religion. All social policy, in one form or another, addresses itself to extending choice. What appears to be critical in political and policy terms is to establish whether, as a notion, it is being used in the pursuit of the goals of individual freedom or social equality.

In the early 1970's the rediscovery of poverty resulted in a flood of social policies aimed at reducing, if not removing, urban inequalities. Less than 10 years later the poverty and inequality bubble had well and truly burst. By the end of the decade public attention had been shifted to the subject of personal freedom. Individuality rather than inequality returned to the centre of the social policy arena. However, despite the massive shifts in emphasis that had taken place politically and economically during the decade, the pursuit of 'choice' had remained as a more or less constant and central part of all government policy changes.

This is largely explicable in terms of the different contexts in which such 'choice' was framed. In one context it was inescapably linked with structural explanations of injustice and inequality. Set against this was the sense in which it was used as a focus upon the *individual* as the prime mover in tackling inequalities in their own situation. However, the very nature of housing provision in this country makes it doubtful that large scale 'individual' solutions are possible within a social framework which, by its very nature, requires losers to exist on an extensive scale.

It is, however, the individual solutions which have often found most favour in housing policy formulation. In his most recent work, Townsend has argued that an approach which so patently fails to effectively tackle housing impoverishment, does not emerge by accident:

> "The housing market must be perceived as an institution which is doing far more than mediating housing supply and demand. It reproduces, and indeed creates, inequality within society."

> (Townsend, 1979, p.505).

Moreover, the denial of equality of opportunity and differential restrictions on the scope for 'choice', have persistently been concealed by the way in which discussion and evaluation of housing problems have been 'tailored', by suc-

The limits of choice: tomorrows queues today's housing prospects . . .

cessive governments, merely to fit the solutions currently on offer.

> "Social perceptions of housing problems are very restricted. They are conditioned, and in effect distorted, by the rules and fashions accepted in Parliament, the press and elsewhere, by which housing is discussed. Housing problems come to be defined in ways which are acceptable to ruling elites, particularly the government, and are measured according to procedures devised by government and local authority services.
>
> (Townsend, 1979 p.478).

However, such an assertion has not often found ready acceptance in housing policy discussions either in government or all academic circles. Gray for example, has critically pointed out (Gray 1975, p.229) that within the discipline of 'urban geography' much of its thinking has been based upon the assumptions that people are in fact free to choose the type and location of housing they most prefer; that patterns of residential segregation result from individual household decision making; and finally that such a focus upon the individual household provides the key to an understanding of urban processes. How starkly this compares with the positions taken up either by Townsend or by the government sponsored Community Development Projects of the mid-1970's,

. . . Children around the Radford flats.

"problems of multiple deprivation have to be re-defined and re-interpreted in terms of structural constraints rather than psychological motivations . . . the symptoms of disadvantage cannot be explained adequately by any abnormal preponderance of individuals or families whose behavior could be defined as pathological."

(CDP, 1974, p.8).

This is, though, the sort of explanation which is frequently advanced to account for concentrations of racial minorities in poor and stigmatised housing. Local councillors and housing officials alike seem particularly vulnerable to such explanations. This might, in part, be because they are often caught in the immediacy of reconciling an inadequate supply of good quality council housing, with an excess demand of those having justifiable claims to it. Faced with such pressures you can see how the inadequate supply can easily become taken for granted, and the outcome of allocation's become associated with judgments of the status and characteristics of applicants. Thus allocations to poor, unpopular properties become defended, not in terms of inadequate housing finance or shortages in housing supply. Rather, they come to be explained in terms of the *standards* of families who accept such offers. The stigma of the property is then transferred to, or attached to, the individuals who occupy it. Pinker described this process succinctly:

> "stigma becomes an administrative technique for rationing scarce resources."
>
> (Pinker, 1971, p.175).

It is precisely this which works against concentrations of black families trapped in poor housing. In this case, the stigma itself assumes racial qualities which both differentiate and down grade their claims for better housing. Whilst deferring, for a moment, an examination of the position which housing officials might have in maintaining such stigmatised inequalities, it would be wholly wrong to ignore the sense in which housing officials are themselves trapped in this situation. They too are caught at the sharp end of a system in which the level of public housing provision is manifestly incapable of meeting all the justifiable claims for decent housing made upon it.

In so far as such a system continues to exist in any degree of relative tranquility, it is because all the participants in it have accepted that 'that's how things are'. Applicants and officials conform to the roles allotted to them, in an uncritical and largely unconscious way, generally oblivious to the violence that is being done to both parties in the process.

> "The denial of equal opportunity begins in infancy and with it the long process of habitutation to inequality without which society would be forever in a state of civil war."
>
> (Runciman, 1972, p.347).

To talk, as the 1976 Race Relations Act has done, of a commitment to the creation of equal opportunities in our society, is in fact to confront and challenge such a state of peace. It is a challenge which extends to all of the victims of this process not merely those identifiable by race.

In approaching this, one of the things which we ourselves have had to come to terms with is the particular sensitivity of housing department officials to suggestions that they may have a significant effect in actually maintaining inequality. Only at senior management level has there been any apparent understanding of the Department's role as "urban gatekeepers', and even then it has been the exceptional officer, rather than the majority, who have gone on to develop a positive working response to the inequalities entrenched within the allocations process. The difficulties of raising this issue are liable to touch on a variety of sensitive feelings within a local authority. The reactions that have been noticed amongst officials include their being — hurt and indignant at the thought of being seen to be prejudiced; reticent about fully analysing the way in which the system affects ethnic minorities, on the grounds that that this in itself would be discriminatory; angry that a focus on race shifts the balance of discrimination positively against white people; self righteous about blacks only getting the housing they deserve, thereby reflecting merely their less than equal *right* to whatever decent housing exists; defensive about the validity of 'judging' people on the basis of standards which are monumentally 'English', (i.e. dress, habits, manner, marital status, family size, etc); and often adamant about the virtues of 'queuing' as a yardstick of housing need.

Even amongst staff who recognized the structural constraints under which they were working, the acknowledgement that they could neither allocate houses which did not exist, nor conjure up decent properties in areas where the Council had not improved its stock, did not appear to result in the development of any sense of solidarity with the public, in opposition to an overall system which was manifestly unjust. Rather, such a recognition seemed to invoke a state of helplessness which, though not justifying them, presented the injustices of the system as immutable.

Council housing is an articulation of the *public* committment to housing provision. This is not simply the relation between private ownership or private renting, but also its relationship to other aspects of public policy such as spending on defence, law and order, roads etc. In addition, it is itself determined by policies relating to taxation and housing finance, and to approaches to income redistribution in general. The localised administration of public housing provision can only be as sensitive, compassionate or humanitarian as the framework of central government policy allows. No amount of tinkering with the mechanics can correct a system which is profoundly indifferent to the inequalities it creates.

A recognition of this makes it necessary to weigh carefully the extent to which the responsibility for such inequalities can be directed at the level of local officialdom. It also raises important questions about the value of traditional pre-occupations with the 'human face' of housing departments, as anything more than a partial solution to housing problems . . .

"At one level of analysis it is the inefficiency and idealogies of the officer structure in the various bureaucracies that restrict resource distribution. People do not get their rights because officers cannot or will not deliver them . . . (however, such) inefficiences and cussedness are not individual faults or errors, but rather instrisic characteristics of the same system of resource allocation . . . only partial change will occur if better advice is avialable to individual people. What is required is a process of politicising groups of people and demonstrating publicly that whole sections of the population do not receive the benefits that are promised them by the Welfare State. Politicisation and subsequent action would then seek fundamental change in the basis on which the system of resource distribution depends, not just adjustments in the discretionary or formal rules governing officers."

(Lambert, Paris & Blackaby, 1978, p.30).

This does not in itself invalidate an examination of the ways in which individuals express preferences or make decisions about housing options which they see as being open to them. It does, however, require a recognition of the extent to which the boundaries of such 'choices' are, already, narrowly pre-determined by public housing policy.

The individual — and the limits of personal choice

"To conduct research into choice, voluntariness and preference in so constrained and competitive a market situation, is merely the indulgence of an ideology which promises what it cannot deliver."

(Lambert & Filkin, 1971, p.332).

The historical inequalities in private sector housing have always made it reasonably easy to see the part that wealth, status and personal connections have played in determining people's housing circumstances. The public sector, with its association with the 'poor' and 'needy' has often been sheltered from such critical analysis. However, differential access to power and influence exists as much within the public sector of housing as outside it. Here too the bargaining position of those seeking housing varies enormously. In the first place the rules and priorities set by a local authority ensure that some people have greater claims to the available housing than others. Nottingham provides as good an example of this as anywhere else. Clearance tenants were in a more powerful position than waiting list ones. Secondary and Supplementary Waiting List applicants were only eligible for flats complexes. The homeless had to take what they were offered. Given a shortage of council housing, this is what an Authority is required to do. Insofar as such differentiation equates with housing 'need', it is an entirely defensible position for an authority to take up. However, both between and within priority categories significant inequalities exist which ensure that some people are permanently at a disadvantage in their ability to 'play' the allocations game. This would appear to be so, irrespective of how high a priority group they were in or how great was their housing need. There are considerable grounds for suggesting that the major constraints which effect individuals in the pursuit of decent public sector housing, are disproportionately experienced by black people.

Knowledge

Clearly the more you know of how a system works the more easily you are likely to find your way around it. The more you know what you want the more likely you are to get it. In this respect black families started at a considerable disadvantage. The residence qualifications required by many local authorities meant that most black families, when they came to this country, were ineligible for council housing. Accommodation was found by either privately renting (from those who would have them) or buying (from those who sell to them). In either case the properties which they found 'open' were by and large, in those declining inner city areas rapidly being abandoned by the indigenous white population. It was a process which, at the same time, both concentrated and segregated black families.

However, the large scale clearance programmes undertaken by local authorties in the mid 1970's transformed, in theory, the position of large numbers of black families. Sud-

denly significant numbers of them were whisked from in-
eligibility to top priority for rehousing. And yet, as we have
seen, many of the black families made only limited advances,
in terms of the quality of housing they obtained.

One part of the jig-saw explaining this was outlined by the
Cullingworth Committee:

> "The 'choice' of an area may face a coloured immigrant family with a
> particular difficulty since they may not know the names of council
> estates, and may accept a poor house in a run down area through ig-
> norance of the alternatives. Sometimes no alternatives are presented to
> them."
>
> (Cullingworth, 1969).

Such a lack of understanding of the workings of the public
housing system have to be seen in terms of 'race' rather than
in straight forward 'class' explanations. Amongst white,
working-class families in clearance areas there was a much
greater prospect of them:—

a. having contacts (family, friends, workmates, etc) spread
   across the range of existing council estates,
b. being able to draw upon an accumulated knowledge of
   'how to deal with the Council' in terms of rehouing
   negotiations, and
c. possessing much clearer notions about their 'rights' within
   a clearance programme.

In relation to the first of these points, the geography of
people's networks of friends and relatives exerts an extremely
important influence on the racial and spatial patterns which
emerge in the rehousing process. This was well illustrated by
Flett in her study of rehousing in Manchester. At one point,
when considering the reasons why white families cleared from
the Moss Side district looked for moves out to the outer areas
of Wythenshawe and the overspill estates, whereas black
families looked in greater numbers to the adjacent area of
Hulme, she commented:

> "The significance of wanting to live near friends lies in the location of
> the friends and relatives. For white people, the presence of relatives and
> friends is the commonest reason for choosing Wytheshawe and overspill
> . . . The presence of friends is never given by black people in relation to
> Wythenshawe, though it is the commonest reason for choosing Hulme.

Friends and relatives draw white people away from Moss Side, but keep black people there. Their networks differ. The spatially wider networks of white households has to do with their more established position in the City. They may have friends or relatives already rehoused by the council in Wythenshawe; older residents may have children who have bought their own houses in the Cheshire fringes; younger residents may have grown up in Wythenshawe. Their networks are not confined to Moss Side.

The immigrant population has had Moss Side as its focus for over twenty years; few black people became council tenants and those who did were mostly rehoused on inner city estates. Unless they had networks of (scattered) white friends, black people had little reason to get to know outer estates . . .''

(Flett, 1977 p.41).

The social as well as physical segregation of black families has meant that many households only really knew the area close to their existing accommodation. In addition, it was certainly true of Nottingham (and probably a common pattern elsewhere) that the various tenants based organisations of working class people in clearance areas, many of which sprung to life in the 1970's, failed to reach or include black people in any significant numbers. Thus at a time of sharing and learning within the tenants movement, the exclusion of the black community meant that, in this respect, they shared little and learnt nothing.

One additional factor, which has often been mentioned as contributing to the difficulties faced by the black community, related to the perceptions of the original migrants. Many came to this country believing it to be commited to fairness and justice. Often it was only after a considerable 'waiting' time, and with great misgivings, that they accepted that the system did not always work in this way. As such this often made black applicants for council housing particularly vulnerable to the pressures under which housing allocations staff themselves had to work — viz, to let as much of the 'difficult' property as possible and at the same time retain as much of the decent housing for those with particular requirements in top priority rehousing categories. It is probably not unreasonable to suggest that no present or future generation of black people will enter the public housing market with such widespread naivety. In particular, the second generation of black applicants appear to be more substantially aware that:

> "The existing system or resource distribution is inegalitarian but permits, at least in principle, many benefits as of *right*. Rights, however, often need to be fought for in order that the principle be translated into practice."
>
> (Lambert, Paris & Blackaby, 1978 p.30).

Expectations

It is worth nothing that a person's attitude towards their 'rights' in any given situation strongly influences their expectations, not of how they will be treated, but of what they *feel* they can bargain for. For black households in many parts of the country, the years of exclusion from public sector housing, and the frequency of their experiencing direct discrimination in their search for private sector housing, will certainly have helped to generate an expectation that their rights to council housing were equally limited.

The pattern of inequality established in the private sector housing market, in which black families at first only had access to, and then became synonymous with, poor housing, works against black households when they try to enter the Council house system. This does not require direct discrimination and racial prejudice to be a key feature in the housing allocation process. It merely recognises the way in which people's current housing position may serve as 'an index of achieved life chances' (Haddon, 1972, 1.2) and as such constraints both *their own* expectations about their eligibility in the council house system and also their eligibility for better housing *in the eyes of those dealing with allocations*.

There can be little doubt by now that many blacks feel that they *are* discriminated against in the housing market, and that such discrimination is no less in the public sector than in the private one. In this respect, Nottingham appears to be no different from anywhere else. Writing in 1974, Danny Lawrence was able to point out from the responses to one his survey questions ('do you think that immigrants have as much chance of getting council houses as anyone else, or do you think they find it more difficult?') that of all the black people interviewed only 12% considered thay had the same chance. A majority of 54% thought immigrants found it more difficult. Forty one per cent said that coloured people were only allocated old houses in poor areas, and in addition to this 42% voiced much stronger criticisms of the Council's treatment of coloured people:

> "The only ones that get them (i.e. good houses) are guinea pigs — just to pretend there's no prejudice."
>
> "They do register our names but we're ignored when the houses are allocated. If some immigrants do get them it's just to hoodwink people."
>
> "Even if our name is registered they do not have to let us have our turn. They say that we cannot keep them clean so they try their best not to let us have them."

(Lawrence, 1974, p.95).

The significance of such comments if fourfold. They are indicative of the fact that black people often enter the area of public housing *expecting* to be discriminated against. They support the notion that, in the past at least, such expectations have been coupled with a *passive acceptance* of such treatment. They conform to the actual *pattern* of housing allocations being made to blacks in Nottingham. And finally, they touch one one of the sensitive areas of Nottingham's approach to housing records. This is that ethnic identity has not been recorded until *after allocation*. Thus, there is no ethnic breakdown of those who are still 'waiting' for council accommodation. Such an omission has made it impossible for the Authority to refute the allegation that black households are 'registered' on the waiting list, but then systematically ignored, or given only poorer properties.

Housing stress

In the rehousing process, there is a direct correlation between the strength of a persons 'bargaining' position and their current housing conditions. This is particularly true in clearance areas where the Council is itself under pressure to rehouse families quickly so as to minimise the financial costs they incur in advance of rebuilding. If there is water running down the inside of your walls; if bare wiring is exposed in your room; if the sewers are backfiring — it's not the housing department which experiences this as stress . . . it is the family living there. A certain amount of this stress can in fact be transmitted to the department by the irreverent tenant, but ultimately it is the person living in those conditions who is under greatest pressure. Inevitably the worse those conditions are, the more prepared the tenant is likely to be to accept the first offer to come along. Not, as Nottingham's Director of Housing suggested earlier, because the tenants have lower standards, but because they know they have no choice. What this invariably ensures is that those in the most desparate housing conditions can command only the most limited advancement in the council house system. There is a painful logic in the fact that those needing urgent rehousing are generally only able to choose from amongst the least desirable parts of the council's housing stock — in Nottingham's case the multi storey complexes or unimproved 'aquired' properties. It is, however, a logic which is invariable rather than inevitable; a direct product of local allocation policies, rather than an act of God. The effect of this is often that the status of 'slum tenants' simply shifts its venue, as the individuals or families concerned, become caught in a meteoric journey around the bottom of the barrel of public housing. So where does race came in?

A sense of community — the Meadows.

The whole host of studies on race and housing in the late 60's and early 70's spelt out the precise way black families disproportionately suffered from housing conditions of this kind. The PEP studies, carried out up to the point at which our own examination of the housing allocation process began, perhaps illustrate this most readily:

> From the 1971 Census we know that 3.8% of households in England and Wales are occupying shared dwellings, and, from our own survey, this compared with 30% of West Indian households and 22% of Asian households.''
> "Among the general population the lower socio-economic groups tend to live at a higher density, but this does not account for the difference between the minorities and whites. Within each job level, density of occupation is higher among minorities than among whites. The biggest difference is at the lowest job levels; . . . working class Asian and West Indians have far worse accommodation than working class whites.''
> "Each of the minority groups tends to be substantially worse off for housing amenities than the white population . . .''
> "Housing amenities, like other aspects of housing quality are worst in the areas of high immigrant concentration.''
> (David J. Smith, 1975, p.231-4).

To accept, in principle, the notion that people in the worst housing conditions also have the greatest limitations on their scope for exercising 'choices', requires, in the face of the evidence quoted above, an acknowledgement that this, more than anything else, defines the position of black households in search of council housing.

Follow up studies concerned with how much choice people actually *felt* they had, confirm this view. The CRC study — Housing Choice and Ethnic Concentration (1977) revealed, for instance, that:

> "It is disturbing to note that half the black people in areas of low ethnic density and one quarter of black people in areas of ethnic concentration stated they had no choice in where they chose to live.''
> (CRC, 1977, p.31).

Even a study of an earlier phase of Nottingham's clearance programme, and written almost in a spirit of golden optimism, revealed that one household in four had been rehoused in a district *not* of their first choice. (Coates & Silburn, 1980). Although there was no indication of the proportion of black people in their sample, it is significant that, even in this highest priority category in local authority rehousing, many people moved to areas not of their 'choice' in resignation or resentment rather than in any positive sense:

> "They accepted a house in another district, thinking that this would be a temporary measure and that in due course they would be able to move again if they wished, presumably into the area of their first choice" . . . "they moved because they could not bear to live in St Ann's a day longer" . . .
> "they moved into another district from the one they wanted because they felt that they had little alternative."
>
> (Coates & Sillburn, 1980 p.57-8).

Even here, though, it is worth remembering that to be housed in the area of your (declared) first preference does not guarantee a major improvement in the *quality* of housing open to you. We shall return to this point in a moment, but first it is necessary to touch upon one further example of the way in which greater degrees of housing 'need' actually reduce 'choice' rather than increase it.

The major contradiction in the attempts of local authorities to direct their rehousing programmes towards those in greatest 'need', emerges in relation to homelessness. Our own study identified an over representation of black households in an albeit limited number of homeless families in the City. In so far as this is consistent with the findings of reports done elsewhere in the country, it is only remarkable in so far as it identified a *continuing* incidence of relative disadvantage.

Homeless families have by and large only received offers of properties which are in least demand from other categories in the Council's priority list. In Nottingham's case, the Authority actually avoided even nominating such families to the national housing associations actively building and letting properties in the City. In this context, 'choice' often approximates to a 'take it or leave it' situation, in which the 'de facto' absence of choice reflects, not a recognition of housing need, but a punitive gesture towards those who have been so feckless or careless as to become homeless. Such an approach is often also seen as a deterrent to those gathering hordes who would, at the drop of a hat, do likewise to jump the queue.

This sort of stereotyping merely legitimates a process which exploits the extremes of housing stress. In response, we would merely echo the comments of Lambert and Filkin about London's homeless:

> "These are not problem or pathological families, but the poorest of (the) unemployed, the most powerless in the highly competitive market for housing."
>
> (Lambert & Filkin, 1971, p.332).

Choosing — friends or houses

It is appropriate to include in this section a look at the one positive context in which concentrations of black households in poor housing conditions can be a reflection of choice of a sort. In so far as black households express a preference for living in reasonable proximity to each other this may, in part, explain the continuing significance of the inner city in their pattern of relocation.

> "The desire to live amongst friends is a natural one. This applies to all the minorities, and it's as true for the Italian Community in Nottingham as the Asian or West Indian ones."
>
> (Carroll, April 1980).

However, the notion of living amongst friends takes on a special significance where aspects of race are concerned. The open hostility expressed by the white community towards black immigrants, from the moment they arrived here, was in itself a major influence on the grouping together of black households. Minority groups under threat do instinctively close ranks both physically and psychologically. The racial hostility which they experienced was not a temporary phenomenon but one which has persisted. To this day it is an hostility which has changed often only in terms of subtlety. Even as the patterns of settlement were being established, attention was drawn to the fact that the majority of West Indians were resistant to being spread out throughout the suburbs "because of the risks involved in pioneering" (Deaking & Ungerson, 1973, p.241). The notion of such risks is not one which normally has much significance of white households. For black families, developments over the last few years, including the increasing public coverage of groups putting forward openly racist views, have only confirmed their feelings of being under threat. If it is right that "increased support in the mid-1970's for the National Front — at least in local elections and parliamentary bye-elections — may be an indication that scapegoating of ethnic minorities is becoming more potent in Britain . . ."

(Nugent & King, 1979, p.47).

then the pressure to close ranks is one which will only have increased in significance.

A failure to recognise this factor in relation to the position of black families exposes the cultural one-sidedness of suggestions such as:

". . . if for whatever reason there is no accommodation in the district that you really do wish to live in, then any offer of a more or less similar house, in a more or less similar street, becomes (less or more) equally acceptable."

(Coates & Silburn, 1980, p.59).

For black families, the preferences expressed have also to be seen in terms of other variables which limit their 'choices' — the proximity of religious and cultural facilities; the prospect of obtaining a (relatively) multi-cultural education for their children; the availability of specialist food shops; the existence of cultural support networks; as well as some (mutual) protection from the politics of racial hatred. A more profitable base for understanding and examining the importance of such 'non-housing' considerations is perhaps the recognition that

"in a situation of very limied choice, black households will opt for unpopular types of housing in areas which are familiar or convenient; white households will accept the unfamiliar for the sake of a house or cottage flat."

(Flett, 1977, p.27).

There are, however, two points here which ought not to be confused. On the one hand there is the positive recognition of the value of living in supportive communities which allow ethnic minorities to retain and enhance their cultural traditions. Set against this must be an unequivocal recognition that *there is no logical reason to equate such facilities with poor housing conditions*. This may reflect the price that black households have to pay for such 'privileges', or the necessary outcome of local housing policies, but it ought not to be mistaken for a positive preference by black families for slum housing. In many ways it is more clearly undstandable as the end product of the piecemeal and half-cock 'urban policies' of the 1970's under which money was directed into the central areas of cities to strengthen (in a multi-cultural way) the educational, recreational, and social facilities there, whilst specifically excluding similar (and larger scale) initiatives in housing. (See Edwards and Batley, 1978, — *The Politics of Positive Discrimination*).

Whatever the origins of this, and whatever the virtues of existing cultural support networks, the ultimate judgement about the nature of individual 'choices' expressed by blacks in this way remains the same,

> "the persistent reluctance on the part of black and brown minorities to take the social and economic risk of dispersal from the inner city must be, in part, the consequence of the climate of race relations in Britain."
> (Deakin & Ungerson, 1973, p.242).

If this is so then real choices only emerge when real and substantial housing initiatives are taken by local authorities to provide high quality council housing within traditional areas of migrant concentrations.

We have already made it clear that applicants for council housing differ considerably in terms of knowledge, expecta-

Environment and choice — the pressures of waiting (Hyson Green).

tion and housing need, and that these factors structure and limit freedom of choice. Combined with the pattern of priorities laid down in housing policies, and the limited availability of favoured and appropriate kinds of housing stock, these factors go a long way to explain the pattern of allocations outlined earlier. What has not so far been taken into account is the possibility of conscious or unconscious discrimination on the part of those responsible for making council house allocations.

Although we made no specific investigation into this aspect of the allocations process, it cannot be ignored entirely when evidence exists of the effects of cultural and racial bias on the part of allocation staff in other housing authorities. Whether or not comparable bias exists in Nottingham we are not in a position to say. What is certainly true is that the staff have a role which could influence the prospects of racial minorities. It is, therefore, essential that they be as much beyond criticism as possible. Moreover, however sympathetic such staff may be to members of racial minorities, it is still possible for bias to arise unconsciously. Amongst any group of people dealing face to face with an increasingly heterogeneous general public, where a great deal rests on the quality of information provided and the assessments reached, there is an obvious case for monitoring of the processes involved. This seems especially necessary when those on either side of the divide come from widely differing cultural backgrounds, and where many of the applicants may be uncertain, diffident, and frequently uneasy about expressing themselves in the everyday language of the officials concerned.

The work of Allocations staff is often fraught with difficulties. Inevitably they are required to make some element of subjective assessment of applicants. In Nottingham at least it could be argued that, given this, the Housing Department has neither provided sufficient, continuing, in-service training or support for them, nor established the monitoring which would publicly affirm the role and integrity of its Allocations staff.

Indeed, during the one training session held in recent years, one member of the section specifically complained that they often had to "rely on the local paper for information, particularly about sudden policy changes."

(Gallagher, 1980, p.2).

Allocations staff can, and do, come under continuing pressure from local councillors, doctors and social workers; all with interests in particular cases. Yet Allocations staff have no real control over the properties available for letting; and they obviously operate for much of the time in difficult and uncertain cirumstances. It is perhaps not surprising that, in her account of the training session held in 1980, Gallagher claims to have observed a degree of defensiveness amongst Allocations staff when faced with criticism.

Allocations staff are, in a very real sense, the Housing Department's front line troops. Not only are they amongst the least well paid and most vulnerable members of the Department, but they are faced with the impossible task of reconciling legitimate demands for housing with an obviously inadequate supply. Moreover, the effective exercising of what little choice is actually open to individuals, can be very much affected by the way in which Allocations staff relate to the members of the public they deal with. There is considerable opportunity for them, consciously or unconsciously, to influence both the eventual pattern of housing allocations, and the reputation of the Housing Department within the community.

Within the context of this study, there are at least 2 aspects of the Department's allocation procedures which warrant closer examination. Between them, individual differences, and the limits of available housing stock, do not seem to adequately explain why it should be that, in every category of allocations, blacks went in greater proportions than whites to the particularly unpopular deck-access maisonettes. They also seem insufficient explanations of why, having gained access to the system, blacks should then have received transfers at only *half the rate* at which whites did so.

Accounting for such obvious disadvantages or inequalities requires careful examination rather than a hasty pursuit of someone to blame. What we would argue is that such an examination needs to be carried out within a framework which fully appreciates how complex and constrained the notion of choice actually is. Any such examination would have to move away from the cosy simplicity of descriptions which suggest that Nottingham's council housing is based on

> ". . . elaborate processes of choice which . . . would have been quite inconcievable had the Corporation not been a landlord on a vast scale, within whose empires lay easy permutations of exchanges of houses, a widespread choice of locations and addresses, and a rather simple set of mechanisms for exercising such choices."
>
> (Coates and Silburn, 1980, p.116).

To begin from such a position would only be to manifestly misconceive how limited a notion choice actually is, for *all* of those involved in the rehousing process.

Housing Policy

6

Housing Policy and the Structuring of Disadvantage

". . . council housing has fallen far short of its potential. It has largely been used as a safety net to compensate for the failures of the private market, and has been hamstrung by having to compete for land in the market place; by having to borrow money from the City institutions and banks in order to pay for construction work; and by its reliance on private construction firms which are aiming to maximise their profits. Council housing has been a major target for cuts in public expenditure; and poor design and paternalistic management have led many tenants to make legitimate criticisms of the way in which the allocation and management of council housing operates."

(NUPE/SCAT, 1978, p.2).

The various aspects of racial disadvantage emerging in this study do not necessarily result from the prejudices of housing department staff and/or the short comings of its allocations system. Such an assumption would tend to ignore the extent to which allocations staff, as much as council tenants, are the victims of housing policies which (in effect if not in intent) actually require racial discrimination to take place.

In this section we want to spend some time in examining the impact of successive housing policy changes on Nottingham's council housing stock. In so doing we hope to identify the extent to which the root responsibility for racial discrimination in public housing lies at a policy making rather than an administrative level.

To achieve this, in the context of this study, it is necessary to outline the make up of the city's housing stock, its condition, and changes in policy which affected its quality and availability during our research period. Each aspect can then be assessed in terms of its influence upon the allocations *opportunities* which existed at the time.

One of the biggest difficulties which we faced in trying to do this was the extent to which previous research has tended to treat housing policy and allocations procedures as distinct and almost unrelated fields of study. It was as if an unwritten law existed which required those who examined *allocations* to take main housing programmes as given. Discrimination on a basis of race or class then became a matter of micro-processes — so that a little oil here, or a slight adjustment there, could make the allocations machine run smoothly, fairly and impartially.

On the other hand, studies which focused upon the macro-processes of central government housing policy, invariably pulled up short of any useful analysis of the impact of such policy changes on local allocation procedures; the one outstanding exception to this broad rubric being Stephen Merrett's — *State Housing in Britain*.

It is hard to avoid a feeling that such a 'de facto' division of investigation resulted in each approach 'short-changing' the other. Simply arguing the case for council housing conveniently ignored the very real way in which such a system itself brought into existence a range of *public housing classes** — principally distinguished by differential points, and rates, of access to the council house system, and by their subsequent movement within it. Moreover, studies of allocations procedures within any framework which was politically myopic (i.e. which failed to take into account the nature and scale of housing finance, the programme of clearance, house building and improvement, policies of council house sales, or the ambiguous position of housing associations) ignored many of the greatest sources of discrimination ultimately manifested in patterns of local authority housing allocations. Houses which do not exist cannot be allocated. Slums had to be removed by clearance or improvement programmes, not by ignoring or redefining them. To make any real sense at all, structural and textural influences on the pattern of housing allocation must be drawn together into a common fabric.

* The general notion of housing class was originally outlined in J. Rex and R. Moore's *Race, Community and Conflict* (1967) although in their work public sector housing tended to be treated as a single homogeneous unit. This study subjects public sector housing to the same class based analysis as Rex and Moore applied to the private sector.

What follows is an attempt to do so.

Compared with many larger cities Nottingham has a much greater proportion of its housing stock in public ownership. In broad terms the housing stock at the beginning of the research period is outlined in Table 6.1 below.

TABLE 6.1*

Nottingham's Council Housing Stock, April 1975

Property	Houses	Flats/ Maisonettes	Bungalows	Total	%
1 Bedroom, Council built	—	6,417	630	7,047	14.5
2	2,586	4,581	1,311	8,478	17.4
3	29,460	659	331	30,450	62.5
4	870	—	—	870	1.8
Acquired properties	1,848	—	—	1,848	3.8
Total	34,764	11,657	2,272	48,693	
% of all stock	71.4	23.9	4.7		100.0

*Collated from figures in Nottingham's Housing Revenue Account as at April 1975.

These figures bear no necessary relashipship to the propertions of different types of property actually *available* for letting at any point in time. Nor do they give any clue to the *condition* of the properties themselves. They do, however, provide a basis upon which we can begin to build up a fuller picture of the properties in Nottingham's housing portfolio and the policies which have subsequently affected them.

The major characteristic emerging from Table 6.1 is the large number of 3 bedroom houses owned by the Council. These accounted for roughly 60% of its total stock, and for the vast majority of all houses. There were almost 3 times as many 3 bedroom houses as there were of all types of flat/maisonette accommodation. At the very least this is an indication of the extent to which Nottingham missed out on the planner's multi-storey jamboree in the 1960's — a feature which stands-out even more clearly in Table 6.2 below.

It is also important to emphasise that larger properties may have accounted for only 2% of total stock: all of these being houses. To some extent this figure is probably an underestimate since it does not include any larger houses incorporated in the category of 'acquired properties'. However, this heading gives little clue to the nature of properties included in it; nor their condition or reason for acquisition. Such speculations as can be made about these houses can have no great precision. Even if the majority of such properties were 4 bedroom houses we would still be talking about little more than 5% of the total housing stock being suitable for large or extended families.

Nottingham is by no means unique in being short of larger properties. The significance of this is, however, as profound as it is common place:

> "The council sector contains the smallest proportion of dwellings of 3 or more bedrooms of all the tenures. Because the public sector contains a dispoportionate number of large households there is, in absolute terms, more overcrowding in the council sector than in other tenures."
>
> (Merret, 1979, p.199).

The data in our own allocations study not only gives weight to this conclusion but adds to it a racial dimension which often passes unrecognised. Even restricting the focus to households of 6 or more persons, we are faced with a picture in which, during the study period, these accounted for *25% of all Asian households receiving allocations, 14% of West Indian ones, and only 5% of the white sample.*

Taking out the elderly from these figures (in order to compensate for their disproportionate involvement in the pattern of white allocations) changes the percentages only marginally (i.e. they become 25%, 14% and 6% respectively).

Still life (?) — the Wharfdale Estate, Wollaton.

TABLE 6.2
Nottingham's Council Housing Stock, April 1975 — Pre-war and Post-war breakdown

Pre-war

Properties	Houses	Flats/ Maisonettes	bungalows	Total	%
1 bedroom	—	656	—	656	3.5
2 ..	946	—	—	946	5.0
3 ..	15,294	—	185	15,479	81.7
4 ..	332	—	—	332	1.8
Acquired property	1,523	—	—	1,523	8.0
Total	18,095	656	185	18,936	
% of pre-war stock	95.6	3.5	0.9		100.0

Post-war

Property	Houses	Flats/ Maisonettes	Bungalows	Total	%
1 bedroom	—	5,761	630	6,391	21.5
2 ..	1,640	4,581	1,311	7,532	25.3
3 .	14,166	659	146	14,971	50.3
4 ..	538	—	—	538	1.8
Acquired property	325	—	—	325	1.1
Total	16,669	11,001	2,087		
% of post-war stock	56.0	37.0	7.0	29,757	100.0

In broad terms we already know that larger properties were of greater importance to the black community (because of their greater involvement of large families) and smaller ones to the white community. In part this was because a large proportion of white allocations were to the elderly and that, conversely, pensioners barely figured in the pattern of black allocations. From Table 6.2, we can see that the bulk of smaller units of accommodation were post-war properties. Virtually all bungalows were post-war. Almost half of all post-war council built properties were 1/2 bedroom, and just less than 90% of these were flats, maisonettes or bungalows.

Three bedroom houses divided almost evenly between pre-war and post-war categories and, though the number of 4 bedroom properties built since the war was greater in numerical terms, the proportion of such properties (both pre- and post-war) remained constant at 1.8% of total stock.

An important difference emerged in relation to properties 'acquired' by the council. In both numerical and proportional terms, the majority of these were built pre-war. If, as we suggested earlier, the bulk of such properties were large family houses then it would follow that the quality of this stock would constitute a major influence upon the position of large families in Nottingham's council housing.

If such a supposition is not true (and the acquired properties were *not* predominantly large family houses) the conclusions to be drawn would be bleaker still. In that case, larger families coming into the council house system would have been competing for a supply of suitable pre-war or post-war properties which were more in a state of famine than scarcity.

On balance, however, we are inclined to believe that the former assumption is the more credible one. Precisely how old this stock was is hard to ascertain. In the first place, there is no available evidence as to the proportion of these houses built prior to the First World War as opposed to the inter-war years. Given the changes in house building policies prior to World War II, the precise time would have greatly influenced the size and quality of the properties which now make up Nottingham's acquired stock.

Nottingham and the growth of council housing

Prior to the First World War, although Nottingham was one of the few authorities to actually take advantage of the strictly limited opportunities to build its own council houses, the vast majority of housing was privately built and privately owned. It was also concentrated entirely within a tight densely populated central zone. This was mainly because of local difficulties in securing the complete closure of the common fields before 1845. Following this period, larger and more spacious properties were built on land which is, today, considered to be very much a central part of Nottingham's inner city. The large and expensive houses then built on

> "undulating land, overlooking the protected open spaces of the Arboretum and Forest".
>
> (Lawrence, 1974, p.70)

have since become the areas abandoned in flight by the more affluent middle classes. Many were also subsequently used for profiteering by private landlords before ending up under the ownership of the Nottingham Council.

The absence of any really large scale clearance programme

in Nottingham up until roughly 1960, meant that these properties constituted a major part of the central area housing stock during a period in which improvement programmes were little more than an afterthought to public housing policies. Even when Nottingham did embark upon large scale slum-clearance, many of these properties remained in pockets by-passed by the bulldozer. As Danny Lawrence accurately commented:

> "The pattern of housing which had emerged by the last quarter of the 19th Century can still be recognised today."
>
> (Lawrence, 1974, p.70).

Although such properties will have offered the greatest scope for accommodating larger families (particularly those wishing to remain in the central areas) they will also have been the ones in greatest need of rehabilitation. The importance of this part of the council's housing programme, which we examine shortly, is only reinforced by a clear picture, by 1975, of the post-war trend towards smaller housing units, and the possible concentration of larger properties amongst the older housing stock.

Some comment must also be made about the council's own purpose built stock built during the 'pre-war' period. It was then that the first flood of major changes in housing policy began to emerge on the statute books. Not all of these changes creditably reflected upon the quality of municipal housing. To *its* credit, Nottingham built the majority of its pre-war estates during the phases in which it was possible to build good quality housing stock, under favourable subsidy conditions, and avoided phases in which local authorities had to build under shabby, mean-minded funding policies.

It is worth briefly re-capping on the pre-war period as a whole if only in order to appreciate how far Nottingham's situation differs from other cities. By a long way, the best and most desirable council estate properties were built within the era of the Wheatley Act of 1924. Such houses were part of a vast expansion of a municipal housing in the 1920's and were significant both in terms of their number and quality. The building of these houses was underscored by a generous flat rate building subsidy, the repayment of which was spread over forty years. It was then that Nottingham undertook the construction of the bulk of its pre-war estates.

It was really only in the wake of the First World War that subsidies became an accepted part of public housing provision. The Addison Act of 1919, (more properly titled the Housing and Town Planning Act) confirmed and extended the basis of rent controls which had been introduced during the war. In the same year, provision was also made to provide state subsidies for both public and private house building. However, brief this flirtation with 'home fit for heroes' turned out to be, it did introduce an element of state intervention into public housing provision, which had hitherto been insignificant.

Council housing's most important filip during this period came five years later in the Housing (Financial Provision) Act, 1924 — the Wheatley Act. This raised the fixed grant subsidy in urban areas by 50% and doubled the period over which it was re-payable. The dismantling of this Act and its subsidies from 1929, and their complete abandonment in 1932, marked an important qualitative transition in the nature of municipal house building.

From the mid 1920's to the early 1930's, when Nottingham's main pre-war estates were constructed, local authority house building had been able to cater for increased numbers of working class families and with substantially built and often substantially sized houses. The cuts introduced in 1932 were not merely in the scale of municipal house-building, nor in tying it once again to clearance programmes. They were, as much as anything, an attack upon the stand-dards of council house building. Beneath the guise of providing houses which were 'within the means' of poorer workers, the changes in policy sought to reduce the unit costs involved in public housing provision. The instruction to local authorities to concentrate upon building small houses was actually explained in more forthright terms by one of the senior civil servants in the Ministry of Health:

"It was directed in fact less to the benefits of the working classes than to the limitation of the number of houses to be erected and the avoidance of expenditure on houses of substantial size."

(Quoted in Merrett, 1979, p.57).

The impact of this can hardly have been judged more precisely or unflinchingly than Merrett's declaration that

"many of the estates built in the 1930's were to become the ghettos of the 1960's in strong contrast to the housing approved under the full Wheatley subsidy."

(Merrett, 1979. p.57).

The extent to which this accurately describes the national picture of public housing provision is also the extent to which it distinguishes Nottingham's situation. Few of the city's pre-war estates even approximated to the slums of the 1960's and 1970's. This is really where the sting in the tail comes in. The council's housing efforts, made in the 1920's and 1930's, did result in the development of a number of low density council housing estates on the outskirts of the city. The trouble was, as Burney pointed out, that the

". . . clearance of the worst slums still left Nottingham with thousands of others as bad as the worst in many other towns . . ."

(Burney, 1967, p.187).

Thus, from the pre-war period, it was the housing conditions that were ignored rather than new estates poorly built, which were the problems in Nottinghams housing legacy of the 1960's and early 70's. An appreciation of that part of the legacy which has been carried through to the 1980's, can perhaps best be derived from one of the city's own assessments of its housing finance needs. In February 1980 it was reported locally that;

"Some 2,300 council owned houses have officially been declared as unfit for human habitation. And 9,600 houses lack one or more of the basic amenities of bath, hot water, and inside toilet. There are many more in the private sector . . . (in addition) over 15,000 council houses are in need of renovation."

(*Nottingham News*, 29th February 1980).

All of the 15,000 council houses needing renovation were part of the council's pre-war stock. It is almost certain that all council houses which had been declared unfit, or which lacked basic amenities, would have been in this category. In other words, at least two thirds of the councils pre-war stock was seriously sub-standard by early 1980. It would have been unlikely that the proportion of such properties during the years 1975, '76 and '77 would have been any less than this. On the contrary, given the council improvements which actually took place during the period, their original proportions may well have been significantly greater.

In qualitative terms then, the picture of the city's pre-war housing stock would be one of extremes — the best being soundly built, often by the Authority itself, and having limited renovation needs; the worst urgently needing clearance or wholesale rehabilitation.

As a result of similarly varied public housing polices which have been pursued over the last 25 years, the same sort of disparities can be identified in the character of post-war properties. Almost certainly the most substantially built houses were those constructed in the immediate post-war years. This was again a direct consequence of an enormous, if unsustained, commitment from central government to build a large number of high quality council houses. Not only were standards of space and amenities in council house design improved, but the scale and proportion of central government subsidies rose dramatically. For those who still retain any notion of what 'old money' actually was, the following account highlights the extent of these changes:

> "The existing subsidy on a standard three-bedroomed house, granted on a forty year basis, was £5-10s from the national exchequer and £2-15s from local rates. The new bill* lengthened the period from forty to sixty years, and raised the subsidy to £16-10s from the exchequer and £5-10s from local rates — thus altering the pre-war proportions of national and local contributions from two to one, to three to one. This was the major substantial alteration, but a host of others was added to deal with special cases . . . No such far-ranging and meticulous effort had ever been made to use subsidies as a spur over the whole field of public housing policy."
>
> (Foot, 1973, p.75).

*The Housing (Financial and Miscellaneous Provisions) Bill, 1946.

In Nottingham's case this resulted in the building of estates such as that at Clifton. Such stable and popular estates have already been identified in our study as offering important rehousing opportunities to the white community; opportunities which were not paralleled in West Indian or Asian allocations.

Nationally and locally, the post-war flirtation with quality was a short lived one. It gave way first of all to a reduction in standards, in order to churn out greater number of housing units, then to a tightening of the subsidies system and finally to curtailments in the number of council houses which the government was prepared to see built.

This trade off between quality and quantity found its embodiment in Macmillan's 'Peoples Houses' of 1952 onwards. Soon these two faced severe pruning through a reduction of 'general needs' subsidies, and the winding up of the Public Works Loans Board (which had given local authorities access to housing finance at protected, low interest rates).

> "Such steps, at a time when building costs and interest rates were beginning to rise, put great pressure on local authority housing financies. Their only recourse was to the slum clearance subsidies, and these offered differential rates to encourage flats and high rise building, a factor which was to prove very significant in reducing council housing standards."
>
> (CDP, 1976, *Whatever Happened to Council Housing*, p.19).

At least some of Nottingham's 15,000 council houses currently in need of renovation will have been spawned during this period of large scale reconstruction.

One of the most distinctive features emerging both from tables 6.1 and 6.2 is the limited amount of flats/maisonette accommodation built in Nottingham during the post-war period. Were these figures to be broken down even further they would reveal a distinct lack of *high-rise* flats complexes within the council's housing mix. Without doubt this representes a markedly different response to that of the majority of urban areas in post-war Britain. Its explanation lies less in terms of any particular municipal disinterest in council house building at the time, than in the peculiarities of the city's historical development. For a long time the city's housing had been confined to the central areas. Then, suddenly, large areas of land around its former boundaries were released for housing development. Indeed, as Lawrence has pointed out, the council during this period, sustained a generally high level of involvement in all house-building in the city. The critical factor seemed to be that land was perhaps less of a premium in Nottingham than in other cities. Thus, Nottingham's need/desire for flats complexes only surfaced at a time when, nationally, widespread doubts were beginning to be voiced about the extent of their virtues:

> "In Nottingham, between 1919 and 1940, 66% of all new houses were built and let by the Corporation with the aid of government subsidies. Between 1945 and 1964 the proportion was 75%. Most were intended to supplement existing stock rather than replace slum property. For this reason, and because of the shortage of land within the main body of the city, most of the building took the form of distinct low density estates around the city's boundaries. Only as recently as 1960, when Nottingham's first multi-storey block was completed in Denman Street (Radford), was a real start made on slum clearance."
>
> (Lawrence, 1974, p.73).

It was, then, only in the 15 years or so prior to our study that the major upheavals associated with clearance re-housing, and the subsequent reconstruction of parts of the central areas, took place. That this should have coincided with the major movements of black families into the city has been of lasting disadvantage to them. The inescapable necessity of completely clearing many of the worst parts of

Team games — Balloon Woods.

these slums was often lost in more facile explanations of clearance in terms of racial prejudice. Rather than recognising the inevitable culmination of poor design and structural neglect, it was the qualities of the newest incumbents which gave folklore its most popular and malicious explanation of the need for wholesale clearance.

It was the black immigrant, who finding himself

"defined as a man who overcrowds and destroys good houses",

(Rex, 1968, p.214).

remained the symbol of slums long after the particular buildings had been cleared. Such a mythology also dangled the same fate in front of any subsequent property or area that they were able to move to, and provided the same convenient misinterpretation of its shortcomings. The nature, quality and location of Nottingham's council housing stock in 1975, to some extent guaranteed that the larger families, characteristic of both Asians and West Indians in our study, were most likely to be offered properties of a type and/or location which would only serve to perpetuate such public maledictions.

Changes during the research period

The make up and condition of Nottingham's council house stock in 1975 helped determine the properties which were coming available for letting during our research period. It was, however, by no means the only, or necessarily the most important, variable which made up the supply side of the allocations equation.

There are bound to be changes in the stock of council housing over any three year period. However, when we looked at Nottingham's council housing in early 1978, on the surface, little appeared to have altered since 1975. The actual number of houses within the council's portfolio had increased from 48,493 to 52,675 (April 1975-April 1978). As can be seen from table 6.3 below, most of the proportions outlined in tables 6.1 and 6.2 seemed to have remained fairly constant.

TABLE 6.3
Nottingham's Council Housing Stock April 1978

Pre-War Stock	Houses	Flats/ Maisonettes	Bungalows	Total	%
1 Bedroom	—	656	—	656	3.5
2 ..	860	—	—	860	4.7
3 ..	14,503	—	166	14,669	79.9
4 ..	308	—	—	308	1.7
Acquired	1,942			,1942	10.5
TOTAL	17,613	656	166	18,435	
% of pre-war stock	95.5	3.5	1.0		100.0

Post-War Stock	Houses	Flats/ Maisonettes	Bungalows	Total	%
1 Bedroom	—	6,704	700	7,404	21.6
2 ..	2,248	5,132	1,308	8,688	25.4
3 ..	15,354	1,051	136	16,541	48.3
4 ..	745	—	—	745	2.2
Acquired	862	—	—	862	2.5
TOTAL	19,209	12,887	2,144	34,240	
% of post-war stock	56.1	37.6	6.3		100.0

All Stock	Houses	Flats/ Maisonettes	Bungalows	Total	%
1 Bedroom	—	7,360	700	8,060	15.4
2 ..	3,108	5,132	1,308	9,548	18.1
3 ..	29,857	1,051	302	31,210	59.2
4 ..	1,053	—	—	1,053	2.0
Acquired	2,804	—	—	2,804	5.3
TOTAL	36,822	13,543	2,310	52,675	
% of all stock	69.9	25.7	4.4		100.0

The most noticeable changes during the period may be sum-marised as follows:

1. a decrease in the *proportion* of 3 bedroomed properties from 63% to 59% (even though their numbers rose by almost 700).
2. an increase in the overall *proportion* of flats/maisonettes from 24% to 26%.
3. an increase in the *number* of 3 bedroom flats/maisonettes, all post-war, from 659 to 1,051.
4. an increase in the *number* of 1 bedroom flats/maisonettes, from 6,417 to 7,360.
5. an increase in the total *number* of 2 bedroom houses from 2,586 to 3,108.

6. a decrease in the *number* of pre-war, 3 bedroom houses from 15,294 to 14,503.
7. an increase in the total *number* and *proportion* of acquired properties from 3.8% to 5.3% (accounted for by the acquisition of additional pre-war houses, and new properties from private built estates).

Such changes, spread over a 3 year period, might seem to suggest a fairly static situation. However, what would appear to be only marginal changes in housing stock, mask the wholsale upheavals in housing policy which were taking place at the time. These changes, which were taking place nationally and locally in public housing policy, were to have far reaching consequences not only for council tenants in general, but for racial minorities in particular.

Life rarely allows for a neat dovetailing of all the variables influencing social change. This research is no exception. It has had to take account of changes in policy during the period which were clearly pulling in opposite directions. Similarly, a clear recognition has to be built in to the analysis, of the 'hereafter' effect of some of the changes in the housing policy — particularly the way in which changes in the building programme were often not felt (in allocation terms) until some years after the original decisions were made.

In Nottingham's case we have, first of all, to allow for the change in local policial control which took place in May 1976. The new Conservative administration acted swiftly to 'up-end' some of the previous housing policies. The out going Labour council had, for example, operated an arrangement known as the 'X' scheme, whereby families were invited to find for themselves, suitable property for sale in the private sector. By purchasing such properties the council thereby extended the notion of choice in clearance rehousing. Such acquisitions, principally during 1975, would have accounted for most of the increase in acquired properties between 1975 and 1978. After the 1976 local government elections this was one of the first measures to be abandoned. Privatisation rather than municipalisation became the order of the day. As such the only other additions to the council's stock of acquired properties would then have come from within Housing Action Areas, where private landlords, or owners, rather than improving their own properties, exercised a right to compel the council to purchase their houses. In this way the responsibility for improving them would have been transferred directly onto the local authority. Acquisitions of this sort will have been few in number, and undertaken not as a positive choice but because the council had no other option.

Similar about-turns took place in relation to the building programme, improvements policy and council house sales. These, along with important policy shifts in relation to rehousing practices, housing associations, and the treatment of empty properties, warrant separate consideration.

The Building Programme

Before the 1976 local government elections the council was committed to an extensive public building programme. This was intended to tie in closely with the clearance schemes which were still in full flow in the older central areas. This was not only part of a committment to extended council ownership, but also one which opened up, as widely as possible, the rehousing options of the poorest of inner city, clearance area tenants. The scale of this committment was seen as an indispensable pre-requisite for maintaining a high rate of clearance.

The policy had a double-edged success. On the one hand, the extensive and on-going building programme clearly increased the standing, status and acceptability of council housing amongst clearance families. By June 1974 this had become sufficiently clear for the Chief Executive to comment upon it in a progress report to council . . .

". . . it was assumed in the estimates that 21% of families from clearance areas would find their own accommodation and not require to be rehoused by the council. During the June quarter, very few families rehoused themselves."

(Hammond, June 1974, p.1).

By April of 1976 such a pattern had become sufficiently common to have brought about a major shift in the local authority's planning approach to clearance:

"Experience has shown that over the last few years the proportion of families making their own arrangements (for rehousing) has dropped considerably. For the purpose of forward programming it has been assumed that all occupants of clearance areas will require to be rehoused by the council."

(Hammond, April 1976, p.6).

However, this growth in popularity of council housing itself raised problems. Maintaining the rate of clearance was of paramount importance to the Authority. In order to do so, increasing proportions of the available council housing stock were having to be allocated to clearance families. This was particularly true of the point in time that our allocations study began.

"Satisfying the clearance programme . . . will necessitate about 64% of all available property being taken up by families from clearance areas."

(Hammond, November, 1974, p.2).

The steady flow of new houses being completed and handed over to the Authority was an important component in making this possible, whilst still allowing for other forms of movement both within and into the public housing sector.

One recurring feature of the Chief Executive's progress reports had been a reminder, to the Labour controlled council, of the importance of having sufficient land upon which new development could take place. In the year leading up to the local elections a large number of sites, outside the city boundaries, were being investigated. Whilst not being the only areas which the Authority was planning to incorporate into its building programme, these sites would have provided space for some 7,000 council houses, which were to have become progressively available for letting, up until the early 1980's.

In 1976, almost as soon as the Conservative administration had taken office, all of these development plans were stopped. On 21st May 1976 the new administration also decided to stop all acquisitions from private developers. These had been expected to produce in excess of 150 new houses per year, which would then have been available to the Authority. Purchases of older housing for improvement, or merely as straightforward additions to stock, (expected to add a further 180 houses per year) were also prohibited except where the Authority had a statutory obligation to do so.

The policy of the new administration was as succinct as it was stark. The motto 'It is not our policy to build council houses', was one of the unequivocal flags under which the new council took office. In the short term at least, the impact of this policy shift was inadequately recognised. The new houses which were then coming available to the Authority had, after all, been set in train at least 2 years earlier. In many cases the gestation period for such houses had been considerably in excess of this. The real impact of the new policy was not to become practically apparent until after that particular administration's term of office had ended. Instead there was an Indian Summer of housing provision for the new administration — basking in its ability to dramatically cut expenditure on new council house building, whilst at the same time having an apparently unaffected supply of new properties available for clearance families.

The retreat from a continuous building programme of any

significant scale, gathered further momentum when, in March 1977, the Housing Committee decided to defer approval of all new council house schemes. This decision did not simply remove any future commitment to council house building and land acquisition, it included a resolution not to go ahead with existing schemes; many of which had already passed the stage of detailed design and layout. In place of these schemes the council declared themselves willing to sell all of these sites either to private developers, who could build houses for sale, or to housing associations. At the very least this decision caused a considerable delay in any new properties becoming available on such sites; even begging the question of whether any then became available for renting by people at the top of the council's waiting lists.

Although, in Nottingham's case, such an about turn was conducted with positive relish, it would be misleading to suggest that other authorities under different shades of political administration, were not also forced some way along this path from the mid-1970's onwards. The undermining of public sector housing provision was a national phenomenon rather than an entirely local affair.

> "In 1974-5 the national economy was in the most critical condition. The rate of inflation was well into double figures. The balance of payments was deeply in deficit, much of it because of our inelastic demand for imported energy sources. Unemployment followed a strong upward trend to levels not seen since the 1930's and by the beginning of 1976 had reached 1.2 million persons or 5.2% of the labour force."
>
> (Merrett, 1979, p.265).

That this now appears as little more than a watered down version of our plunge into the 1980's may make it an easy scenario to grasp. However, it ought not to dull the sense of high anxiety in which our economic plight was then perceived. The state of crisis brought with it a renewed interest in monetarist economic ideas. These largely revolved around regulating the money supply by directly controlling (i.e. cutting back) public expenditure. Housing provided a prime target for this.

Such control found its embodiment in the Labour government's 1976 letter of intent to the International Monetary Fund, in which part of the price for financial support was the setting of definite target limits for controlling the money supply. The public expenditure cuts of £1 billion which the Chancellor of the Exchequer, Dennis Healey, announced in July that year were the translation of this commitment into practical terms.

£150m of this sum was to be clawed back from local authorities' housing budgets. As a direct result, local authority expenditure on municipalisation and new building fell by 23% in the 2 years after 1975/6. This contraction in terms of restricting the availability of council housing in subsequent years was unmistakeable and dramatic. Labour and Conservative controlled local authorities alike would have been affected by the Labour government's changes in public housing policy.

> "Total public sector starts in 1975 were 173,800, compared with 112,800 in 1973, the last full year of the Health government. But with the 1976 economic crisis, building was cut back to a total of 107,200 — i.e. below the last year of the Health government."
>
> (Webster, 1980, p.117).

Such figures severely dent the credibility of Labour's long standing claim to be the champions of public sector housing. The estimates, now being examined, of as few as 25,000 council houses being started in the first 6 months of 1980, do not make Labour's housing policies any more admirable. In many ways the Labour government's growing interest in general monetarist policies, and disinterest in council house building, merely prepared the ground for the Conservative government of 1979.

For those who, with increasing difficulty, have sought access to, or movement within, the council house sector since the mid 1970's, there can be only the most perverse satisfaction in recognising that the economic ideas tentatively fondled by the Labour government in 1976, were precisely those pursued with greater ardour by their Conservative successors since 1979.

Whatever other conflicts of interest or policy existed between the, then, Labour government and Conservative controlled local authorities, there can be little doubt that the cuts in expenditure on council housing provided an effective screen behind which council's like Nottingham could make the large scale withdrawal of investment in public housing that they so fervently desired. The extent to which they proceeded to do so can be most graphically illustrated by the city's own figures of the amount of money even being *applied for* from central government for new council house building. In the 3 full years which the Conservative administration budgeted for, their own building target fell as follows:

Year	New Building Estimates in the Housing Investment Programme
1977/78	£25,620,000
1978/79	£12,812,000
1979/80	£2,725,000

(Taken from Notingham's Policy & Resources Committee Minutes 20/9/77 and 21/2/78).

The changes in political control of both central government and (in Nottingham's case) local government in 1979 have to be understood clearly in the extent to which public housing provision had already fallen from grace. The sense in which such changes locally afforded grounds for optimism or despair is something which we will return to shortly. It is simply worth stressing that the commitment to maintain the clearance programme (continually stressed by the Conser-

The great divide? The bridge between Balloon Woods flats and housing association properties (Wollaton).

vative administration in the city) will have increasingly pressed upon the margins of housing supply as the building programme ground to a halt.

Housing Associations

The 1974 Housing Act, devised by the outgoing Conservative government but implemented by their Labour successors, enhanced the role of housing associations in the provision of rented accommodation.

> "The main objectives of the 1974 Act in respect of housing associations were that they would be able to fill some of the gap left by the diminishing private landlord, particularly in areas of severe shortage of rented accommodation such as the stress areas of inner cities, and 'provide a third choice to prevent the tenure system polarising into the two monoliths of owner-occupation and council housing'."
>
> (Lansley, 1979, p.192).

The nature of this alternative was outlined more fully in the Department of the Environment circular 170/74. In essence, this circular spelt out the ways in which:

> ". . . the government saw housing associations playing a variety of roles in helping to meet housing need, especially in stress areas, including

catering for specific categories of need such as the elderly and handicapped, in providing smaller-scale and less remote management than that provided by local authorities, in providing a base for co-operative management, and in experimenting in tenant participation.''

(Lansley, 1979, p.192).

As part of this initiative, massive increases in grant aid were made available through the Housing Corporation. The price for joining in on this bonanza was that the money was only to be made available to associations who became 'registered' with the Corporation. In this way associations of more dubious pedigree were to be weeded out: sobriety and respectability were to become central qualities of this up-rated 'third arm' of housing provision. Many local authorities and housing associations responded quickly to take advantage of this and, between 1973 and 1976 the annual amount of housing association 'starts' more than doubled (for both new build and rehabilitation work).

The Nottingham City Council was not immediately impressed by such legislative changes. The local Labour council of the time appeared to have two major objections to housing association involvement. The first was a deep rooted suspicion of the extent to which professional self-interest (of estate agents, architects and solicitors) entered into the programmes put up by housing associations (despite the vetting of the Housing Corporation). Such feelings crystalised around accusations about the lack of direct democratic accountability of the associations. The second objection, held equally strongly, was on the grounds that, nationally, the Labour and Conservative parties had colluded in taking this initiative without giving any serious thought to channelling the money through local authorities themselves, i.e. by allowing councils to experiment directly with alternative management systems or specialist 'needs' provision.

Only with the election of a Conservative Council in 1976 did the position of housing associations, under go any radical change in Nottingham. The independence of housing assocations, as well as the funds available to them, appealed to the ideological commitment of the new council to move away from direct public housing provision. Neither the lack of close accountability of housing associations, nor their generally higher rents, afforded grounds for hesitation. Land was being sold off; housing associations had access to finance. In offering them land (particularly sites for which private developers were not making offers) the council would get houses built at a much reduced cost to themselves. Such properties would also have the double attraction of being available for lettings (the council having certain nomination rights) whilst it would be virtually impossible for any subsequent Labour administration to take them back into public ownership. It was no surprise then that the Chief Executive, in the first housing progress report following the local elections, reported a change in the council's housing policy, such that:

> "in future greater reliance will be placed on their partnership with Housing Associations for the provision of dwellings to let."
>
> (Hammond, April 1977, p.7).

In pursuing this line Nottingham faced a number of technical problems. Of the housing associations which had grown up locally, only two were of any significant size. Both of these had, however, concentrated upon improvement work rather than new building. They had, though, also catered for the specialist needs groups which had been identified by both the Department of the Environment and the Housing Coroporation, e.g. the homeless, single parent families, black adolescents etc. This proved an insufficient attraction for the city council, who instead invited some of the larger national housing associations to make offers for the land they had available. Only slowly did the Authority recognise that their lack of control over the building schedules of such associations, as well as the complexities of funding via the Housing Corporation, caused considerable delays in the supply time for new properties. Whilst this was not an area which greatly troubled the new administration, it clearly had an impact upon the prospects of those seeking rented accommodation through the Council.

In addition to this, the new partnership arrangements with housing associations were undertaken without any credible system to monitor their effectiveness. The consequences of this were wide ranging. Neither the Housing Department nor the Housing Committee knew what proportion of their nominations to housing associations were successful, why nominations were not accepted, or what proportion of total properties were going to council nominees. In addition to this, it meant that the council's housing visitors and counter-staff were invariably ill-informed about the extent of housing association properties which were available.

The associations themselves made little attempt to publicise their presence, and even less to ensure that black residents in the clearance areas, or on the waiting list, knew that the associations offered a rehousing possibility. There was almost a cloak of secrecy or disinterest worn by the Authority and the associations. This ensured that those who were least knowledgeable about the council's allocations system also stood the least chance of obtaining housing association accommodation.

However, even those who did manage to find out about housing associations were not necessarily successful in getting accommodation through them. The liberal and progressive management arrangements evisaged by the Department of the Environment, and facilitated by staff/tenant ratios far better than local authorities have had to work to, did not always materialise. One recent study of housing associations operating in Nottingham was highly critical of most of their lettings policies. In particular, the report drew attention to the importance which associations attached to applicants being 'of good character'. In interpreting this, the report concluded that it was usually taken to exlude:

> "people with rent arrears or debt problems in the past, people with a prison record, and even people whose housekeeping standards are not up to scratch — in other words many of the people in the most acute housing need. In fact, all except NCHA* were very wary of tenants with a history of rent arrears and tried their best to exclude such people."
> (Nottingham Housing Rights Group (NHRG), 1980, p.13).

In addition to this, the report made reference to another piece of research in which the director of the City's Homeless Families Unit was quoted as commenting that the council:

> ". . . would not expect large (i.e. National) housing associations . . . to house . . . such groups as; households on low incomes, households

(*Nottingham Community Housing Association — the largest of the local housing associations.)

whose breadwinner was unemployed, and one parent families.''

(NHRG, 1980, p.13.)

Such an approach to housing allocations had obvious, and far reaching, consequences. Even though the current stock of housing association properties in the city is unlikely to exceed 2,500 houses, the contradictions between their lettings policies and the rehousing responsibilities of the city council are disturbing. In addition, they raise real questions about the extent to which, in such a role, associations contribute more towards the housing problems of the urban poor than their solution.

We need to be clear, however, that the grounds on which the associations were criticised, in this report, were very precise. They did not in any way relate to the quality of new-build or rehabilitation work carried out by the associations, On the contrary, the report concluded that:

"Their building, improvement and maintenance work is *usually* . . . of a better standard than local authorities achieve. They are also the main providers of good quality older rented housing in the city . . ."

(NHRG, 1980, p.19).

It is in this respect that the aspect of race is most strongly linked to the role played by housing associations in meeting the city's housing allocations objectives. It was an enormous step to take in designating housing associations as the major vehicle through which new rented accommodation would be provided in the future. This was, however, the step that the Conservative administration decided to take in 1976.

The manner in which this was done raises doubts as to the administration's interest in rented accommodation of any kind during our research period. The 'agency responsbility' which the city placed on housing associations was not in any way constrained by equivalent measures to ensure 'agency accountability'. At best the city only followed through 'liaison' work with the associations (in terms of their lettings procedures). The clearly defined 'nomination rights' held by the city council with each housing association, have in the main been ignored or abused. One report, only recently published, described the allocation processes operating at the time quite starkly:

"In the past (under the Tory council) the system of nominating people to associations was a chaotic one. The association itself would put forward a family to the Housing Department, asking if that family could count as a Local Authority nomination. Such a system gave associations a high degree of control over the nominations system, and they could if they wished, avoid taking their fair share of what they might see as 'problem families', by not putting such families forward as Council nominations. Associations were also not always notifying the council about nomination rights over relets."

(Thorpe, 1981, p.19).

Such a system has now changed, with the local authority making nominations from its own priority lists for rehousing. However, this was certainly not the case during the period of our research, and even now all of the associations retain the right to veto nominations wherever they wish.

What does not seem to have changed is the council's lack of interest in ascertaining the extent to which the allocation policies of housing associations contain any degree of racial equality.

". . . there has been no real attempt by the Corporation to see how allocation policies operate with regard to ethnic minorities. None of the associations interviewed have ever been asked by the Corporation to supply figures relating to the ethnic origins of applicants or tenants."

(Thorpe, 1981, p.18).

That this should have been so in an authority whose Director of Housing was also the Housing Commissioner of the Commission for Racial Equality, can hardly auger well for the prospects of close monitoring of housing associations being pursued elsewhere in the country. That the city has since then changed the political complexion of its administration and also appointed a new Housing Director, does not appear to have reduced the scale of official disinterest in monitoring. Housing associations are still not required by the local authority to keep or monitor any ethnic records of their allocations. Though the Authority itself has a section on its nomination form where ethnic origin can be recorded, it appears that this has only symbolic relevance:

". . . the Local Authority has no intention of monitoring this data, and will not therefore be in a position to state the number of black nominations in proportion to white ones, and the success rate of black nominations as compared to that of whites. The Director of Housing said 'I am not interested in knowing whether some Housing Associations house more blacks than others', and it is clear that the policy makers are not interested either. The leader of the Housing Committee said, 'this is not a matter that the Committee has discussed and as yet we do not have any plans to discuss it in the future'."

(Thorpe, 1981, p.21).

The far reaching consequences of this approach to allocations responsibilities must, however, be tempered by a clear recognition of the time scale within which our own evaluation has to take place. As was pointed out earlier, the commitment to provide future rented accommodation primarily though housing associations, was only taken in the middle of this allocations study. The actual impact of it will not have been apparent until some time later. Essentially it is an issue of the early 1980's rather than the late 1970's. Recognising this, however, does not make it any less of an issue. Whatever criticisms can be made of the Authority's direct handling of housing allocations, these can only be compounded by the steps which were taken to divest itself of these responsibilities during the period of our research.

Without any attempt to monitor the lettings policies of housing associations it is hard to see how the local authority (or, for that matter, the housing associations themselves) could comply with the law which requires that equality of opportunity be a *demonstrable* part of its housing programme. Furthermore, such an approach did nothing to dispel the popular notion that housing associations, particularly the larger national ones, are inclined to 'cream off' the most respectable housholds seeking accommodation. Indeed the attitude of the local authority would have encouraged any such tendancy.

In Nottingham, the provision of good quality rented accommodation, particularly in central areas of large older housing, was intended to become the domain of housing associations. Such a policy shift was of particular importance to black families if only because of their need for larger properties. The actions of housing associations, both in terms of their own improvement policies (i.e. retaining in large single units or converting into smaller ones) and in their lettings policies, will have profoundly affected the rehousing prospects of black families in the city.

There is a degree of irony about an examination of housing association policies in relation to the improvement of properties for larger families. The irony lies in the fact that official recognition of the shortage of such improved properties came in the same council report as the declaration of a new found faith in the capacity of housing associations to provide them. Yet an examination of the size of improved properties being offered through housing associations makes it clear that they have manifestly failed to do so. One of the reasons most readily advanced for this failure was in fact touched on in the council's recognition of the shortage in 1976:

> "A review of the need for more 4 bedroom dwellings by conversion is at present being undertaken, but the future programme of conversion will be dependent upon the availability of finance."
>
> (Hammond, April 1976, p.6).

Though housing finance was not then in the same absolute state of scarcity as it is today, government cost yardsticks imposed very real constraints on the sort of improvement and 'new build' work being undertaken. What must be recognised is that, directly and indirectly, the structuring of central government housing finance 'encouraged' housing associations (as much as local authorities) to undertake work which catered for small families. It is behind this constraint which some of the local housing associations have explained away their failure to provide rehousing opportunities for larger families. The Housing Corporation (which is in most cases the body through which housing association finance is channelled) has not entirely accepted this explanation. Rather it has suggested that where housing 'need' and cost-limits clash, then it ought to be the cost-limits which are challenged. This becomes doubly important when the unmet need can be identified as having an additional and distinct, though not necessarily intentional, racial bias. If such financing institutionalises a discrete form of racism, then to fail to challenge it is not to be neutral. As the Nottingham CRC's report on housing associations commented:

> "It is important therefore that housing associations do not simply say that their property is not suitable for many black families, but make positive efforts to cater for such housing needs, by expanding their stock of larger houses and applying to the Housing Corporation for

higher cost limits where necessary."

(Thorpe, 1981, p15).

Whilst supporting this, it must be recognised that by now a good deal of the damage has already been done. Such a response would have to relate to future policy. The present government's fervent disinterest in the provision of rented accommodation of any sort, makes it debatable as to when this might even become a serious prospect in the immediate future.

What demands a more immediate evaluation is the current role of housing associations in the provision of rented accommodation. In Nottingham they have been given an increased role and responsibility in areas and categories of housing which are of particular importance to black families. Yet no associations give any adequate information about the extent to which black people gain access to their properties. Whilst the significance of the associations has increased, their accountability has remained ethereal and evasive. Successive governments, in bolstering the support for this 'third arm' of housing provision, have consistently failed to clarify the nature of the body to which it was intended to be attached. Whether any future government choses to expand this provision further, or to curtail it, local authorities will still have to grasp the nettle of accountability, if only for existing housing association properties. That the current leader of the city council can state that:

> "We should really be able to ensure that housing associations act in accordance with out own approach to equality of opportunity. We, and they, ought to be able to prove that discrimination does not take place."
>
> (Carroll, 1980).

merely underscores the extent to which such a commitment has not existed in the past. For our part we have been able to find no grounds for presuming that the transfering of improvement and new-build responsibilities to housing associations has improved the rehousing prospects of black families. On the contrary, there appear to be stronger grounds for presuming the opposite.

The most direct responsibility for this must be borne by the local authority itself. At the very least, it must be said that in adopting such an important change in housing policy without firm and continuing ties of accountability, the Authority conducted itself with much the same degree of moral integrity as Pontius Pilot. To this must now be added doubts about its legal probity in relation to compliance with Section 71 of the 1976 Race Relations Act.

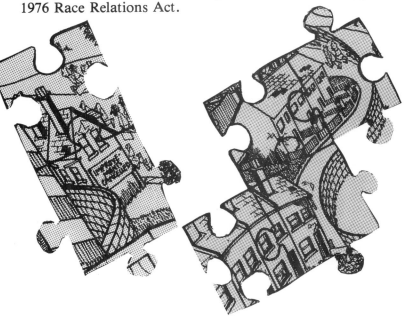

The Council's own Improvement Programme

Whatever hopes were pinned on the housing association movement it was clear that major rehousing responsibilities during this period still had to be borne by the local authority itself. Even if housing associations had had money and administrative capacity sufficient to take over all the housing stock that the city wished to 'off-load' (which they did not), it is doubtful that they would have necessarily wished to do so. As it was, the local authority remained unchallenged as the major possessor of rented properties in the city.

Their approach to housing associations, however, raised important questions about improvements within the council's own stock. It was one thing to talk about 'widening the choice of tenure patterns' by supporting housing association

work in the city. It was entirely another to do so directly at
the cost of those remaining within the council housing sector.
The dangers of such an approach can be sketched out quite
simply. If improvement initiatives were to be directed entirely
through housing associations, then those receiving (or currently occupying) council properties would increasingly be
confined to the poorest of the remaining housing. The logic of
such a two-tier renting system would ultimately be that of
American 'municipal housing': residual accommodation being provided for residual families. In this case, the residual
families would be those who, for one reason or another, were
not accepted by housing associations. Such a polarised
scenario would clearly depend upon the extent to which the
local authority curtailed improvements to the housing stock
which it could not dispose of.

At the start of our research period it must be said that no
such scenario existed in relation to the councils improvement
programme. The council had in fact only recently carried out
a re-evaluation of its housing policies in which the improvement programme had been given a significant boost:

> "In 1974 the city council drew up a programme for modernising council
> houses. The schedule identified the areas and the number of dwellings in
> need of modernisation . . . the programme was for about 1,500 dwell-
> ings per year up to 1978. The programme was to be carried out in two
> ways; firstly, modernising vacant properties before re-letting, and
> secondly, modernising whole streets at a time . . ."
> (Nottingham Housing Action Group (NHAG), 1977, Section on
> 'Council and Private and Improvement').

This was a formidable commitment by the local authority.
It was, however, the logical one to make in so far as the city's
slum clearance programme called out for a similar policy initiative in relation to improvements. Six years later, there is a
discomforting starkness about having to state that the initiative died in its infancy. Table 6.4 shows just how short lived the initiative acutally was.

The responsibility for reversing this commitment to improving the Authority's own property will almost certainly be
disputed. There are, however, only two major contenders
between whom blame can be apportioned. On the one hand
there was the Labour government which invoked (as we have

TABLE 6.4
Renovation of City Council owned dwellings*

Financial Year	*Number of dwellings improved*
1974/75	597
1975/76	1161
1976/77	609
1977/78	215

* Taken from the city's 1978/79 and 1979/80 'Housing Strategy Appraisal'. These renovations form an important part of the local authority's annual application for financial support from central government for its proposed housing programme.

outlined above) cuts and constraints which even the most committed local authority would have found difficulty in resisting. On the other hand, the people of Nottingham elected a new local council in 1976 which was committed to keeping the rates down, extending home ownership and curtailing public expenditure. The new council was, at best, ideologically indifferent towards the improvement of its own stock.

No great purpose would seem to be served in pursuing this search for a single culprit any further than we already have done. However, there would be some value in outlining the

Ships that pass . . . spending cuts guaranteed that many of those in the worst housing conditions were denied improvements (Hyson Green).

mechanisms through which the Labour government and the Nottingham council, between them, managed to mutilate the improvement programme.

The 1974 Housing Act was originally a Conservative Bill, which became adopted by the Labour government with very little amendment. The main focus of the Act was upon improvement programmes and an important part of this gave the Secretary of State for the Environment the power to direct local authority spending. During 1975 the Nottingham City Council (then Labour controlled) was informed that the government would be exercising greater control of local authority improvements and spending under Section 105 of the 1974 Housing Act. The City Council was not ecstatic about this, and brought in the local Members of Parliament to seek clarification as to whether their programme was being cut, and if so to what extent. Replying to the MP's, Mr Ernest Armstrong, Under Secretary of State at the D of E, in a piece of majestic understatement tried to make the point that:

".. . one cannot talk about reduction in funds when passing from an uncontrolled to a controlled situation."
(Quoted in NHAG, 1977 as above).

The rest of his letter, however, made it abundantly clear that this was precisely what he was talking about. The control which was to be introduced had two distinct objectives. The most laudable one was that which sought to direct local authority improvement work towards those properties most desperately in need of structural renovation. In the main these were thought to be the older housing which had not been part of any purpose-built council house programme. Rather they would be ones which the council would have acquired from the private sector. Such a policy would not necessarily have disrupted the city's improvement programme.

More substantial, however, was the second tenet upon which control was based. This was that the economic situation, or rather the government's interpretation of the economic situation, made it necessary that there should be controls on the *level* of rehabilitation expenditure.

Despite this, Nottingham's improvement figures for

1975/76 were well on their way towards the target of 1,500 council houses per year. However, overlapping with the local elections of May 1976 came the increasingly severe restrictions in housing finance from central government. Locally, these were received with some degree of resignation. It was reported that the national economic situation:

> "has brought additional restrictions and revised procedures giving increased control by central government in capital expenditure. These measures are beginning to take effect and several projects have suffered delays."
>
> (Hammond, October 1976).

In many ways such a comment understated the extent of the restrictions being imposed by central government. It had, in fact, been the case that in its 1976/77 budget the Authority had been instructed that there was to be no further expansion in general improvements work (private and council). Improvements in the council house sector were even more curtailed and only the granting of special D of E approval made it possible to see through the improvement programme in at least one council estate during that financial year.

Unfortunately, the response of the Labour government went from bad to worse:

> "By February 1977 the government again notified the city council that Section 105 money would be reduced, and that the money was to cover not only improving private dwellings and structural repair to council flats but also the environmental works such as landscaping and play areas in improvement areas (this had before come out of different funds)."
>
> (NHAG, 1977, as above).

This pattern of progressive cuts in local authorities' own improvement work has, like the cuts in the building programme, merely increased as the decade drew to a close. The advent of a Conservative government merely accentuated the process. If anything saved the government from having sole claim to the mantle of palpable indifference to the conditions in which many council tenants had to live, it was local authorities such as Nottingham. The newly elected council in 1976 pushed this level of disinterest further than most. In their first full budget they set out upon a new approach to their own improvement work:

"We shall look increasingly to the rehabilitation of suitable houses and shall encourage the sale of them, when improved as providing a source of reasonable low price houses."

(Conservative policy statement, (in Hammond, April 1977, p.3)).

The consequences of such an approach, for the council's own allocations system, can not be ignored. In prospect at least, it denoted an abandonment of council tenants living in older poorer property. Older improved properties which came available were to be offered for sale in the first instance. The older properties available *for letting* were then, presumably, those which had either not been improved or which had proved difficult to sell. In either case such lettings would have had difficulty in escaping the hall mark of 'leftover' properties; with all the ensuing stigma that would be attached to those who occupied them. This has to be hammered home if we are to fully appreciate the impact of the remaining allocations policies upon black families. The increasing concentration of black families in older central area housing will have made them the group most directly affected by the policy relating to council house improvements. What appears to have happened in Nottingham is that, by the end of the research period at least, the policy which existed was a derisory response to those in, or seeking, older central property to rent from the council. In the light of a policy commitment to sell off those older houses which were improved, even the dwindling figures outlined in table 6.4 must be a significant over-estimation of the number of improved propeties acutally *remaining* within the public sector.

The figures quoted earlier on, about the number of properties which the incoming Labour council of 1979 would need to substantially improve or demolish, are themselves ample testimony to the failure of any coherent improvement programme during the late 1970's. As such, it is important to recognise the extent to which such unimproved and structurally neglected properties were being let, in greater numbers, to black families.

Council house sales

To discuss Nottingham's housing allocation policies in the

late 1970's and fail to relate them to the policy changes in relation to sales, would be as fruitful as a football team planning out team tactics whilst the directors were in the process of trying to sell off the whole club — kit, balls, boots, players and ground. The sales policy which Nottingham introduced in 1976 did not achieve quite this level of total disposal. It did, however, manage to get rid of some 10% of the council's housing stock in the three years which followed — analagous to selling off 1 in 10 of the best players without any equivalent replacement. Only one Authority in the country managed to dispense with a greater proportion of its public housing stock during this period.

The origins of this particular sales drive ought now to be well known. The local authority elections of May 1976 saw the Conservatives sweeping the board in many urban areas. In Nottingham they did so on a platform which was as much a commitment to home ownership as to a general reduction in public expenditure. Although central government approval was required for the sale of council houses the, then, Labour govenment chose not to intervene in any serious or effective way. The scene was then set for what was heralded in London as the council house 'sale of the century'. The new Nottingham council responded with much the same enthusiasm. Within a month of the May elections the initial sales programme had been worked out. The Council's June meeting of the Policy and Resources Committee resolved:

"1. that all Council dwellings be offered for sale except flats, maisonettes, elderly persons dwellings, temporary dwellings, dwellings subject to service tenancies or let with shops, houses in clearance and redevelopment areas and houses purchased in future redevelopment areas;
2. that purchasers have the choice of buying at market value or at a reduced purchase price as follows:

Market value less 15% for tenants with less than ten years occupation.
Market value less 20% for tenants with more than ten years occupation.

3. that the above reductions in market value be subject to a condition prohibiting the re-sale of the property at a higher price within a period of five years and also reserving the right of pre-emption to the City Council which would prevent a re-sale within that period unless the owner first offered the property back to the City Council at the original purchase price;
4. that mortgages of up to 100% of the purchase price (less £1) be offered in appropriate cases at the City Council's current lending rate and a further report be submitted on possible alternative mortgage schemes;
5. that houses be sold only to sitting tenants except for houses purchased from the private sector and not yet occupied, which should be offered to:

i. people in clearance areas;
ii. tenants of Council dwellings not eligible to purchase (e.g. tenants of a flat, maisonette, etc) who qualify under existing conditions to be allocated a house;
iii. people on the waiting list who have qualified under existing conditions for an offer to tenancy of a house through the Council's allocation scheme."

(Minutes of the Policy and Resources Committee June 1976, item 23).

In terms of council house allocations, the impact of this move was painfully simple. The only properties which, in the first instance, were available for *lettings*, were the least desirable ones in the Council's portfolio. Increasingly, from mid-1976 onwards, the council properties being made available for letting were the residual ones excluded from the sales programme or unwanted by the buying public.

The earliest impact of the policy was seen in respect of newly built houses at Nethergate and Grotto Farm. Tentative offers had been made to let some of these houses to clearance area or waiting list tenants. Such families were then told that unless they wanted to acually buy the properties, the offers were withdrawn.

This was inevitably going to be the first area in which lettings were to be affected. Initially the sales policy was restricted to sitting tenants. The only sales not confined in this way were of unoccupied houses which had been bought from the private sector, and these were still restricted to households who satisfied the conditions of points 5i, ii, or iii, outlined above.

Despite the discounts being offered to sitting tenants the expected cavalry charge of prospective buyers did not materialise. At least one of the reasons was that the cost of buying any of the new houses was prohibitive; particularly so if the sale price had to be related to the cost of building the house rather than its market value. Fortunately for the local council, the Labour government got them off the hook, in the sense that the Department of the Environment approved the selling off of new properties at *less than they cost to build*, and without requiring the local council to make good the deficit out of its Rate Support Grant (the source of housing subsidy to local authorities). These costs were effectively paid for out of national taxation. Those involved in pressing for greater expenditure on public housing at the time will have gained little comfort, and even less amusement, from a recognition that, financially, this sort of sale resulted in the public sector having to continue interest repayments on housing which it no longer possessed.

Of more immediate consequence for those seeking to rent council property was the change in council restrictions as to who was entitled to buy. By early 1977, with the rate of sales still not satisfying the new political regime, important alterations were made to widen, not only the categories of eligible buyers of council houses, but also the types of properties being made availabe to them.

The revised policy meant that:

a. new houses, which were not purpose-built council houses, which had not been sold within 3 months would be made available for anyone to buy;
b. all new council houses coming available were to be offered for sale to anyone on the waiting list or living in a clearance area;
c. all re-let houses were to be offered initially for sale to waiting list or clearance area families. (No time limit was specified before these reverted to being available for renting).

Such changes had an important effect upon the lettings side of the housing department's work. One of the earliest arguments in support of the sales policy had been that it would not interfere with lettings because sales would be over-whelmingly to sitting tenants. Table 6.5 below shows the extent to which the argument became increasingly vacuous. The month by month sales breakdown makes it clear that, at most 75% of sales went to sitting tenants. This was, however, an erratic instance right at the very beginning of the sales cam-paign. Towards the end of our research period it is obvious that the rate of sales to sitting tenants plummeted to a low of roughly 16% of all sales. By no stretch of the imagination can such a situation be said to have had no effect on council house lettings.

The light at the end of the tunnel? — Victoria Centre flats.

TABLE 6.4

Nottingham's Council House Sales 1976 & 1977

Date	Houses originally purchased from the private sector or built for sale	Council Relets	New Council Houses	To sitting tenants	Monthly Sales	Percentage of sales to sitting tenants
1976 Aug.	1	—	—	—	1	0.0
Sept.	4	—	—	4	8	50.0
Oct.	13	—	—	38	51	74.5
Nov.	60	—	—	84	144	58.3
Dec.	53	—	—	56	109	45.9
1977 Jan.	48	—	—	92	140	65.7
Feb.	30	—	—	78	138	56.5
March	66	—	—	122	188	64.9
April	50	—	—	103	153	67.3
May	54	—	—	65	119	54.6
June	35	7	—	37	79	46.8
July	26	26	—	33	85	38.9
Aug.	23	85	—	22	140	15.7
Sept.	18	77	—	18	113	15.9
Oct.	27	111	—	44	182	24.2
Nov.	29	37	38	39	163	23.9
Dec.	50	64	19	60	193	30.6

Sales to sitting tenants became a smaller and smaller part of total sales, particularly once relet properties began to be more widely available for general purchase. The impact of this has generally been assessed in terms of its effect on the Council's total housing stock. For those seeking rehousing at the time it will have been the effect of sales upon the stock *which would otherwise have been available for letting*, which would have been felt most acutely.

By the end of 1977 some 2,000 council properties had been sold — less than 4% of its total stock. When we set sales in the context of 'total changes in council occupancies' (i.e. sales + total new lettings + transfers) a very different picture emerged. By the end of 1976 roughly 1 in every 6 properties which the council could have let was being sold (NB excluding sales to sitting tenants). One year later the rate had increased to almost 1 in every 3. However gloomy this might seem for those seeking rehousing by the council, it must be remembered that such figures seriously *understated* the extent to which those tenants remaining within the council house system faced increasingly restricted choices, in terms of the most desirable properties. (The major flats complexes had always been excluded from the sales programme — adding further confirmation of their low status within the City). Increasingly, as houses were sold off, the council's own allocations will have been concentrated upon flats complexes. This proposition is merely reinforced by the housing department's estimates that, at any one time, some 60% of their available properties were within flats complexes (even though these constituted less than 20% of its total stock). It was becoming increasingly true to say that the only way to get a council house was to buy one.

The point was most succinctly made by the Director of Housing, in reply to a woman with two children seeking a transfer from one of the citys notorious flats complexes. Despite her priority rating (viz the policy of transferring families with children out of flats complexes) the Director was unable to offer her any prospect of a move closer to her family on the Clifton Estate. He could only comment that:

> "a number of people have expressed an interest in purchasing a house in Clifton, as well as other areas, and these applications are being given priority over lettings to the waiting list, clearance rehousing and all other categories of rehousing including transfers . . . I am sorry that this will be a disappointment to you, as it will be to all other similar outstanding cases . . . Should you be interested in purchasing a house I will be pleased to register your name."
>
> (M. Campbell-Lee, quoted in Forrest and Murie, 1978, p.172).

During the second half of our research period (and for a considerable time after it) council house allocations need to be seen in a very specific context. The families involved will have been ones who lacked the interest in (or finance for) home ownership. The choice of properties that they were confronted with will have been made up of flats complex properties, plus the leftovers of the sales programme, plus the minimum number of houses needed to keep the clearance programme on schedule. The rest of the City's housing stock was up for grabs.

The extent to which the new council's desire to sell off its housing stock exceeded its sense of accountability to the local population was soon demonstrated by Thames Television.

The Council had argued that the sales policy did not really alter the local demand and supply situation for housing. After all, the houses which the council was selling were going to families on the waiting lists. These, it was argued, were precisely the families which the council, would in any case have been trying to rehouse. Much to the chagrin of the local Conservative party, a *T.V. Eye* production team soon demonstrated that this was patently not the case, and that it was perfectly possible for complete strangers to by-pass the waiting lists if they wished to buy a house.

> "In a single day, a journalist from Thames Television with a temporary address in the city, visited the Housing Department, registered on the council waiting list, went to another department, paid £5 and was given the keys to inspect a council property with a view to buying it. In practice, sales to those on the waiting list amounted to sales on the open market."

> (Forrest & Murrie, 1978, p.172 above).

Such a free-for-all for public housing only further undermined the position of those waiting to *rent* a council house; as well as making it increasingly difficult for the housing department itself to attempt to allocate housing on a basis of need.

Table 6.6, taken from the City's 1979 HIP submission to the Department of Environment, illustrates how extensively the sales programme was *expected* to cut into the stock of council houses.

TABLE 6.6*
Expectations of Council House Sales

Financial Year	Built for Sale	Other
(Actual figures)		
1975/76	30	—
1976/77	161	618
1977/78	76	1,575
1978/79	65	1,956
(Expected figures)		
1979/80	86	1,920
1980/81	100	1,423
1981/82	100	1,423
1982/83	100	1,408

* Taken from Section 1 of Department of Environment form 16314, submitted in September 1979 by the Nottingham City Council.

There is a certain degree of irony about the similarity between the level of expected sales in later years, and the target rate set by the Council in 1974/75 for improvements in its own housing stock. Both sets of expectations were rudely interrupted by local authority elections which dislodged the party in power. Unfortunately, for those remaining in (or seeking) council tenancies, the level of sales far outstripped the level of improvements within the retained council house stock.

So far, the impact of council house sales has been dealt with only in general terms. The extent to which there is a racial dimension to this has, once again, to be seen in terms of the nature of the properties which were being sold. We were unable to obtain the sort of property breakdown we required, simply covering our own research period. Fortunately, most of the spade work for this breakdown had already been done by the Nottingham Alternative Publications group in their report — 'Where have all the assets gone?'' The information, set out in Table 6.7, is drawn directly from their work and, though covering a wider time period than our own research, allows important conclusions to be drawn out concerning the rehousing prospects, of larger (and frequently black) families seeking council housing.

TABLE 6.7
Sales of Council Houses built under different Housing Acts*

ACT —	1919/23	1924	1930	1935	1946	1956/61	1967
Numbers available for sale	2,200	7,200	4,400	1,600	11,000	5,000	12,000
Total Sold 1967-78 (March)	194	509	187	70	1,690	598	442
% Sold	9%	7%	4%	4%	15%	12%	4%
Typical Estate	Sher-wood	Aspley	Best-wood	Brox-towe	Clfton	Best-wood Park	St. Anns

* Taken from Nottingham Alternative Publications, (NAP), 1979, Appendix E, p.48.

Even allowing for the much greater time period covered, what this table shows is that the highest proportion of council house sales were in estates built under generous subsidy conditions (i.e. the 1924 Wheatley Act and the immediate post

World War II period). This was also the housing which had been given the most generous standards of space as well as subsidy. Selling off such properties will only have narrowed the arena in which black and white families were forced to compete for an increasingly limited number of properties for rent. The additional popularity of early 1920's housing only adds to the impression that it was the larger older properties which were proving to be the most popular in the sales campaign — as well as being the most sought after by the black community.

This is not the place to go into an extensive and detailed argument about the uneconomic nature of council house sales. Others have in any case already presented powerful arguments in support of such a case. We would, however, merely want to register the point that if there was *ever* an appropriate time to sell council housing, it would *not* be one when the council's own building programme had been cut to shreds; or when house building and private improvement programmes were in disarray. Within the sphere of industry a comparable policy would be criticised as assett stripping; in the arena of public housing it deserves precisely the same acclaim. The whole thrust of the sales programme will have merely compounded the conditions of scarcity and neglect which the cuts in the building and improvement programmes set in train.

Voids

The issue of council houses standing empty during this period is one which only adds insult to the general injuries already done by the preceeding policy changes. Councils always have some empty properties. Such 'voids' form a necessary part of a council's ability to offer movement within its own housing stock and facilitate its clearance rehousing. Within limits, a range of vacant properties also offers a degree of choice to those who have reached the top of the waiting list. As a matter of course, however, it is in a Housing Department's interest to limit these numbers. The more it restricts the number of voids it has, the more effectively it can claim to be carrying out its housing responsibilities and the more it reduces its own loss of income (i.e. through the obvious absence of rent and rates payments).

Nottingham's sales policy had the effect of increasing the number of 'voids'. This was particularly so in relation to the sale of relet properties (existing council properties which for one reason or another became vacant). To all intents and purposes, relets could not be put on the market until they were vacated by the previous tenant. This differed considerably from new house sales, or private sector ones, where the transactions could begin much earlier. The effect of this was to create a significant increase in the number of properties which were standing empty at any point in time. The Housing Department's void analysis, up to the end of our research period, showed that within the last 6 months of 1977 (when relet properties were first made available for sale) voids had increased to about 2,000 properties at any one time. The actual increase was in excess of 500 properties over the six month period. As far as we have been able to ascertain, the increase in properties standing vacant because of the sales policy continued throughout that period of Conservative administration in Nottingham.

It was not simply that, at any point in time, a larger number of council houses stood empty. In other circumstances this could have been associated with a large amount of movement within the council house system. In this context, however, this was clearly not so. In fact, the limited movement within the public rented sector was exacerbated by the increasing length of time that relet properties were kept empty, in the hope of finding a buyer. Despite official protestations to the contrary, this aspect of Nottingham's sales policy was increasingly recognised by outside observers. In November 1978, Forrest and Murrie commented that:

> "Nottingham currently has about 1,300 dwellings available for sale. It is policy to return dwellings to the lettings pool if they remain unsold after 3 weeks. What has happened, of course, is that some houses have lain empty for months before the sale finally fell through. By that time the property can be in a serious state of disrepair . . ."
>
> (Forrest and Murrie, 1978, p.172).

Just how commonplace this was, and how extensive the time for which properties stood empty, was not fully understood until much later. Not until political control of the council again changed in 1979, did information about the extent of abortive sales transactions become widely available. The new leader of the city council subsequently commented that:

"One in every five applications fell by the wayside. In theory a house which was empty for three weeks went back into the pool. But they defined this as being a time when no 'interest' had been declared in the property. Therefore if a house was empty for one day and then someone registered an interest, what would happen would be that there would be at least 3 months legal work involved. Finally, you get to the altar and all of a sudden the bride changes her mind. The deal falls through. Technically, though, the house has still only been empty for one day. This sort of delay could go on and on almost indefinitely, and the house would remain empty for the whole of that period."

(Carroll, 1980).

Thus, it was not simply that, within eighteen months of its introduction, the decision to sell relet properties — to virtually anyone who fell into the Housing Department with enough money in their pocket for a deposit — resulted in an extra 1,000 council properties standing empty at any one time. What also became apparent was that such 'voids' often stood empty for considerable periods of time. The report 'Where have the assets gone?' identified the fact that, from Nottingham's council housing stock:

"around two thirds of relet houses coming vacant from February 1977 to March 1979 were sold."

(NAP, 1979, p.49).

Clearly the families who managed to obtain any of the remaining one third of relet properties, will not have done so before the properties had remained empty for some time. The cuts in the repair and improvement programmes which accompanied the sales drive, also raise doubts as to whether any but the most superficial aspects of disrepair accumulated whilst the housing was left vacant, will have been tended to. Moreover, the importance of this has to be seen in respect of the different types of relet property. In terms of sales, the least popular properties were those built under the most meagre subsidy conditions. These will, at one and the same time, have been the properties most likely to have been returned to the lettings 'pool', and also those most vulnerable to degeneration during the period for which they were kept empty.

Synthesis: Housing Policies in the late 1970s and the Prospects for Council Housing in the 1980s

The mid-1970's marked a turning point away from an expansionist policy in respect of public sector housing. With the ending of many of the major clearance programmes, the emphasis was placed more upon improvement of existing properties. What cannot be avoided, however, is a recognition that such a shift was not merely a transferring of finance from one pocket to another. It was the pretext behind which a major disinvestment in public housing took place. Both political parties must share the responsibility for this. The Conservatives might have pursued it more ruthlessly at a local, and then national, level. But the Labour government, by the end of 1975 was beginning to make similarly sweeping cuts in its own right, and gave their approval to the running down of council house stocks locally.

In Nottingham, the curtailment of the building programme, the sale of land for future development, cuts in the improvement programme, a commitment to sell virtually anything with a door on it, and a prepardeness to leave properties empty for extensive periods in order to do so, had a devastating effect. It would be a mockery to discuss the allocation of council houses during this period without giving due recognition to the derisory conditions in which these were having to take place.

The sales policy offers the most effective touchstone for gauging the declining status of council housing during this period:

> "In Nottingham, transfers fell from 2,300 to 1,000 per year after just two years of their sales policy . . . Allocations of council housing went down by over 25% between 1976 and 1978. In the coming year (1979) the council predict that nearly 1,400 families are scheduled to be rehoused from slum properties — but there will be only 670 council houses for them to move to."
>
> (National Tenants Organisation, 1979, housing action pamphlet).

The arguments justifying such a substantial undermining of public sector housing provision, comprised a mixed bag of half-ideas, cobbled together in order to rationalise away a growing distinterest in council tenants and council housing. As far as council housing was concerned, the arguments were based upon much the same constructive and compassionate intentions as the Viking invasions.

In the first place notions of housing 'needs' were attacked. Nottingham had, for some time, carried a waiting list of some 10,000 households. The appointment of additional housing visitors under the government's Urban Aid programme, had been a recognition of the particular difficulties faced by families still living in the deteriorating parts of the private rented sector; particularly those which were not affected by clearance programmes.

One way that the Conservative council found to make the reduction in allocations acceptable, was to undermine the credibility of the waiting list. As the local paper reported:

"Nottingham's house waiting lists could well be cut from 6,000 to just 1,000 cases of real need, City Council leader Cllr. Jack Green claimed today . . . A year ago the total list stood at 10,000 he said. Half the present list was names of people who might want a house — they were not cases of real need."

(Nottingham *Evening Post* 11/10/76).

Reducing the waiting list to more 'sensible' numbers of those in 'real need' (which was never defined) provided a convenient way of reducing the level and urgency of meeting these responsibilities.

The process of re-defining problems out of existence was also carried through into the presentation of housing statistics. Earlier, as we mentioned, the trend which had been identified by the Chief Executive, was of fewer and fewer families in clearance areas looking to re-house themselves. This resulted in the council having to plan their clearance programmes with a view to rehousing all the families involved. After the change in administration, a notable change in style crept into the way that statistics were presented. The local authority began, in effect, to claim the credit for all those who moved out of clearance areas — irrespective of whether they were rehoused by the council or not. There are real grounds for believing that a high rate of 'self-rehousing' crept back into the clearance programme.

Faced with protracted waiting periods and increasingly dilapidated properties, there will have been considerable pressure upon the poorest families once again, to find themselves other rented accommodation one step ahead of the bulldozer.

Central government itself provided considerable opportunities for the Nottingham City Council to disguise its own lack of commitment to council housing during this period. Labour's collusion with local authority sales programmes was added to by their general cuts in 'improvement' finance for local councils. This was further compounded by their introduction in 1977 of the 'Housing Strategies and Improvement Programmes' (HIP's) system of advance planning for local authority finance. When the Department of Environment introduced this it was, theoretically, to encourage local authorities not to interpret their housing responsibilities too narrowly. The extension of the housing remit of local authorities was to be aided by a larger timsecale within which to plan and implement changes.

> "The HIP's system brings together the forward planning of local housing policies and programmes with the allocation and control of investment resources by central government."
>
> (Bramley, Leather and Murrie, 1980, p.3).

In retrospect such cross-breeding must be seen as having produced a genetic throw-back rather than an evolutionary advance. It introduced a much greater degree of centralised control of local authority programmes, but in an almost entirely negative way. The rolling programmes that council's were to develop, became laden with bureaucracy and riddled with uncertainty. Their popular title became 'rolling probation' rather than rolling programmes.

> "the framework of financial control appears to contribute to a tendency to underspend given prevailing local authority practice in relation to capital programme management. What has been established is a ceiling without a floor, which is a relatively limited achievement and, it may be argued, a costly one in so far as it has allowed resources to be under utilised."
>
> (Bramley, Leather and Murrie, 1980, p.193-4).

It was, however, left to the incoming Conservative government of 1979 to most clearly demonstrate the overwhelmingly repressive bias in the arrangements introducted by Labour. The swingeing cuts which have followed since then rely, to a large extent, upon the more direct controls of local authority housing programmes which were established under the previous government. The re-elected Labour council in Nottingham may well, with considerable justification, grimace at being forced to run a three year housing programme on two years money. What they cannot ignore is the fact that many other Labour councils were expected to do exactly the same by a Labour government during the period of our study. At a national level, the Labour government appeared to accept that description of the political situation

". . . which says that only so much resources have been allocated for housing and the working classes, and let the buggers fight it out amongst themselves, with the local Labour Party playing referee and fight promoter."

(Byrne, 1974, Working Paper in Sociology).

More than any other aspect of policy change during this period, it was the programme of council house sales which increased conflict over the allocation of council housing. The economic arguments upon which the council house sales were justified have since been torn apart: no more so than in Nottingham:

"Nottingham will make a net loss of £75 million in the long term by selling 5,356 houses in the last three years. The initial gain is £1½ million a year but within eight years the gains will have turned to losses."

(NAP, 1979, p.2).

Even if the scale of these losses are disputed, what has become increasingly clear is that a variety of organisations ranging from Shelter to the Institute of Cost Management Accountants have confirmed that, in the long term, the sales policy will result in substantial losses.

However, sales alone cannot carry the whole can for the decline in public sector housing provision.

". . . it is not just sales policies which are called into question but levels of public expenditure, the methods of controlling it and the combination of policies effecting housing opportunity, choice and mobility. The present policies in many areas of housing stress are the very opposite of a systematic housing strategy. They are a muddle of underspending, underhousing, underbuilding, underinvestment and overselling.''

(Forrest and Murrie, 1978, p.172-3).

In the short term, which is what most of us gauge our daily lives by, we must add to this the problems of 'under consumption', namely the losses borne by those seeking to rent

Contrasts in older housing — Radford/Forrest Fields.

council housing. Their loss was in rehousing prospects. In this respect, all of those who sought rehousing *by the council* were discriminated against by the housing policies of the period. So too were the housing department's staff, who had the task of making allocations decisions about those properties which remained. Our specific concern with the racial consequences of this situation, stem directly from its impact upon the sort of properties and areas into which black families were rehoused. For such families, the pursuit of larger houses, predominantly restricted to the older central areas or estates of the early 1920's, will have been doubly frustrating. The supply of properties which they were seeking was more and more restricted to the rejects or leftovers of the sales programme. Even where such properties were obtained the shortage of funds for council house improvements ensured that there was little prospect of the extensive rehabilitation which they increasingly required.

Moreover, the local authority's approach to older housing, specifically in relation to housing associations, only extended the disadvantage confronting black households. The transfer of ownership and improvement responsibilities for many of the larger, older council properties to housing associations, meant that the local authority abandoned direct responsibility for properties which were of specific, and disproportionate, importance to black families. As if to ensure that this was so, the council avoided the establishment of any monitoring system which might identify racial inequalities which might have emerged in the pattern of housing association allocations. This must have been of considerable relief to the various housing associations who showed little or no interest in being able to publicly demonstrate that their allocations were free from racial bias. Neither of these approaches did anything to dispel the notion that housing associations, in fact, are particularly choosy about the families that they accept — and that they are so in ways which work to the specific disadvantage of the black communities.

Within the properties which remained available for letting by the council, West Indian families were additionally disadvantaged by their dependence on the waiting list as a means of access to the system. This will have inevitably restricted them to offers of those parts of the council's housing stock which were not even considered saleable — increasingly the flats complexes which the majority of council tenants sought to avoid, or escape from.

It is hard to avoid the conclusion that the combined effect of housing policies being pursued in Nottingham during this time, in many ways, constituted the most pervasive and insidious discrimination of all.

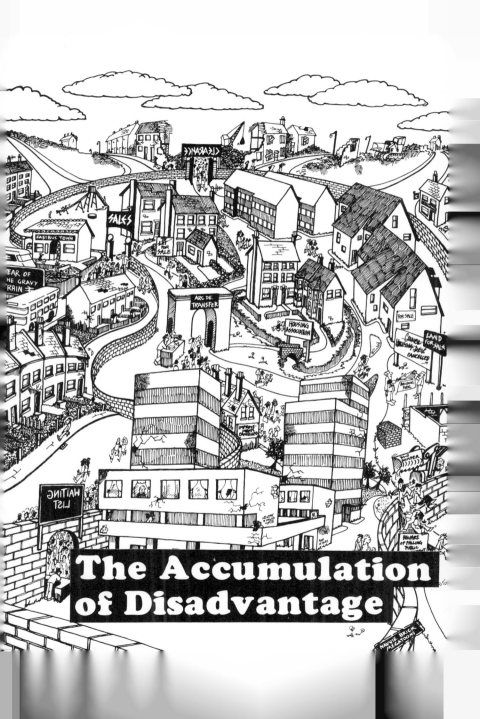

The Accumulation
of Disadvantage

7

The Accumulation of Disadvantage — and the Potential for Change

". . . the relative confinement of West Indians to furnished accommodation is a product of discrimination elsewhere in the housing market."

(Haddon, 1972, p.113).

". . . housing deprivation can be understood and explained only in relation to the full range of inequalities in housing . . ."

(Townsend, 1976, p.98).

In every aspect of this study, from its broadest context to the working of each individual reshousing category, black households have experienced disadvantage, of one form or more, in their pursuit of good quality council housing. It would be naive and blinkered to suggest that they were the only ones to do so — since 1975 all of those seeking decent council housing throughout the country have been increasingly discriminated against; to a degree almost unparalleled in post-war Britain. Such discrimination has been a central feature of successive government housing policies which have maintained or extended housing inequality. Before returning to the internal workings of Nottingham's council housing policies, it is worth focusing upon the changes which would need to take place at a national level in order to make equality of housing opportunity a realistic target for local authorities.

Few would dispute the fact that, during this period we have experienced a considerable economic decline. However, the really problematical aspects of this have been not so much the existence of a crisis in itself, but the way in which we have *perceived* this; and the policy approaches which have then resulted. In most cases these responses have only helped to bring a crisis into being, or make it more intractable. The monetariest policies played with by the last Labour government, and pandered to by the current Conservative one, have actually created a housing crisis when previously they merely had a problem.

How perilous the housing position now is, can be seen from the extent to which organisations of both Labour controlled and Conservative controlled councils, throughout the country, have been urging the government to re-think its housing strategy. In October 1980 the Guardian detailed the conclusions of a report by the, Conservative contolled, London Boroughs Association, in which it was predicted that:

"within five years there will be a shortage of 500,000 houses in Britain and nearly two million families living in poor housing . . ."
(*Guardian*, 23rd October, 1980).

Within months of this the Labour controlled Association of Metropolitan Authorities came to even starker conclusions. Their sense of despondency was partly based upon the swineging cuts in local authority Housing Investment Programmes (1980/81 allocations being a reduction of 42% on the orginal figures for the previous year), but also on the prospect of seeing 1980 produce one of the lowest number of new housing 'starts' since the Second World War. Two of their conclusions were unequivocal in their criticism of existing government policies:

"The switch of emphasis from new build to rehabilitation that has taken place since 1969 has failed to tackle the housing most in need of repair, and a considerable amount of national resources have been expended in a so far unsuccessful effort to significantly arrest the rate of deterioration of the stock. In addition the present rate of demolition is extremely low . . . at this rate it would take over 500 years to replace the stock."
(Association of Metropolitan Authorities (AMA), 1980, p.4).

"The housing situation is rapidly moving to a position whereby it will be beyond the capacity of the construction industry to tackle both major problems, older housing and new build, at the same time. A concentration on new build will lead to an acceleration of the already rapid slide in the disrepair and unfitness. Concentration on rehabilitation would widen the predicted gap between housing requirements and housing provision. The situation is moving to a critical phase and will not be solved by current policies and levels of expenditure."
(AMA, 1980, p.22).

This progressive undermining of the nation's capacity to provide itself with decent housing, gained momentum both during and since our research period. It has also prompted many of those involved in housing issues to do little more than shrug their shoulders in resignation. In doing so, some have accepted the popular logic that destruction of various parts of the country's social fabric is an unfortunate, but necessary, step along the road to economic recovery. For others it has been simply a gesture of impotence; a disbelief in their ability to change or influence the course of public policy. To be fair, looking back at the period since 1975, there has to be some element of despair in any recognition that the best you can say about yesterday is that today turned out much worse, and that tomorrow looks abomnable. This is hardly the fountain of hope.

Yet a basis of optimism has to be established if the social and, more particularly, racial inequalities of our time are not to become the scapegoats for, as well as victims of, such destructive national policies. The process of doing so has to be a two pronged one; involving important changes in the ways in which we perceive housing as well as in the structure of actual housing policies. In the longer term it has to be within this framework that discrimination at a local and national level will be most comprehensively tackled.

At the level of perceptions, housing policy has always suffered from the narrow time scale in which politicians have examined it:

> "Housing problems are seen as temporary aberations which will either pass with increasing prosperity or in the streamlining of existing policies. They are not seen as an inevitable and continuing aspect of structural inequality."
>
> (Townsend, 1976, p.89).

Even at their most full-hearted, the commitments of politicians have often been of a remarkably short-term and 'one off' conception:

> "Many local authorities should be able to solve their housing problems in five years or so." — Harold MacMillan, Minister of Housing, (1954).

> "What we have to do is to mount a *final** assault to clear the slums, end the overcrowding, improve the homes and give real help to the people in

need . . . I can see no reason why local councils should not clear away all the existing slums by 1980." — Julian Amery, Minister of Housing, (1971).

(Both quoted in Townsend, 1976, p.90).

*Our emphasis.

Dramatic lurches in public housing policy between the wildly over optimistic and the cynically disinterested have done little to enable local authorities to develop coherent and on-going renewal strategies. No one would seriously suggest that, in terms of personal health for example, the occasional meal (or even banquet) every few years would constitute an adequate or balanced diet. And yet what we would scorn for individual sustenance we accept quiescently in housing terms. It would be far more realistic to acknowledge that, in one sense at least, the housing 'problem' will never go away. People will always need houses and houses will always need repairing and maintaining. The more houses you build today, the more will need maintaining in the future. Eventually yesterday's housing solutions became today's problems — as they, in turn, require radical improvement or demolition. But this is not a *problem* as such, any more than 'living' is. It only becomes so if public policy seeks to view it in the context of once and for all hand-outs.

The strength of council housing provision lies in the opposite notion — namely one of continuing commitment. One of the great virtues of public housing provision has been the extent to which local authorities have been able to use the diverse age range of properties which they possess, to cross subsidise each other. Thus the income from properties during their 'low maintenance cost' stages has been able to be used to offset the extra costs of maintaining older property and building new ones. The reinforcement of this form of financial load-spreading requires an on-going rather than whimsical commitment.

However, there are two other aspects of perception which also determine the scope for reversing the current direction of public housing policy. The first concerns 'desirability' and the second, 'profitability'.

Over the last few years it has become increasingly popular to suggest that council housing is an unwelcome intrusion upon the rights of people to own their own home. The property-owning democracy to which the world is said to thus aspire, gains much of its rationale from criticisms which need to be responded to in different ways. On the one hand the management, maintenance, and allocation of council housing *have* frequently and justifiably, invited the most strident criticism. The often judgmental and prejudiced manner in which housing departments have sought to divide applicants into the 'deserving' or the 'underserving' *cannot* wholly be explained in terms of the rationing by central government. The standards of space and amenity *have* often failed to provide an acceptable environment for council tenants and their families. The administration of council housing *has* frequently been as dour, lifeless and monolithic as some of its housing. And, within local authorities there *has* been an in-built resistance to experiment with new forms of management, in which decentralished control to tenants themselves, took pride of place over the bureaucratic aspirations of senior housing officials or councillors. These, and the lack of adequate 'rights' of individual tenants over the accommodation that they lived in, are all valid criticisms of the internal workings of the local machinery of council house provision. They are, however, arguments for *changing* the nature of this provision rather than dispensing with it altogether. This is where arguments about the cost and lack of profitability of council housing enter the arena.

The writing on the wall . . . Caunton Avenue flats.

Contemporary folklore has it that council housing is an enormous drain on the national economy; with massive state subsidies being paid out to prop up the whole system. How much simpler then if council housing were sold off. Tenants would benefit by becoming owners; local authorities would benefit from the savings in maintenance costs (which would then be borne by the owners); and the state would benefit by not having to pay out vast subsidies — happy days! What usually remains unquestioned is the extent to which there are losers in this process; for losers there certainly are:

"A policy of indiscriminate sales will reduce the choice open to existing or prospective tenants by reducing the public rented stock in total and handing over the most desirable type of homes within the stock — precisely the sort of housing that is most sought after by the tenants trapped in high rise flats, the inter-war estates."

(Holmes, 1979, p.17).

However, it is not merely those trapped in such estates who are affected by council house sales. Those looking to obtain council housing for the first time are similarly afflicted. One individous effect of reducing the stock of council housing is that:

". . . it can provide potential tenants for tower blocks which are not attracting sufficient applicants."

(Townsend, 1976, p.100).

Both of these features come over clearly in the pattern of Nottingham's allocations. It was the larger, older, central housing which was sold most rapidly. Flats complexes were never included in the sales programme.

The sales policy certainly helped find tenants for the council's flats complexes. But, with increasing disproportion through the rehousing categories, *these allocations maintained or renewed racial disadvantage.* Every category of rehousing saw a greater proportion of black households being allocated to flats complexes than white ones. Having been so allocated, blacks then found themselves receiving transfers at only half the rate of white families. Earlier we referred to a particular statement on this from the City's Director of Housing, suggesting in part, that families who accepted such moves and had come from the poorest parts of the private sector, might have been willing to go there because they had 'lower standards'. Far more precise an explanation would be one which recognised the inherited inequality in their starting positions; the structuring of housing policies geared to maintaining this; and the absence of any real choice faced by these applicants. The argument about whether such allocations were then based upon exploiting the unequal position of black applicants, or upon more direct feelings of racial prejudice, are somewhat academic. Either way their effect was to take the disadvantages experienced by black families in the private sector, and compound or institutionalise them within the public sector.

The ability to alter this situation is further constrained by another 'losers' aspect of any sales policy (or any policy which runs down the finance for council housing). Council housing suffers by being required to function in an area it was specifically designed to avoid. Council housing was never intended to be built for profit; and yet the bulk of its income goes into interest repayments — the 'profit' of private money lenders:

"The biggest cost on any local authority's Housing Revenue Account is interest repayment — the practical outcome of paying for houses with borrowed money. It eats up 70% of all income — from rents and subsidies. It effectively controls the system of council house finance . . . in the end it represents the over-riding control exercised by the capital market over council housing.

(CDP, 1976, *Profits Against Houses*, p.34).

If public interest in council housing were to be genuinely tested, then its links with 'housing as a speculative venture' would have to be completely severed. Whatever form this took it would, in all probability, have to include the withdrawal of public subsidies from the speculative side of housing provision (i.e. private ownership), and the provision of *public* sector housing finance which was not tied to interest repayments to the money market. This would then free council housing to make a much more substantial assault on the housing inequalities which have been historically built in to its provision. Such an approach was patently not a characteristic of housing policies under the Labour government during the period of our study. Nor has it ever vaguely entered into the policies of the Conservative government which succeeded it. Controls upon the level and direction of local authority spending are now so rigorously applied by central government, that the scope for redressing inequalities within council house allocations is severely limited. Even an unequivocal acceptance of the racially discriminatory impact of its allocations during this period, would not provide the Nottingham City Council with any easy options of how to set about redressing this. Merely to introduce changes in its allocations procedures which would enable them to work on a much more even-handed basis, would not necessarily result in any redressing of *previous* inequalities. When councils such as Nottingham lack the powers of finance to buy properties they are desperately short of for larger families; when they can not maintain a building programme offering hopes to those trapped in the worst parts of council or private sector accommodation; when they are unable to maintain or improve the larger, older stock which they possess; when sales of their better properties are forced upon them; and when much of their central area stock has been transferred to housing associations that they have little control over — where is the scope for redressing disadvantage?

In many ways the pressure on the local authority has been to increase inequalities rather than reduce them. As the local paper explained under banner headlines in Feb. 1980:

> "Nottingham's housing policy is in ruins. The government has slashed £12m from the City's housing investment programme. And that means a miserable future for families in clearance areas and housing action areas
> . . .
> Instead of the £31.5m they asked for to cover capital expenditure in 1980-81, they are to receive just £19.8m."
>
> (*Nottingham News* 29/2/80).

What with the rent rises and additional housing expenditure cuts which have followed, it is clear that the catalogue of sufferers now includes virtually all council tenants in one way or another, as well as those stranded in poor housing outside it.

Yet it is within this context that racial inequalities have to be tackled, if they are not to generate their own form of conflict in this already fraught area of public policy. It is here that the responsiveness of the local authority comes to play an important part in determining what might or might not be done. Authorities such as Nottingham, who have thought themselves to be offering a 'colour blind' and 'fair' deal to all their local citizens, may face enormous difficulties in accepting that the effect of their policies has been discriminatory. And yet this is precisely what has happened. The different gates through which people have entered the council house system — gateways often entirely unrelated to housing need — largely determined the housing prospects of those coming.

This is probably best demonstrated in relation to the allocations to deck-access maisonettes. Taking a comparison between the relative proportions of West Indian and white allocations going to these maisonettes through the 4 principal gateways which we examined, the pattern of this disadvantage becomes clear.

TABLE 7.1

Allocations to Deck Access Maisonettes — by Rehousing Category

	Clearance		Transfers		Waiting List		Urban Aid	
	%	100%	%	100%	%	100%	%	100%
West Indian	7.1	294	9.0	155	40.6	360	51.3	121
White	4.5	336	3.4	298	29.6	222	41.1	17

Not only did the proportions of each group going to deck access maisonettes increase as the categories became lower in priority, but they did so in ways which were particularly disadvantageous to the West Indians. First of all, in every category, West Indians went in greater proportions to the maisonettes than did whites. Second, the percentage differences between black and whites increased as the categories become lower in priority. And finally, as the proportions going to these maisonettes increased, the ratio of actual numbers of black and white households reversed. The greatest numbers of whites were rehoused in those categories with few allocations to deck-access maisonettes. For West Indians it was the other way round. Their greatest numbers came into the system where the proportions going to maisonettes were greatest, and where the percentage differences between such black and white allocations were widest.

The position in respect of allocations to houses was virtually a mirror image of this. The differences were perhaps not quite so marked, but again it was the case that even in the higher priority categories, where the percentages of West Indians most favourably compared with those of whites, the *numbers* of West Indians involved were far fewer than those coming in via the Waiting List.

The role of transfers in this situation deserves some additional attention in terms of compounding the disadvantage of black families still further. Had the vast majority of black allocants gone into high quality council housing, their absence from the transfers category might have been less disturbing. Then, at least, it might have been argued that since black families had gone into the best parts of the council's stock, they would have had far less inclination to seek a move. Unfortunately, as the rest of our data showed, this was manifestly not the case. Nor could it be effectively argued that the narrow time period of our study prevented those rehoused in flats complexes from coming into the reckoning for transfers (because their applications would not yet have reached the front of the queue). Even from the much more limited earlier data which was available within the Housing Department, we were able to establish that the patterns which we have identified were consistently present in the period immediately preceding our study. Thus in 1972, 50% of all black allocations were to flats complexes. In 1973, more than 50% of black allocants came in via the waiting list (or via the newly introduced 'Urban aid' category) and some 46% went into such maisonettes or flats. In fact, 27% of black allocations in 1973 went specifically into the deck access maisonettes, a figure slightly higher than our average over 3 years. Transfers for black families during these two earlier years were 12% and 6% of their total allocations respectively.

What seems to be abundantly clear is that during our research (and immediately prior to it) black families were going into flats complexes at a far greater rate than they were able to get out. It is also clear that despite the official policy of not placing families with children in the flats complexes, the sheer number of black, waiting list allocations going there will have ensured that significant numbers of black families with children did actually move into these complexes.

As we established in the section on transfers, those families receiving transfers generally did extremely well in terms of the quality of housing they obtained. The problem was largely one of numbers — or rather the disparity in proportions between black and white transfer allocations. The flats complexes have long provided the thorniest problems for the housing department in its allocation policies. Even before housing cuts began to restrict the supply of new Council houses, the City was becoming increasingly aware of the unpopularity of some of its flats complexes, and the particularly damaging effects that their total environment had on families with children. It is worth recalling the comment made by the leader of the outgoing 1976 Labour Council that:

> "The Labour group is on record as saying that families with children should not have to live in high rise flats, and should therefore be a priority for decant (i.e. transfers). But to where? We're short of 4 bedroom houses and it's even hard to build 4 bedroom houses within existing government cost limits."

(Carroll, 1980).

This situation was doubly unfortunate for blacks. As we have established, a greater proportion of black families who received allocations, required larger propeties than did white families. This seems to have been consistent with the pattern of allocations immediately prior to our study. From one set of Housing Department records covering the period 1968-73, it seems clear that some 30% of the total black allocations during this period were to households of 5 or more persons. In comparison only 18% of the white households came into this family size.

Much of the council's larger housing stock was also its older housing; concentrated within the central areas of the city. This will have been the limited housing stock that larger families were competing for; with 'choice' being already narrowly constrained in terms of both housing quality and location. For black families in flats complexes, as well as those seeking first time entry into the council house system, their housing prospects will have been further undermined by the sales policy and the curtailment of council house improvements (pursued by the incoming Conservative council from 1976 onwards) and their extension to a national level by the new Conservative government in 1979.

Following the introduction of a sales policy locally the rate of transfers declined considerably as did the level of allocations in general. Houses which came available were sold whenever possible. As the sales policy progressed, fewer and fewer of the houses sold were to sitting tenants. Those living in flats complexes were increasingly trapped there, and those coming into the system progressively found flats complexes as the only properties on offer. Tables 7.2 and 7.3 show how this, again, disproportionately affect black families:

TABLE 7.2
Total Allocations from the Waiting List — By Year, 1975-77 inc.

	1975		1976		1977	
	%	N =	%	N =	%	N =
Asian & West Indian	21.0	89	33.9	167	41.9	126
White	12.5	54	9.3	112	19.7	56

TABLE 7.3
Total Allocations to Flats Complex Accommodation — By Year 1975-77inc.

	1975		1976		1977	
	%	N =	%	N =	%	N =
Asian & West Indian	34.5	146	36.7	118	39.2	118
White	22.6	98	20.0	93	19.4	55

As the proportions of blacks allocants coming in via the waiting list increased, so too did the proportion of their numbers going to flats complexes. This was not so for the pattern of white allocations. As the proportion of white waiting list allocations rose (albeit only dramatically so in 1977) the proportion of their allocations to flats complexes actually *fell*. This disparity cannot, in itself, be explained by the sales policy. Rather, it raises again questions about racial inequalities built in to the internal workings of the allocations process. Such questions become even more pressing when you recognise that changes in the *rate* of such allocations in any case failed to account for equally substantial differences in the *proportion* of black and white households, respectively, that these allocations affected.

The absence of any real choice in these initial allocations, and the subsequent dependence of such families upon an extensive stock of council housing to which transfers were are least possible, was simply sketched out by one tenant in a letter to the local paper.

"I have lived in a council house for three years. Before that my children and I lived in a council flat for five years. The noise was so bad that to get a good night's sleep we had to use earplugs. There was no garden. The central heating, pleasing layout of the flat, and extra room were, however, a vast improvement on our living conditions compared with our accommodation before reaching the top of the council housing list.

Then we shared a flat with another family at the top of a house. We doubled up in bedrooms, carried shopping up three flights of stairs, suffered from lack of privacy and felt trapped by circumstances. We were very well off compared with some other people waiting to be rehoused.

As I sit in my house with enough bedrooms for every member of the family, a kitchen to myself and a garden to sit in and hang the clothes out (no more bus trips with suitcases to the launderette) I contemplate the fact that if the council were selling, or being forced to sell council houses three years ago, we would never have got out of our block of flats."

(In *Nottingham News*, 13/6/80).

The woman who wrote this letter was perhaps even more fortunate than she realised. In the first place the council *were* selling houses around the time that she obtained a transfer. True, the government of the day was not forcing them to do so, but the sales campaign had already become part of Nottingham's new 'pioneering spirit'. She was one of the fortunate ones to get a transfer to a house on the new St. Ann's estate. The second part of her good fortune was that *new* houses were not selling as rapidly as the older *relet* properties, and that her requirements were in any case for a medium sized property rather than a larger one.

The disproportionate number of black families seeking larger properties will have found no such joy. As was explained earlier, the more substantial discounts on older council properties made them much the most attractive proposition to prospective purchasers. These relets included most of the council's larger central area housing stock. The best parts of this stock were sold first and, of the remaining houses, increased numbers stood empty, awaiting offers of purchase. The supply of these larger older properties *for rent* slowed to

a trickle. Even then it will have been the least saleable ones
which eventually became available for council tenants. Even
the fortunate black households who transferred from flats
complexes will, then, not necessarily have found themselves
blessed with the housing of their dreams. The impoverishment of the older relet housing was compounded by dramatic
cuts in the council's improvement programme for its own
stock. Between 1975/6 and 1977/8 the rate of improvement
of their own stock plummetted from 1161 to 215 properties
per year. The 12% of black transfers which were actually *into*
flats complexes (most notably to the Balloon Woods estate)
during this period were almost certainly from council properties effectively abandoned because of the absence of an effective improvement programme.

Individuality — in Basford flats.

The grinding in of disadvantage was taken a step further by
the extensive tranferring of responsibilities for rehabilitation
work to housing associations. No housing associations keep
ethnic records of their allocations, and many appear defensive about how their allocations policy works in practice. All
retain the right to veto council nominations wherever they
choose. In building up the role of housing associations in this
way, without retaining any effective ties of public accountability, the local authority left itself wide open to criticism of

conducting its affairs with a degree of wanton irresponsibility. They certainly did nothing to counter any of the general misgivings that housing associations (particularly the larger national ones) 'cream off' the most financially and socially acceptable tenants from the council's nominations, and ignore the rest. With two important exceptions it has never been obvious that housing associations in Nottingham have shown any particular sensitivity, or sympathy towards the housing needs of black families.

In this way, black families were discriminated against by virtue of their disproportionate need of larger housing. This was a situation that in the short term the council could have done little about. At the beginning of this period the outgoing Labour council did have a scheme whereby they would purchase houses from the private sector in order to rehouse council tenants. However, this was the first of the housing policies to be scrapped when the change in control took place in 1976. Since that date all of the housing policies pursued by the Authority have only served to increase the degree of structural discrimination which the housing department has been required to practice.

In a situation of such widening inqualities, it is hard to see how the local authority could seriously claim to be offering equality of opportunity in its rehousing programme. Whatever the legal judgement turned out to be, there would appear to be strong grounds for the Authority refusing to sell off any of its larger housing stock on the basis that this would place it in breach of the 1976 Race Relations Act: the sale of such properties making it impossible for the Authority to offer equality of opportunity in access to public housing (or, more unequivocally, requiring them to pursue policies which were in effect, racially discriminatory).

This would, however, be a containing measure rather than a comprehensive solution. Substantial problems, arising from inequalities in the housing and allocations policies of the past, would still remain to be tackled. One of the things which this study had attempted, has been to draw attention to the various ways in which the hidden hand of local authority housing policies actually *produced* concentrations of black families in the poorest parts of public sector housing. In the highest of priority categories 51% of Asian families and 38% of West Indians were in households of 5 persons or more. This compared with no more than 15% of white allocants in such family sizes. The concentration of larger properties in the older central areas defined the boundaries of the best choices that the council could offer. It also played a major part in accounting for black clearance families being rehoused in the central areas at almost twice the rate of white ones. When we examined the declared preferences of families moved from the 'Meadows phase 3' and 'Raleigh Street' we noted the similarity between the most popular black and white 'choices' respectively. When these did not then correspond with the pattern of actual allocations, we were able to establish that much of the outward migration of whites was to properties which met all the 'house' requirements of the applicant, though in different (but equally high status) housing areas. In part, this again has to be related back to family size. Even at the front of the queue for council housing, the margins of flexibility are narrowed the larger your family is. Higher priority in itself cannot conjure up bigger houses; nor can it improve them. It was the twin restrictions of qualitative and locational choice that guaranteed concentrations in the first place, and branded them as slums in the second.

The concentrations in flats complexes, however, have a different aetiology. Black families coming in via the waiting list were little different in family size from those of white allocants. And yet they still ended up going to flats complexes in greater proportions than did whites. It may well be that black families coming in in this way had been living in much the most oppressive private sector housing conditions, and were thus more desperate for re-housing. This does not, however, adequately explain the allocations themselves. When the GLC undertook a review of their own allocation methods, they came up with one interesting finding which possibly applies as much to Nottingham as it did then in London:

> ". . . the average quality of first offers accepted is significantly lower for the non-white applicants than for white . . . It is the quality of the first offer which is the all important factor."
>
> (Parker & Dugmore, 1976, p.56).

What they found was that in every category of allocation (with the exception of the homeless), the first offer made by housing officials to black families was, on average, of inferior quality housing than that which was offered to whites. It was this which established differential allocation patterns between black and white applicants. Discrimination of this sort is often camouflaged behind suggestions that the allocations are merely a reflection of individual choices. Table 7.1 helps to illustrate how far this is manifestly untrue. The different proportions of black or white families going into deck access maisonettes from the various rehousing categories, would never lead you to deduce that all waiting list applicants found these maisonettes more *desirable* than did clearance households. Clearly more waiting list families went there more numerously than did clearance ones because, by and large, these were the only properties on offer. Because discrimination between categories is institutionally acceptable, this sort of revelation is fairly uncontentious. However, to use the same logic to explain racial differences in allocations *within* categories, sets all sorts of cats amongst the pigeons. Despite the probable unacceptability of this to the local authority, we could not avoid the possible explanation that differential allocations to flats complexes (in every rehousing category), arose because housing department officials were more inclined to offer such poorer properties to black applicants, in the first instance, than they were to white ones. Thus, (and this remains to be tested), whether it was done on a conscious basis or not, it would still have constituted discrimination in the working of the council's rehousing process.

Before moving on to possible alternative approaches to council housing and allocation, we ought to briefly mention 3 aspects which have received scant attention in this study. First of all, very little rehousing of the homeless took place in Nottingham during the period of our research. We have been conscious that other areas of the country faced far more substantial problems of homelessness than Nottigham appeared to do. Strong and conflicting views are often expressed locally about the interpretation of such low figures. However, the very limited numbers of the homeless in our study prevented us from shedding any extra light on this area. All that we can say is that the recent housing department estimate that about 15% of its 'house' allocations now go to homeless families. This would seem to make homelessness a more important aspect of housing department policy in the 1980's than it was at the end of the 1970's.

What we know was important at the time, but have been unable to follow through, was the position of single parent families in the allocations process. No systematic recording was ever made of single parent families, and certainly none which would have allowed for comparisons between black and white single parent families. The data which we had would only have allowed us to draw the most tentative conclusions based on broad, and frequently unsubstantiated, generalisations. Rather than ignore it entirely, though, we would simply want to record a belief that this was an important variable in the allocations matrix which we were unfortunately unable to follow through.

The third aspect is an ommision of a very different nature. At the start of our period of study the Chief Executive was reporting to the council that for planning purposes the Authority were assumming that they would have to rehouse all those living in the designated clearance areas. This seemed largely due to an increase in the popularity of Nottingham's council housing during the mid 1970's. The change of political control locally brought with it a change in the way in which information about rehousing was presented. The Authority began to talk more vaguely in terms of the number of households *moving out* of clearance areas rather than the number actually *being rehoused by the council itself*. Families who found the waiting, or the offers, unacceptable were encouraged to feel free to rehouse themselves. Pinpointing the precise numbers who did so was an almost impossible task. We estimated, however that by the end of our research period something between 15% and 20% of the households moving out of clearance areas were rehousing themselves. The nature of this 'self-rehousing' could have important implications for the city's future housing policies. The assumption that these families were relatively stable and financially secure might lead to a belief that they found themselves comfortable rehousing by purchasing a house. The opposite assumption would envisage poorer families moving into other equally poor parts of the private rented sector; one step beyond the bulldozer. Such a step would, before long, present the Authority with renewed questions about how it was to respond to these poor housing conditions. The racial characteristics of those who rehoused themselves are as uncertain as the quality of their eventual rehousing. All we can do is, again, to register this as a variable which might represent itself sooner rather than later in the council's future housing programme.

Different sides of the tracks . . . Meadows, old and new.

In the midst of the various criticisms of Nottingham's council housing system, we ought not to overlook many of its extremely good features. For it is upon these that any present and future changes would have to be built. To begin with the city still has an extensive stock of council housing. Much of this stock is in very good condition and was soundly built in the first instance. Though late on the scene for clearance programmes, Nottingham has been remarkably efficient in ensuring that rebuilding began swiftly after demolition had been completed. The council managed to avoid accumulating vast tracts of derelict land which have so often characterised the larger urban areas across the country. In the main, it also missed the high-rise bandwaggon, and has thus inherited a far smaller flats-complex legacy than might be the case in other cities. In addition to this it has, at this point in time, human assets of an extremely important kind, particularly the quality of its most senior staff in the allocations section. Having directed so much critical attention at the Department's allocations processes, we are particularly fortunate in being able to observe that this currently provides an important focus around which political commitment and administrative restructuring might take place.

Many of the suggestions which follow, concerning the internal structuring of council housing, are aimed at making the allocations process more open and intelligible to the general public. For this reason record keeping comes in for particular attention; not simply in itself, but in the sense of it being an empty and futile gesture if such records are not regularly monitored and subject to public review. In addition to this, the actual basis of allocations *criteria* are reviewed in order to suggest the sort of principles upon which these might be based. It is for this reason that we have suggested a points system as the means of identifying rehousing priorities, rather than a more informal one based on priority categories and officer discretion. Enough evidence exists already to make it clear that a points system is no guaranteed panacea. It will not, after all, produce any more houses. Nor does it prevent discrimination from taking place. What it does is to bring the issues much more into the open; giving both the public and elected councillors a more effective and on-going role in the process of reviewing the adequacy of the allocations procedures. The suggestions made in this respect have been designed so as to separate the broad principles, upon which such an approach might be based, from the actual details of Nottingham's existing arrangements and their shortcomings.

Ultimately, however, it will be the nature of a council's housing stock which will most determine the prospects of both black and white applicants of finding a decent home to live in. We have already gone to some length in making out the case for extending rather than curtailing finance for public housing provision. Even if this were to be forthcoming two other points would still need to be made. The first is in relation to transfers, and the second in relation to the notion of dispersal.

In the recommendatins which follow, the high priority of transfers as such would no longer apply. However, this should not be taken to imply that under any new arrangements the level of transfers would necessarily drop. To begin with, the demands cannot be ignored of those who were lead to believe that their acceptance of a council tenancy would quickly enable them to transfer to somewhere better. Meeting such claims would necessitate an increase in the rate of transfers rather than a decrease. To do so would place additional pressures upon an allocations section already burdened with internal reorganisation. At the best of times this would present considerable problems:

> "Housing departments, in view of their other commitments, cannot cope with the large number of tenants wanting to move."
>
> (Bird, 1975, p.33).

Coping with these additional demands would necessitate extra staff as well as revised working procedures. To attempt to do all this on existing staffing levels would be to invite any restructuring to dissolve in chaos.

Dispersal, as a notion, has been floating round for some considerable time. For some uncertain period in the early 1970's, a version of this was practiced in Nottingham, though it appeared to be neither coherently thought out nor systematically carried through. The official wisdom in respect of dispersal policy has normally been taken to be Cullingworth:

> "Dispersal is a laudable aim of policy, but this policy needs pursuing with full respect of the wishes of the people concerned. Dispersal of immigrants from concentrations should be regarded as a desirable consequence — but not the over-riding purpose of housing individual immigrant families on council estates. The criteria of full, informed, individual choice comes first."
>
> (Cullingworth, 1969, paragraph 412).

Dispersal policies over the last decade have however become thoroughly discredited, and eventually illegal. The only reason for citing the notion here is in the value it serves if

A question of access — new housing and the Caunton Avenue flats (St. Anns).

its suppositions are reversed. The problem about dispersal policies has always been that they ascribe stigma to those being dispersed. As Rex pointed out in the field of educational dispersal:

> ". . . to declare that a child has to be moved to another school helps to emphasise, either that he is a problem, or that his neighbourhood is a problem, thus drawing attention to his inferior status."
>
> (Rex, 1973, p.85).

Rather than stigmatising the individuals by removing and dispersing them, it would be more productive to define the area (and its residents) as *victims* of structural neglect. The response would then be to direct substantial capital into those areas in order to provide high quality housing and social facilities within the area for its existing residents. Traditional 'Housing Action Area' or 'General Improvement Area' strategies would have only limited use in this context, since it would need to be based primarily on direct intervention by the local authority; and in a manner which brought about rapid, large scale improvements in housing conditions. Increased, rather than reduced, public ownership would be called for.

One important aspect of such an approach would, be its acceptance of existing area concentrations. In doing so it would, however, seek to ensure that these concentrations become associated with high quality housing rather than slums. As well as removing the forms of structural oppression under which black families have had to live, this would also help to break down the psychological oppression which has equated concentrations of black families 'per se' with problem areas. There is an urgent need to develop the concept of the desirable black estate: 'desirable' in the context of both black and white applicants being anxious to enjoy the housing amenities that that (predominantly black) area had to offer. Only then would we be approaching equality of status and esteem; and only then would a more flexible basis of interchange and integration appear possible.

Towards an
Alternative

Towards an Alternative Approach

Within the field of race and housing, there is always the temptation to simply tinker with the internal mechanisms of the system; or merely to tailor recommendations to fit what you believe is possible in the here and now. Even more specifically, there is the temptation to confine proposals to those areas where there would seem to be the political or moral 'will' to introduce changes. Succumbing to this invariably sells people (and issues) short. Its attraction, however, is that policy makers are less likely to summarily dismiss the recommendations as mere pipe dreams and propaganda.

Within a rapidly deteriorating economic environment — where government initiatives more often resemble 'last rites' than healing hands; where poverty, unemployment and urban decay have re-emerged on a scale altogether unforseen by the general public; and where the politics of hatred and despair find increasingly fertile ground upon which to grow; issues of race and inequality cannot, however, be left to such safe, if acceptable, window dressing.

In housing (as in employment, education, health, or whatever) race has all too often emerged as the convenient scapegoat explanation used to conceal more deep-rooted failures of public policy. This is certainly true of council housing. It is also the principal reason why the sort of changes which we set out, relate to public housing policy in its broadest context. It is not sufficient to say that blacks are discriminated against in council housing. To a large extent *all* council tenants are discriminated against in current housing policy. Blacks may be *more* discriminated against than most (both directly and indirectly), but to seek solutions merely in terms of finding another group to take their place as housing scapegoats, would be as futile as it would be divisive. Lasting solutions will only come through equally real improvements in the whole position of council housing.

Fundamentally, recommendations which are aimed at reducing racial inequalities in the allocation of council housing must, then, begin and end with a reappraisal of central government housing policies. To do otherwise would be to ask of local government what it cannot possible provide. It is certainly not the workers in the Allocations Section of a City's Housing Department, who determine the level of public housing finance, the building programme, the interest repayments which have to be made, or policy commitments involving the sale of council houses. To expect them to redress racial inequalities which arise in this way is about as appropriate as suggesting that cholera would be prevented if medical-workers were only more proficient in dispensing asprins and sympathy. If local Authorities are to redress racial inequalities which have resulted *directly* from the constraints on public housing provision, then they must have the tools to do so. The framework within which such structured discrimination might be tackled would itself require a number of distinct components:

At a national level — there would need to be a re-direction of current government policy in respect of council housing. Revised policies would need to:

1. Substantially increase the level of expenditure on public sector housing, both for new building and improvements (possibly along the lines outlined in 9. below).
2. Curtail the policy of council house sales.
3. Make housing associations directly accountable to local housing authorities in respect of their allocations policies. (Ultimately, this should include Authorities having the power to take properties back into public ownership, where housing association could not demonstrate that their allocations policies and/or management practices were consistent with those of the Authority itself).

4. Give local Authorities greater powers of acquisition for improvement in housing stress areas. This would enable them to ensure that those living in the poorest parts of the *private rented sector* could be provided, quickly, with improved housing by the Authority itself. Such powers would, on the one hand, need to significantly shorten the existing compulsory purchase procedures, whilst at the same time conferring upon tenants clear rights of involvement in the drawing up of improved plans. Even a concession which allowed the existing owner/landlord the right to buy back or retain the property after improvement, would not interfere with the rapid improvements which the local authority would then be able to guarantee tenants. The retention of any such ownership ought, however, to be conditional upon the Authority being repaid, in full, for the cost incurred in renovation. (NB Compulsory purchase powers for 'improvement', would *not* be extended in this way to acquire owner-occuped properties. Local authorities should only be entitled to engage in such purchases by agreement with the owners).

5. Make it possible for local authorities to develop and/or increase their own 'improvements workforce' (including the planning and management aspects). To do so would not only involve a rolling programme of commitments from the local authority (which would be outlined in its HIP submissions) but also a reciprocal commitment from central government. The latter would need to guarantee that, within the annual revisions of such a programme, any reductions of, say, more than 5%, (in real terms), in the Authority's direct improvements budget, would require a 2 year 'lead time'. This would enable authorities to develop coherent improvement programmes (including training and apprenticeship schemes) which were not constantly undermined by vascillations in central government policy. An even sounder basis could be developed if such local authority workforces were additionally allowed to competitively tender for private improvement work (but only to the extent that their obligations to public sector improvements were being satisfied first).

6. Review the cost yardsticks which have made it increasing-

ly difficult for Authorities to build or improve, houses for large families.

7. Alter the system of HIP submissions in order to present a more effective 'social audit' of local housing conditions. Such an audit would need to require authorities to identify their housing stress areas on a zonal basis (wider than the boundaries of existing Housing Action or General Improvement Areas) and in the knowledge that property size, age, and condition would form important elements in the 'weighting' of competing claims for improvement finance. This Audit, which should include council built, council acquired and private properties, would then provide the basis for a shift in improvements policy towards a more direct public sector responsibility for improvements, consistent within the points in 4. above. This would shift the balance of improvement finance in favour of the public sector as opposed to the private one.

8. Include an additional element of weighting within the 'needs' element of the Rate Support Grant, which would be based upon the degree of concentration of ethnic minority groups in any of the identified housing stress areas.

9. In a very practical sense, draw distinctions between public sector housing (as a social asset) and speculative house building and/or ownership. This would entail restructuring public housing finance in order to remove it from the money market. The money for council housing would then need to come either direct from taxation (as opposed to borrowing) or, at nominal rates of interest, through a re-organised Public Works Loans Board. Whatever the ultimate source(s) of such finance, some areas from which substantial inputs might be drawn would include — a public housing, pre-profits tax on banks, building societies, insurance companies and pension funds; the reduction or removal of mortgage relief on housing purchase; and a direct funding through part of current North Sea Oil revenues.

Irrespective of the actual mechanics of this financing, a massive re-investment in public housing provision is now desperately needed if we are to prevent the decline in council housing from becoming irreversible. If this is not done, then the disproportionate numbers of black households stuck in the worst parts of public and private sector housing, have little chance of finding a decent home to live in. It is within this context that changes at a local level have to be set.

At a local level — given central government support, the challenge to local housing authorities is to be able to *demonstrate* that their policies and practices are geared towards redressing and removing racial inequalities in public housing. Practically, such a challenge would focus on at least 4 areas in which discrimination and/or racial disadvantage might emerge:

  i. the relative priority given to different means of access to, or movement within, the council house system,
 ii. unfavourable assessment and treatment by housing officials,
iii. inappropriate structuring of the main council house building and improvement programmes, and
 iv. inadequate record-keeping and monitoring procedures through which the existence of racial bias might be detected.

Before offering proposals in relation to these, it is worth setting out the two broad assumptions upon which the proposals are based. These assumptions are ones which housing authorities nominally subscribe to, but often fail to comply with in practice. The first assumption is that *council housing allocations ought to be based on 'housing need'*, and the second is that *allocation processes should themselves be open, intelligible, and publicly accountable*.

'Housing need', as a working concept, presents considerable difficulties. It is, after all, a *relative* rather than an absolute concept. Its assessment will change from area to area, and from time to time. What we would argue strongly is that existing housing conditions should play a central part of any such assessment, whereas 'waiting time' is only useful in distinguishing between equally meritorious claims. Within such an approach, it would also follow that families living in poor housing conditions would not simply find themselves at the front of the housing queue, but would do so without finding themselves eligible for only the poorest parts of the Authority's housing stock.

In whatever way Authorities then set about evaluating 'need', what becomes important is that the procedures they adopt for doing so are open and accountable. It is for this reason that we have eventually come to believe that a *points system* for allocations is the most useful means of offering such accountability. There is enough evidence around to be absolutely certain that a points system in itself does *not* guarantee that racial discrimination/disadvantage will be removed from the process of council house allocations. On the contrary, some points systems have been shown to maintain or increase racial disadvantages in council housing. The principal virtue of a points system, however, is that it puts the issue of relative priorities into an arena of more open public scrutiny — and more directly in the laps of elected officials who bear the ultimate responsibility for housing policy decisions. The alternative approach (usually broad priority *categories*, linked with a large degree of officer discretion) offers no such comeback. The results of Nottingham's allocations have made it clear that discretionary procedures have failed to produce equality of attainment for black families in council housing. A points system would not necessarily have prevented this, but it would have provided a useful tool to examine where such inequality originated from. What housing authorities have yet to realise is that it is not merely the 1976 Race Relations Act which makes it essential for them to be able to *demonstrate* the equality of opportunity that they offer. Their own standing and credibility within the eyes of the black communities is becoming increasingly tenuous. Bland assurances about the 'colourblind' nature of council house allocations now provide more of a basis for derision than confidence. One way or another, proof-positive will have to supercede liberal rhetoric.

We shall return to the question of a points system in a moment. To begin with though, it is important to stress that the changes being advanced are not aimed at offering a better deal to black families simply because they are black. The proposals are aimed at making the whole system of assessment and allocations fairer; in the belief that blacks, as well as disadvantaged whites, will benefit as a result.

Let us begin with *eligibility*. Many Authorities still retain rules which prevent people from even registering on their waiting lists until they have lived in the area for one year (or in some cases much longer). There really seems to be little justification for this exclusion. As anyone who has spent time on a council house waiting list will inform you, being eligible to register has very little to do with your immediate prospects of being actually allocated a house. Removing this sort of exclusion should also encompass the differential treatment of households coming in from different tenure backgrounds. Thus it is suggested that,

10. an Authority's waiting list should be 'open' in the sense that no prior residence requirements should be needed before people are entitled to register on the list.
11. eligibility for registration should extend to everyone living or working in the area who is over the age of 18 and, in the case of an owner-occupier, who does not own more than the one property in which they live.

In addition to this it would seem to be important that

12. eligibility should also be extended, in special circumstances, to groups of people not living or working in the area but who can prove a strong local connection. Such groups could include those serving in HM Forces as well as persons aged 60 or over.

In the main, such an open basis for registration would help to remove the often unfavourable distinctions which have been drawn between tenants and lodgers in furnished, unfurnished, and part-furnished accommodation. It would also remove the trap of exclusion in which owner-occupiers in the poorest of properties are often caught. (There would still be considerable advantages to such owner occupiers even if the Authority made it a condition that the allocation of a council property to that household, would have to be linked to the sale of the existing property *to the Authority itself*).

This however, only brings us to the more thorny problem

of relative *priorities* given to all those who register for council housing.

In Notingham, the system of priorities remained substantially unaltered throughout the whole of the late 1970's. Theoretically the order of rehousing priorities was — Clearance, Homeless Families, Statutory Overcrowding, Special Cases, Transfers, Lodgers Waiting List, and finally the Secondary, Supplementary, Forces, and Aged Persons waiting lists. However, from the treatment of homeless families it is clear that the *priority* for rehousing was not always linked to the *quality* of housing allocated. The problem with the system of priorities was that it did not always recognise housing 'need', or, in some of the cases where it was recognised, the system itself maintained or compounded disadvantage. Thus, whilst the clearance programme substantially tackled the poorest housing conditions, it by no means encompassed all of them. The increasing concerns of central government about those in the poorest parts of the remaining private rented sector attest to this. Poor housing conditions in themselves, therefore, did not necessarily offer grounds for rehousing, unless linked with another characteristic (i.e. statutory overcrowding, extreme ill health, or location within a clearance area).

This was particularly important for the black families in our study because a large proportion of them entered the system from the private rented sector, via the lodgers waiting list. The low priority of the waiting list compounded their problems by ensuring that, in the main, they were then only offered deck-acess accommodation, or the least propular houses left over after clearance and transfer demands had been satisfied.

In order to begin to construct a more equitable basis upon which allocations might take place we would argue that

13. Authorities should adopt a unified lettings policy in which all existing 'lists' are amalgamated.

Within this, it would then be completely self-defeating for an Authority to proceed to reintroduce new categories of priority subdivision within this common list. Equally inappropriate would be the practice of then assessing rehousing claims mainly on the basis to date order of application — a criterion almost entirely unrelated to housing 'need'. What should be a central feature of any allocations framework, irrespective of the precise form of evaluation which might be used, is that

14. a unified allocations system should work on the basis of assessing all applications in terms of their degree of housing need; relative weighting being determined primarily by differences in current family and housing circumstances.

This would have been particularly important to black families in Nottingham if it had applied during the period of our study. West Indians were substantially under-represented in the (high priority) transfers granted by the Department, and over-represented in the (less favoured) allocations from the waiting list. Blacks would have been less disadvantaged if transfers had not been treated on a preferential basis. However, such a change would not have removed the possibility of discrimination occuring *within* the transfers process itself. The small proportion of West Indians receiving transfers during our study period means that such an explanation cannot be discounted.

This in itself raises concern about the extent to which, in Nottingham and other housing authorities, allocations systems are still based upon a large degree of officer discretion. This raises particular difficulties for the black community who have historically experienced widespread discrimination in housing. The belief, or expectation, that such discrimination also forms a part of public sector housing is not something which our research findings were able to dismiss. Black households did regularly fare much worse than white ones in the allocations process. In this sense *the commitment to a more flexible but discretionary system encouraged the belief that the system itself was discriminatory.* To the general advantage of all council applicants, as well as a boost to the confidence of black families, we would recommend a priority system for allocations which was more open and intelligible to the general public.

To begin to do this housing authorities could:

15. adopt a points system for allocations,
16. ensure that the basis for awarding points is clear and open for public appraisal,
17. make it possible for applicants to know precisely the points that they have and where this leaves them within the general waiting list,
18. retain some limited element of officer discretion, but closely define the number of discretionary points which may be awarded by the allocations staff in special circumstances: (the awarding of such discretionary points being subject to ratification by the Head of the Allocations Section),
19. retain the possibility of additional discretionary points being awarded in circumstances where the normal maximum number of discretionary points was insufficient to meet a particular case of acute housing need. The decision to award these further discretionary points would rest with senior officers and/or the Housing Committee itself (or a specially designated Sub-Committee thereof).

Such procedures would not, in themselves make discrimination impossible nor necessarily make allocations less contentious. They could, however, reduce the possibility of direct discrimination occuring. A points system could also make it easier to identify indirect discrimination within the allocations system, and thereafter to counter it by making adjustments in the number of points awarded for different aspects of housing need.

All of the variables — such as overcrowding, health, family size, length of waiting etc — which are normally considered when looking at an application for rehousing, can be included in such a process. Nottingham's experience, however, highlights several aspects which require specific attention. To an extent, the city's use of the 'Urban Aid' allocations category was an attempt to assist those living in the worst conditions in the private rented sector to gain access to council housing. This was of particular importance to black households. Where the initiative backfired was that it only really succeeded in projecting such households into the least desirable parts of the council's housing stock. If such 'need' is to be recognised then it must be done in a way which does not further penalise or stigmatise the recipients. It is not sufficient to be able to rehouse such families quickly. This must be matched to the quality of housing that they might choose from. If such access is linked to a points level then,

22. the current housing conditions of applicants should figure as a distinct and highly rated variable in any points system. (NB — This would be an assessment of the physical living conditions, *not* the state of the interior decoration or the applicant's furniture).

Consistent with this, would be the notion that,

21. there should be no time restriction upon the rights of council tenants to apply for a transfer.

We make this point because, in Nottingham, there has been the suggestion that all tenants should be denied the right to register for a transfer within a year of being initially rehoused. This seems to be both divisive and destructive. It would be so because of the extent to which such measures actually work against the interests both of tenants and the council itself. On the one hand it denies tenants the right to pursue any valid, continuing claims for better housing. At the same time, far from realising any misconceived desire to

"encourage a better atmosphere on estates"
(Nottingham City Housing Department, Dec. 1980, p.23). .

it would seem just as likely to achieve the exact opposite. To chain someone to a wall for a year on the pretext of giving them the chance to grow to like it there, runs a greater risk of increasing their sense of resentment and alienation. The encouragement of a better atmosphere on estates must be seen as coming largely through the improvement of services to and in them; including the services of housing management and/or maintenance. In addition to all this, the volume and distribution of unrestricted transfer *requests* provides a good indicator for an Authority, as to where such attention needs to be directed most urgently.

In most respects transfer applications can be evaluated in much the same way as any other housing application. The possible exception to this would be in the event of an Authority pursuing a 'strategic lettings' policy of one form or another. In Nottingham this has been the practice in relation to transfer requests from households under-occupying larger properties. Having identified a particular shortage of these properties the Council, quite properly, sought to make the most of its existing stock by giving priority, in transfers, to those seeking moves from such larger properties into smaller ones. Such allocations would not necessarily follow from a points system based largely upon housing need. Specific points would need to be allocated in order to account for this. We would recommend therefore that:

22. specific points should be designated by an Authority as part of any 'strategic lettings' policy which it adopted in order to free specific types of property; the number and permanency of such points being precisely defined and subject to regular review by Committee.

Reviewing any such lettings policy is essential. The analysis of our research data showed quite clearly that the pattern of giving transfers to white elderly people did not succeed in freeing larger properties in any of the major areas into which black households were being allocated. Both the Housing Department, and its Committee, ought to be particularly concerned that such a strategic lettings policy so clearly failed to reach the black families who were disproportionately represented amongst those seeking larger houses.

The third specific aspect of a points system which requires comment, relates to the treatment of the homeless. How many points should you be awarded when your housing conditions are so poor that they are non-existent? A local authority has a statutory duty to re-house homeless families. However, such a responsibility does not necessarily guarantee that those families will be rehoused in good quality council accommodation. Indeed there are pressures upon local authorities to respond to homelessness on a somewhat punitive basis — 'deterring' others who might see it as an easy way into council housing. Equally the Authority might have little choice of the properties available, at any point in time, for the emergency rehousing of a homeless family. A points system could offer a simple but positive way out of these immediate problems. Thus,

23. once rehoused, homeless families should be entitled to apply for a transfer in exactly the same way as any other council tenant, (as outlined above).

In a system of priorities in which points were largely allocated on a basis of housing need, families who had been allocated poorer properties simply as a result of the urgency of their position, would not necessarily then find themselves trapped there. The inadequacies of their new accommodation would, themselves, be reflected in the points position of the family. The worse the accommodation provided for the family, the more likely they would be to find themselves again amongst the top priorities for rehousing.

The fourth aspect requiring specific attention is the treatment of those with rent arrears. In Nottingham, as in some other cities, rent arrears have constituted an automatic barrier to re-housing. In addition, a family have had to be clear of arrears for a period of 12 months before any rehousing application would be considered. At a time when unemployment is widespread and rising, such an approach seems unduly harsh. If Authorities feel that arrears simply cannot be overlooked then a more flexible approach would be to:

24. treat arrears on a 'negative points' basis, *varying with the circumstances leading up to the arrears* Decisions about the awarding of any 'negative points' ought to be taken only at senior officer level, and should be open to appeal to the Housing Committee.
25. exclude altogether any rule making rehousing conditional upon a period of arrears-free rent payments.

With urban poverty re-emerging at an altogether unprecedented rate, we cannot over emphasise the importance of local authorities adopting a sensitive (rather than punitive) approach to the subject of rent arrears.

The next point which a local authority might need to evaluate separately relates to initiatives which it might wish to take in important, but narrow, areas of housing need. This would apply both to groups whose housing requirements were not normally in demand — such as the severely disabled, or the elderly in search of sheltered accommodation, and to those where family circumstances constituted inadequately recognised pockets of housing need (i.e. single parent families, the single juvenile homeless, students, etc). Thus, it may well be that:

26. for planning purposes, distinct means of evaluating group-specific 'needs' might have to be developed where an Authority is assessing the claims of groups requiring particular sorts of housing intervention. In a very precise and accountable way these might be areas where the general restrictions upon housing associations (recommended later) might be relaxed in order to pursue specific, but limited, housing initiatives. However restricted these initiatives may be, the position of individuals within the groups should be no less clear and open than anyone else's within the mainstream of the allocations system.

Additionally, it perhaps simply needs stating that:

27. in establishing a points system, the Authority need not be prevented from accommodating 'key workers'. Such allocations should, however, be kept within clearly defined limits and be subject to Housing Committee approval. (This should also apply to any, reciprocal exchanges with other Authorities).

It has certainly been a central part of our assumptions that in putting forward any precise scheme for a points system, a local authority would first of all offer this, for comment *and amendment*, to as broad a cross section of the community as possible. It is important simply to state this as a working proposition; namely that

28. any proposed points system should be extensively discussed with representatives of tenants, ethnic minority and other organisations, to ensure that (as far as possible) it enjoyed widespread public support.

In Nottingham, one problem which has worked against an effective dialogue between the black communities, Housing Department Officials, and Housing Committee members over the whole field of council housing policy, is that no one has really grasped its relevance to racial equality. Although the Department has been keeping ethnic records for over a decade, these records have been analysed so rarely that they have been virtually useless. Beyond this it must be said that, with reports to the Housing Committee based on these records being even less frequent, *Nottingham's ethnic record keeping has had no influence on housing policy formulation during this whole period.* Yet without regular monitoring, the keeping of ethnic records becomes an empty and hypocritical gesture towards racial equality. Why Nottingham has never made any formal application for central government funds for such monitoring remains a mystery — especially since Section 11 of the 1966 Local Government Act has, in the past, consistently made such money available.

The absence of adequate monitoring begs the whole question of the value of keeping ethnic records. Our own belief is that ethnic identity *should* form a part of the information gathered by a local authority; and against which the impartiality of its services should be measured. In this context we would recommend that:

29. ethnic identity should be part of the information included in housing department records, in order to provide a necessary planning tool for housing policy (as well as enabling the local authority to comply with the 1976 Race Relations Act),
30. the keeping of records which include ethnic identity must be part of a commitment to regular monitoring by the department and the Authority as a whole,
31. ethnic identity should be recorded at the point of *application* rather than allocation (otherwise discrimination in the initial selection process can pass undetected),
32. as well as distinguishing between Asian and West Indian households, the categories of ethnic origin should be extended to include those of Middle Eastern, Far Eastern, European, or Old Commonwealth origin. Within this framework applicants should be offered the right to define their own ethnic identity, including the country of birth.

At a more mundane level some confusion in records can usefully be avoided if Authorities ensured that

33. where name changes take place in a council tenancy, which do not result in any move (i.e. where the wife takes over a tenancy from her husband, or a woman retains the tenancy in her new married name), these should *not* be recorded as allocations. Such changes would not then distort the actual allocations data,

34. the coding of records should itself provide greater information about the condition of the housing to which people are allocated.

Given the acknowledged unpopularity of deck-access accommodation,

35. it must be possible, within any framework of record keeping, to identify allocations to flats complexes and other stigmatised or unpopular estates.

This was the case in Nottingham until 1978. This particular part of the coding was then dropped as part of a rationalisation of computer time for the department. Neither here, nor anywhere else, would this appear to be an adequate justification for obscuring the allocations data relating to such unpopular accommodation.

Finally (in respect of record keeping), in order to ensure effective, on-going, monitoring of the racial impact of council housing policies,

36. the detailed analysis of racial inequalities both in allocations and outstanding applications, ought to be regularly discussed and reviewed *with the black communities themselves.*

Such discussions could have an obvious and beneficial effect on the relationship between black applicants and the Housing Authority. For this to be so, however, senior housing staff will have to find effective means of developing an increased understanding, within their own department, of black community needs. From our limited involvement in Nottingham's Housing Allocations Section, and on one of the Housing Department's training courses, it was clear that

allocations staff often felt anxious and uncertain about inter-
viewing black applicants. Their expectation that the interview
was going to be difficult will, in many cases, have actually
made it so; thereby reinforcing their stereotypes of black applicants as 'difficult tenants'. In addition, different styles of
communication between Asian, or West Indian applicants
and the Allocations staff, have often increased these difficulties. In order to reduce such problems,

37. housing allocations staff and housing visitors should
    regularly be involved in training sessions in which the
    complexities of working in a multi-racial, multi-cultural,
    urban environment are systematically explored.

To the best of our knowledge, all of Nottingham's housing
personnel who are currently in direct contact with the general
public are white. The credibility of a multi-racial housing service within a local authority would be greatly increased if its
own staffing policy *visibly* reflected this. Therefore,

38. an Authority should encourage staff recruitment, at all
    levels, on a multi-racial basis.

It would not necessarily follow that all Authorities should
pursue this by appointing a Housing Advisor on Race. Experiences in other parts of the country sometimes suggest that
such appointments can serve to restrict the involvement of the
black community in housing policy discussions, rather than
extend it. *If there is the political will to face, honestly, the
racial disadvantages and discrimination which appear within
the council house sector, then it is with the organisations
representing black communities themselves that the most
fruitful basis for consultation and re-appraisal exists.* An
Authority which lacks this commitment will find the appointment of a token black to be little more than a temporary
respite which will, in many cases, be more likely increase
rather than reduce their problems.

A commitment to equality of opportunity would not,
however, only encompass an on-going review of allocations
and a multi-racial staffing policy. As a matter of course it
should follow that,

39. information on the Authority's housing services should

be available in translation, for members of ethnic minorities.

This would be particularly important if, as we suggest later, all the Authority's nominations to housing association property also go through the main Allocations Section. Last of all, on the subject of communication,

40. the Housing Department must ensure that comprehensive and detailed information is available to staff in the Allocation Section in order for them to effectively pass this on to applicants.

All too often we heard compliants from Nottingham's allocations staff about the inadequacy of the information that they had on properties which were available for allocation. Properties which the staff genuinely believed to be in good condition frequently turned out to have major (and obvious) defects. This created unnecessary friction with the applicants who went to look at these properties and who, understandably, then felt that they were being insulted.

It is, however, on the subject of housing conditions, housing stock and housing choice that we must finish. The position of all applicants, and the Allocations Section itself, will be largely determined by the broader housing policies which have had an adverse effect upon all allocation possibilities.

In so far as this is also true of many other parts of the country, then if Authorities wish to halt or reverse the situation, they may need to

41. deflect, divert, or delay as far as is possible, all pressures to sell council housing stock.
42. 'invite' housing associations to forego their right of veto on local authority nominations to their properties. (In Nottingham, at least, such an invitation would need to be reinforced by the prospect of sanctions: including one which would deny unco-operative associations the prospect of any future work or assistance in the city). The Authority's nomination rights, for both new and relet housing association properties, should then be handled directly by the Allocations Section of its Housing Department.

This is, perhaps, of particular importance in Nottingham, given the nature and location of housing association properties in the City. In addition Authorities ought to

43. retain as extensive a direct building and improvement programme as central government policy will allow. Of necessity this would require the retention (or acquisition) of substantial development land for future council house building.
44. acquire, wherever possible, larger properties which become available in their locality, particularly those in central area locations.
45. ensure that, within the building and improvement programmes which do exist, particular emphasis is placed upon the provision of accommodation for those household types whose choices within the council housing sector are even more restricted than is normally the case.

Such measures would obviously make an important impact not simply upon black households, but on all people in search of council housing.

To a large extent, many of these proposals would be constrained by the reponsiveness (or otherwise) of central government. This would not, however, apply to all aspects of local authority housing policy. Even where central government constraints do apply, an Authority still has considerable autonomy in respect of its existing stock.

Our research into Nottingham's allocation policies confirmed the quantitative and qualitative significance of central area housing stock to the black community. Of particular importance then is the extent to which Housing Action Area and General Improvement Area policies do not appear to have significantly improved the rehousing prospects of the larger black families looking for inner-city *council* housing. In this respect the Council's whole approach to its older central area housing — usually categorised as 'acquired' or 'corporate' properties — needs re-evaluation. That these properties are viewed by the local authority as low status ones, can be seen clearly from their Allocations Review proposals of December 1980. Corporate properties were one of only two sections of the City's housing stock to which homeless families with a history of rent arrears were proposed to be allocated (see 'Review of Allocation Policies' Nottingham City Housing Committee, 4/12/80, agenda papers, p.23). Such policies (which relate to the very houses which, in terms of location and size, were most important to black families) only serve to reinforce those stereotypes which have characterised black families as slum dwellers and problem families. This is not an argument for 'dispersal' but for 'enrichment'. It is an argument for taking the locational 'preferences' of black families and directing substantial resources into these properties and areas, so that they become synonymous with high quality council housing — sought after by white households as well as black.

To pursue this end a local authority might, of its own accord,

46. establish a central area Housing Audit (broken up into zones and/or with specific identification of housing stress areas) in which the whole balance of housing was under continuing scrutiny. As outlined in 7. above, this should include readily available information on property sizes, age and condition, as well as the family size and racial characteristics of those living in each area. The Audit would need to cover private sector as well as public sector housing.

47. use the experience which has been accumulated in the local authority Housing Action Teams as a basis for extending, and speeding up, the council's housing improvement programme. Such a move would probably require that Teams be given substantial executive (rather than advisory) powers. The effects of such a policy would help to shift the focus towards much greater public sector responsibility for improvements (by voluntary or compulsory acquisition of empty properties and private rented ones). Compulsory Purchase Orders (CPOs) could be served immediately an area was 'designated' by the Authority — with negotiations for voluntary purchase or private improvements being conducted between then and the government's decision to confirm the CPO, or to hold

a public enquiry. (If improvements had been completed to the Authority's and tenants satisfaction before confirmation of the CPO, the Order could of course be withdrawn). This process itself would be more effective if central government were to support a streamlining of the existing CPO procedures — particularly in shortening the waiting time before decisions are made. Such an approach would specifically *not* apply to owner-occupiers in such areas. Again any purchase by an Authority from owner-occupiers should only be done by voluntary agreement.

The Authority should then

48. identify, within the Audit, the numbers of improved and unimproved council houses (and unimproved private rented houses) in each sub-division of its locality. This should also include details of variations in property size in the different areas.
49. include within the Audit, an analysis, by 'race', of the allocations to improved/unimproved properties.
50. use such an Audit as the basis for regular appraisal by the Housing Committee; with the pattern of racial rehousing being one of the distinct variables which the Committee examined.
51. use the Committee responses, and the Audit itself, as supplements to the annual HIP submission to central government (Housing Investment Programme submissions are made by local authorities to the Department of the Environment and this forms the basis of an Authority's housing strategy).
52. adopt a similar approach to the monitoring of allocations to flats complexes and/or other stigmatised estates.

In addition to whatever standing consultative committees an Authority has, which involve tenants organisations in its local consultations, it should also promote public scrutiny of its policies in respect of racial equality. To do this an Authority might specifically

53. include representatives, nominated from the black communities themselves, in the Council's housing policy

evaluation process. This might be done either by extending to them rights as co-opted members of the Housing Committee for those particular sessions. Alternatively, the local authority could establish a separate forum for discussing, with the black communities, the racial consequences of its public housing policy.

These proposals are by no means an exhaustive (or definitive) list of the ways in which racial inequalities in council housing are to be tackled. They do, however, provide a basis against which other alternatives might be tested. What even sympathetic Authorities such as Nottingham can not escape from, is the knowledge that bland declarations of faith, to the effect that 'we do not discriminate', are increasingly being made to look both inadequate and hypocritical. The gut feeling of a great many black households that they *are* discriminated against, demands to be systematically examined. Allocations policies that are obscure, unaccountable and discretionary provide no basis for doing so.

A commitment to offering equality of opportunity in council housing requires that the framework of local authority housing allocations should be an open and accountable one; that the actual allocations are regularly and extensively monitored; that the main building and improvement programmes of an Authority attempt to redress the structural inequalities, experienced by particular groups whose real housing 'choices' have been restricted both in qualitative and quantitative terms; and that consistent and substantial resources are made available to improve and extend the stock of council housing rather than reduce it.

At a time when almost the whole tide of public housing policy is rolling in the opposite direction, the redressing of racial disadvantages in council housing requires a good deal more than liberal sentiments and empty rhetoric.

An Afterword on the Impetus for Change

In this country conflicts between people and the state, workers and emloyers, or simply between different groups in society, have generally avoided large scale violence. In recent years, however, this has become progressively less true of incidents involving race. Lewisham and Notting Hill in 1977 well illustrated the trend towards increasingly violent clashes. They in turn were followed by clashes of equal intensity in Leicester, Southall, at Grunwick, and, most recently, in Bristol and Brixton. Not only has the rate of such clashes appeared to have increased, but so too has their association with more widespread racial conflict. That Nottingham's name was not added to this list in late 1980 is partly a matter of luck and partly due to some uncharacteristically discrete press coverage at the time.

In August 1980 an incident occured which could have had devastating repercussions. In the area around the Hyson Green flats complex a series of clashes took place between a group of white youths and number of West Indians. This was not a straightforward fight between two groups, but rather a series of incidents involving individual blacks and the white youths, spread over a period of a couple of hours. The clashes themselves took place against a background of stories about increasing activity of British Movement or National Front groups in the area. Almost irrespective of the clashes, the level of tension was raised dramatically by what blacks saw as the wholly ineffective response of the local police. The end result was that a number of petrol bombs were made, and some were thrown into the local police station. The bombs which went off did not in fact burn down the police station, but a group of some 50 or so angry black youths then thronged around the station and flats for some time. More established leaders of the black community were hurriedly drawn in to the area to defuse the situation. At the end of the day the white youths, and a number of black youths, were arrested and charged with unlawful assembly.

In a city which had made such a meal of the 1958 disturbances, the press coverage of the whole incident was remarkedly subdued. When it reported the incident on 15th August 1980, the *Evening Post* devoted little more than 3 column inches to the story. As the extract shows, even then it did so in an extremely low-key manner. So much so that race was not even mentioned.

> "Bombs: 6 to be charged?"
> Six people were expected to be charged later today after two petrol bombs exploded in Hyson Green, Nottingham.
> The bombs — bottles containing inflammable liquid — were thrown from the balconies of the Hyson Green flats on to Gregory Boulevard while police were searching garages.
> During the incident a brick was thrown through the window of the unmanned police station.
> Extra officers have now been drafted into the area to work on the investigation.
> *(Nottingham Evening Post, 15/8/80).*

It was not until 7 months later, when the trial of those involved took place, that there was any real public appraisal of the incident. To an extent, the role of the white youths as instigators of the trouble did emerge as part of the press coverage:

> "Accepting that they initially went to Hyson Green 'for a lark' the judge told them: 'You deliberately set out to hunt coloured people — not only in Hyson Green but also in the city. And when you didn't think there were enough of you, you went back to attempt to enlist support."
> *(Nottingham Evening Post, 11/3/81).*

Most of the news coverage, however, focused upon the black response to this, and almost no comment was made about the nature of police-black community relations in the area.

Thus, under front page banner headlines following the first day of the trial, the local paper reported that:

"Molotov cocktails — petrol bombs — were thrown at Hyson Green police station in an attempt to burn it down on a night of racial trouble . . . A number of bottles were thrown at the front and back of the police station . . . When the first sortie failed the youths returned to the flats and made another lot. And when the police arrived at the flats a second petrol bomb was thrown from a level above the officers and landed less than ten yards away and exploded, sending flames into the air . . . Five of the seven police officers were then ordered back and third bomb exploded with such force that officers were driven back by the heat."

(*Nottingham Evening Post*, 10/3/81).

In the event the 4 white youths and 4 of the black youths received substantial prison sentences (mostly of between 3 and 5 years), whilst 4 others have yet to be tried or sentenced.

Since the bombing of police stations is not an everyday part of Nottingham life, it becomes extremely important to consider how close to the margins of social control this incident came. Had the police station actually caught fire and burnt down the scale of the conflict would have altered dramatically. The number of both police officers and blacks converging upon the area would have risen alarmingly. Then, little more than 4 months after the ugly debacle of St Pauls in Bristol, many of the same deep-rooted frustrations and conflicts would have been triggered off into violent expression.

The reasons for mentioning this are not to suggest that the incident was the responsibility of the housing department. It is, however, to clearly establish housing as one (important) part of the matrix within which such community relations are determined. Employment prospects, education facilities, social, shopping, and transport facilities are also major parts; but it would be dishonest or foolish to suggest that housing — council housing — has no relevance in determining how volatile such situations are likely to be. As one important assessment of the Bristol riots commented:

"Finally, and perhaps most importantly, the dimenstion of race was added to the volatile mixture of social need, inadequate infrastructure and unemployment in the inner city. Blacks became associated with squalor and whites with material success. It provided, simultaneously, racially-based idologies of liberation for the blacks and reinforcement for notions of racial superiority among whites. Ambitious whites managed to leave the inner city but most ambitious blacks were trapped there in immobility, and unemployment.

"This is the context in which festering resentment and rage are kept on the boil by constant reminders that white racism remains a potent force in this society — demoralising and dehumanising people, who end up finding that the equal opportunity talked about by the politicians, the love preached by churches, and the brotherhood extolled by the trade unions are alike empty."

(New Society, 10/4/80, p.47).

It is within this total context that the inequalities in Nottingham's council house allocations need to be evaluated. In contrast, one of the most inappropriate responses to this sort of situation, whether it be in Bristol, Nottingham or anywhere else, has been to describe it in terms of 'spontaneous public disorder' — as both the police and politicians have been inclined to do — and then to seek 'solutions' entirely within the context of law and order programmes. To do so fails to grasp both the complexity of the situation, and the extent to which an extension of the mechanics of suppression merely prepares the ground for greater conflict in the future. It is not simply that:

". . . black youth will no longer accept their disadvantage and discrimination without hitting back. When discrimination is compounded by openly racist activities by certain groups, often seemingly protected by the police, then tension can erupt."

(CRE, *The Fire Next Time*, 1980, p.8).

As the leader of the Nottingham City Council discovered during the initiative he took following the Hyson Green incident, the issues are not merely about youth/police conflict, or about clashes with openly racist groups. His meeting with large numbers of black youths revealed how broad a spectrum was covered by their complaints and hostilities. Housing, employment and social provision for the black community as a whole, were as rooted in their frustrations as the more direct conflicts which they had with the police, or with racist groups. If this can be fully grasped and understood by public officials in general, then it provides not so much an impetus for change, but an imperative for change; housing cannot be excluded from this imperative.

Such an imperative only gains weight from the possible alternative consequences for local authority departments themselves. There are already a growing number of groups and individuals who would argue that the only way in which black communities are likely to get any reasonable response from public agencies is by directing their anger and hostility at the agencies themselves. This harassment of public agencies may have a certain cathartic value for those who initiate it; and it may produce some positive (if piecemeal) gains for them. However, the response that it elicted would then hardly constitute a coherent, thought-out shift in housing policy. Nor would it be a particularly profitable or enlightening experience for those on the receiving end — in this case probably the lower grade administrative officers within the housing department. Nor, ultimately, would it represent any credible strategy, within the black community, for securing a more generalised equality of opportunity in the council housing sector. Such a strategy is essentially an alienated reponse to a system which is itself characterised as having little or no interest in racial equality. It is however, a response which gains credibility in the absence of alternative, specific, policy commitments directed at removing racial inequalities in council housing.

The events in Bristol, and the near miss in Nottingham itself, stand as a salutory warning to those who have turned a blind (or colour-blind) eye to such inequalities. The passive acceptance by black communities that such is their 'lot' in life, is a factor which can no longer be relied upon in public policy formulations.

Appendix

Housing Records and Research Methods

Since 1968, Nottingham's Housing Department has recorded the ethnic origin of all those allocated council properties. It is this information, plus the additional details recorded at the points where an offer of a property is about to be made, and is then subsequently accepted, which forms the basis of our study. Although the classification of ethnic origin is not very refined (each tenant is labelled I (West Indian), A (Asian) or X (white), it has been adequate for our purposes. Moreover, its simplicity has had the advantage of reducing the likelihood of mis-classification by the housing visitors who record the information.*

The additional information collected is of four kinds. The first concerns the character of the tenant's route into the allocations process. The form of housing tenure and place of residence prior to re-housing is recorded, as is the basis of the allocation (e.g. from a clearance programme, the waiting list, a transfer, exchange or some other special category). The second kind of information recorded concerns the property actually allocated to the tenant and includes the area into which the tenant moved, the period in which his or her property was built, the kind of property it is, how many bedrooms it has and whether or not the property includes a garage or car

---

* One problem which did arise concerned a small number of Middle East students from Trent Polytechnic who occupied flats in the Victoria Centre complex. These were classified in the same way as Indian and Pakistan tenants heading normal households. This has been fully taken into account in the analysis.

    The fact that the classification has been adequate for our immediate purposes does not mean that we consider it to be ideal. Suggestions for an alternative are included amongst our recommendations.

parking space. The third type of information recorded concerns the tenant, i.e. age group, broad level of income and size of household. Unfortunately, since no distinction in the computerised records is made between the adult and child members of each household, it is not always possible to be certain what kind of family unit has been re-housed. Finally, the housing visitors record their impression of whether or not a family has particular problems which may require further visits or attention.

Throughout the 1970's the Housing Department has sent weekly returns to the Nottingham and District Community Relations Council (NDCRC) containing not only the numbers of Asian and West Indians rehoused but also the computerised codings of the information described above. In the late 1970's the NDCRC decided to examine this body of data and, under the supervision of Daniel Lawrence, a preliminary analysis of it was made by Isobel Tate. Although this indicated a number of points of concern, there was also evidence that this data was not fully reliable, and so a further decision was made to mount a fuller investigation. At this stage a grant was obtained from the Community Relations Commission and Stephen King replaced Isobell Tate.

Since various totals derived from the weekly returns did not correspond with those kept in another form by the Housing Department, it proved necessary re-commence the study by checking the details on the computer-coded returns against those kept on the 'house' and 'personal' card files of the Housing Department. This exercise revealed a large number of coding errors in the period up to 1974 and so the original plan to make an analysis of allocations throughout the 1970's had to be abandoned. Since, subsequent to 1974 the coding had been subject to close scrutiny within the Housing Department, it was decided to begin the analysis with the allocations made in the calendar year 1975. The pressure on computer space, which obliged the Housing Department to subsequently reduce the information it kept on computer (including crucial information concerning the very large number of allocations to the unpopular flat properties), meant that it was necessary to end the period of investigation with the Calendar Year 1977. At this stage it was

also decided that it would be a wise precaution to base the
analysis *not* on the information recorded in the weekly
returns supplied to the NDCRC, but on the *weekly lettings
lists* kept by the Housing Department.

With the exception of the one per cent of cases where the
information available was incomplete, all Asian and West Indians allocated council properties in the years 1975-77 have
been included in the investigations. In total they numbered
1,217. To enable comparisons to be made with allocations
made to those classified X (white) by the Housing Department, a corresponding number of allocations was drawn at
random from the total number of lettings made during the
three year period. This was achieved by generating random
numbers within the range 1 to 18,252 (the total number of
allocations in the years concerned). Where a number produced an Asian or West Indian allocation a substitute case was
drawn using a supplementary list of a further 100 random
numbers. In a small number of cases it was found later that
the information available was incomplete, or incorrectly
recorded, and these cases were then deleted from the study.
Consequently the white sample is made up of 1,183 cases
rather than the 1,217 originally drawn. It represents, 7 per
cent of the total white allocations in the period.

An indication of the extent to which the sample is representative is drawn in the table below. In the top row are the actual proportions of white allocations made through transfers,
exchanges, and to new tenants in the study period. The
figures in the second row are the corresponding proportions
derived from the white sample.

Allocations to white tenants 1975-77 inclusive

	% through transfers	% through exchanges	% to new tenants
Actual proportions	28.0	10.5	60.5
Sample proportions	27.4	11.1	61.5

The task of feeding the data into Nottingham Univerity's
computer to obtain the frequency distributions and cross
tabulations for the analysis, fell to Stephen King. However,
his full-time attachement to the project came to an end

sometime before the analysis was complete and at an early stage in the writing-up. Although the limited support provided by the Community Relations Commission had been generously supplemented by the Hilden Trust, this was not sufficient to maintain a paid research worker for the duration of the study. In anticipation of this, Alan Simpson, the NDCRC Research and Information Officer, was released to work on the study. After the departure of Stephen King he became, under the continual supervision of Daniel Lawrence, primarily responsible for both the analysis and writing-up.

Other information used in the course of the study and in the preparation of this report has been obtained from published sources (national as well as local) but also, in many instances, directly from the staff of the Housing Department whose help has been invaluable.

References

Association of Metropolitan Authorities (AMA) — 1980 — *Housing in the Eighties: prospects in the public and private sectors.*

Bird, Heather — 1975 — Residential Mobility and preference patterns in the public sector of the housing market. (Centre from Environmental Studies, abstract of manuscript, 1 July, 1975).

Bird, H. & Whitbread, M. — 1975 — Council House Transfers and Exchanges (*New Society*, 14 August, 1975).

Bishop, John — 1979 — Report on Nottingham City Housing Policy, (Unpublished), Nottingham Areas Project.

Bramley, Glen; Leather, Philip; & Murie, Alan — 1980 — Housing Strategies and Investment Programmes (*Working Paper* No.7, School for Advanced Urban Studies, Bristol University).

Bull, D.G. — 1971 — Problems of Communication in Redevelopment Areas (*South Western Review of Public Administration*, No.10, July 1971).

Burney, Elizabeth — 1967 — *'Housing on Trial': a study of immigrants and local government* (Institute of Race Relations/OUP).

Byrne, D. — 1974 — Problem families: A Housing Lumpen — Proletariat (*Working Papers in Sociology*, No.5, University of Durham).

Carroll, John — 1980 — Leader of the Nottingham City Council, (extracts from a recorded interview, May 1980).

Coates, Ken & Silburn, Bill — 1980 — *Beyond the Bulldozer* (Department of Adult Education, University of Nottingham).

CDP — 1974 — *Inter Project Report* (CDP Information and Intelligence Unit).

CDP — 1976 — *Profits Against Houses* (CDP Information and Intelligence Unit).

CDP — 1976 — *Whatever Happened to Council Housing?* (CDP Information and Intelligence Unit).

Commission for Racial Equality — 1980 *'The Fire Next Time': Youth in a Multi-Racial Society* (CRE).

Community Relations Commission — 1977 — *Housing Choice and Ethnic Concentration* (CRC).

Community Relations Commission (Housing Section) — 1975 — Local Authority Housing and Race — Discussion Paper: Seminar of Housing Directors, Feb. 1975 (CRC).

Cullingworth, J.B. — 1969 — *Council Housing — Purposes, Procedures and Priorities:* 9th Report of the Housing Management Sub-Committee of the Central Housing Advisory Committee (HMSO).

Deakin, Nicholas & Ungerson, Clare — 1973 — *Beyond the Ghetto: the illusion of choice* (in London: Urban Patterns, Problems and Policies — Donnison, D. (ed) — Heinemann).

Edwards, John & Batley, Richard — 1978 — *The Politics of Positive Discrimination* (Tavistock).

Flett, Hazel — 1977 — Council Housing and the Location of Ethnic Minorities (RUER, Bristol University, *Working Papers on Ethnic Relations*, No.5).

Flett, Hazel — 1979 — Black Council Tenants in Birmingham (RUER Bristol University, *Working Paper No.12*).

Flett, Hazel, Henderson, Jeff and Brown, Bill — 1978 — 'Some Aspects of the Operation of Birmingham's Housing Department, and the factors Affecting Housing Allocation — Discussion Paper for the DoE.

Foot, Michael — 1973 — *Aneurin Bevan, 1945-60* (Davis — Poynter Ltd).

Forrest, Ray & Murie, Alan — 1978 'Paying the Price of Council House Sales', (in *ROOF*, Nov. 1978, p.170-173).

Gallagher, Pam — 1980 — Report to the Housing Department on the outcome of a training course for counter staff, (Trent Polytechnic, April 1980).

Gray, Fred — 1975 — Non Explanation in Urban Geography (in *AREA*, Vol.7 No.4).

Gray, Fred — 1976 — Selection and Allocation in Council Housing (in *Transactions of the Institute of British Geographers*, No.1 Vol.1).

Guardian, The — 1976 — Report on problems in the Old Basford Flats Complex (23 March 1976).

Guardian, The — 1980 Housing report (23 Oct. 1980).

Haddon, Roy — 1972 — A Minority in a Welfare State Society: the Location of West Indians in the London Housing Market (*New Atlantis*, 1,2).

Hammond, Michael (Chief Executive Nottingham City Council) — 1974 (June) — Progress Report on the Clearance and Housing Programmes; 1974 (Nov.); 1975 (April); 1976 (April); 1976 (Oct.); 1977 (April).

Holmes, Chris — 1979 — *Issues of Access and Allocation in London* (SHAC 1979, Policy Paper 2, London Housing Conference Papers).

Housing Services Advisory Group — 1978 — *Allocation of Council Housing* (DoE).

Lambert, J. & Filkin, C. — 1971 — Race Relations Research: Some Issues of Approach and Application (in *RACE*, xii, 3, 1971).

Lansley, Stewart — 1979 — *Housing and Public Policy* (Croome Helm).

Lambert, J., Paris, C. & Blackaby, B. — 1978 — *Housing Policy and the State* (Macmillan).

Lawrence, Daniel — 1974 — *Black Migrants: White Natives* (Cambridge University Press).

Magee, Malcolm — 1980 — Deputy Director, Nottingham City Housing Department (extracts of a recorded interview May 1980).

Merrett, Stephen — 1979 — *State Housing in Britain* (Routledge & Kegan Paul).

National Tenants Organisation — 1979 — *'Selling Council Houses'* — a tenants action guide.

New Society — 1980 — Editorial (10 April 1980).

Niner, Pat, — 1980 — Transfer Policies: A case study in Harlow (CURS Research Memorandum 79, University of Birmingham).

Nottingham Alternative Publications — 1979 *Where have all the asetts gone?* (NAP 83 Beauvale Rd., Meadows, Notingham).

Nottingham City Housing Department — 1976 (Feb.) — 'Old Basford Flats Development', Report of the Director of Housing.

Nottingham City Housing Department — 1976 (Oct.) — Report to Housing Committee.

Nottingham City Housing Department — 1980 — Review of Allocation Policies,

Housing Committee Agenda Paper, Dec. 1980.

Nottingham City Council — 1971 — Evidence to the Select Committee on Race Relations and Immigration (*also* in the Select Committee's own 'Minutes of Evidence' — "Visit to Nottingham in the Session 1970-71, HMSO).

Nottingham City Council — 1977/1978 — Policy and Resources Committee Minutes (20.9.77 and 21.2.78).

Nottingham Evening Post — articles/report — 25 Nov. 1975; 15 Aug. 1980; 10 March 1981; 11 March 1981.

Nottingham Housing Action Group (NHAG) — 1977 — 'It's not our policy to build Council Houses' — Nottingham's Housing Cuts.

Nottingham Housing Rights Group (NHRG) — 1980 — *A Guide to Housing Associations in Nottingham*.

Nottingham News — articles/reports — 29 Feb. 1980 ('Home Truths'); 1 Aug. 1980.

Nottingham Social Services Department — 1975 — Report on Basford Flats (Social Services Committee 8 Aug. '75).

Nottinghamshire County Council — 1977 — Report of the Officers Review Board to the Accounts and Review Committee on Unemployment in the County.

Nugent, Neil, & King, Roger — 1979 — Ethnic Minorities, Scapegoating and the Extreme Right (in *Racism and Political Action in Britain* — (eds) Miles, R. & Phizacklea, A. — Routledge & Kegan Paul).

NUPE/SCAT — 1978 — *Up against a brick wall — the dead end in housing policy* (SCAT Publications).

Parker, John & Dugmore, Keith — 1976 — Colour and the Allocation of GLC Housing (*Research Report 21*, GLC, Nov. 1976).

Pinker, Robert — 1971 — *Social Theory and Social Policy* (Heinemann).

Popplestone, Gerry & Paris, Chris — 1979 — 'Managing Difficult Tenants' (Centre for Environmental Studies, *Research Series 30* Sept. 1979).

Rex, John — 1968 — 'The Sociology of a Zone of Transition' (in R.E. Pahl — *Readings in Urban Sociology* — (London, Pergamon).

Rex, John — 1973 — *Race, Colonialism and the City* — London (Routledge & Kegan Paul).

Rex, John & Moore, Robert — 1967 — *Race, Community and Conflict* (OUP).

Runciman, W.G. — 1972 — *Relative Deprivation and Social Justice* (Pelican).

Simpson, Alan (*et.al.*) — 1978 '*What Jobs for the Boys*' (Nottingham Areas Project, 1978).

Skellington, Richard — 1976 — 'Old Basford Flats, Nottingham' (Open University, Tutors Report — Summer School, May 1976).

Smith, David J. — 1977 — *Racial Disadvantage in Britain* (Pelican).

Tate, Isobel — 1979 — Problem Families and the Creation of the 'Problem' Estate (Postgraduate thesis, Nottingham University May 1979).

Thorpe, Jean — 1981 — *Housing Associations and Ethnic Minorities in Nottingham* (NDCRC).

Townsend, Peter — 1976 — *Sociology and Social Policy* (Penguin).

Towsend, Peter — 1979 — *Poverty in the United Kingdom — a survey of household resources and standards of living* (Penguin/Pelican).

Webster, David — 1980 Why Labour failed on housing (*New Society*, 17 Jan. 1980).